FAMILY REUNIONS:
HOW TO PLAN YOURS

FAMILY REUNIONS:

HOW TO PLAN YOURS

by

HARRY MC KINZIE

McKinzie Publishing Company
11000 Wilshire Boulevard
Post Office Box 241777
Los Angeles, California 90024
Copyright @ 1987 by Mc Kinzie Publishing Company

ALL RIGHTS RESERVED, WORLDWIDE.
Manufactured and Printed in the UNITED STATES OF AMERICA.

LIBRARY OF CONGRESS CATALOGING-IN-PUBLICATION DATA:

Mc Kinzie, Harry.
    Family reunions: How to plan yours.

    Bibliography: p.
    Includes index.
    1. Family reunions--United States--Planning.
I. Title.
GT2423.M35 1987   390   87-19615
ISBN 0-86626-013-7

CONTENTS

CHAPTER I
I. ORGANIZATION AND PLANNING

A. INTRODUCTION

B. ORGANIZING THE FAMILY REUNION

    1. To Establish the Permanent Board

    2. Letters and Forms

C. PLANNING

    1. Why We Should Have a Family Reunion

    2. Special Occasions for the Family Reunion

    3. Committees

        a. Establishing the Host Committee

        b. List of Committees

        c. Commitee Letters and Forms

ORGANIZATION AND PLANNING

A community is only as strong as the families that reside within it.

The family is only as strong as its weakest members.

HARRY MCKINZIE

INTRODUCTION

The full moon was larger than the mountains that it hovered above, and certainly wider than the highway that I was driving upon while on my way from the Sixth Annual Family Reunion of my father's immediate family. At first, it seemed all too easy, no accidents or serious car trouble.

All the others were asleep during my turn at driving. Yes, there was my oldest brother and his girlfriend, my sons, my girlfriend, and cousin-in-law. I reflected for a moment trying to reminisce upon the things that were included in the planning stage that made this a successful trip and a happy family reunion. I realized that all of the planning was an essential ingredient in the overall success. It was no coincidence that the spare tire was adequate to get us to a gas station for repair of a flat tire that was punctured by a nail picked up on the way home. It was not by accident that the day was not ruined by ants and mosquitoes because of the insect-repellent sprays and creams we had thought to provide.

The fun of traveling along the highways with my family and friends was without a doubt more enjoyable than traveling alone. I could remember the time that I was in Delphi looking at the clear ocean and the time the Acropolis was being dissected by a tour guide. What marvelous sights to see but they did not compare to the splendor of family and friends traveling together to greet other members of the family tree.

I started to wonder to myself about the way the world seemed to place less significance on the family structure. What has happened since the time the pilgrims traveled long and treacherous journeys across the Atlantic searching for a new homeland? The trip was slow, the journey long, and the task was arduous with no certainty of what to expect but the challenge that loomed ahead. The family was closer then, each to the other, if for no other reason than sheer survival.

Even though communication was antique compared to the present split-second means, the family kept in closer touch than it does now. We can travel from one coast to the opposite coast today in the time it took neighbors to go to each other's houses or to leave the home to purchase necessary food and hardware from the town's general store. Everyone knew each other and all were able to tell when a stranger came to town.

What happened to all of the unity that the families used to have toward one another? Have we become a selfish and divided society with no concern for the basics? If we have become selfish and unconcerned for our family, what hope is there for the nations of the world? Our society is a lost society which is performing surgery on the symptoms and not on the causes of our problems. We must return to basics and strengthen the family.

While I was driving, I thought of how much fun we had had looking at the marvelous Grand Canyon in Arizona's mountains. I was completely amazed at the beauty of the canyon, so much more impressive than all the pictures I had seen. It seems strange to me now that all those pictures, apparently taken from the bottom of the canyon looking upward, had given me the impression of a mountain looming overhead rather than a canyon tunneling deep into the earth. What a revelation the actual sight was, of a crevice deeper than the tallest building looms above. It must have taken eons to develop such a canyon.

It took me seven years to get my reunion started, going home Christmas, during the summer, talking about it to various members, and finally the seventh year my oldest sister said if she was made chairperson she would help with the family reunion. So I said, "Yes." When she became chairperson she called my older sisters and brothers and got them involved. This was really about 80% of my immediate family, including my two older brothers and four older sisters and their kids. There are 13 children in our family and when she called the oldest six together they had about 30 kids and about 50 grandchildren between them. So when she got the first family reunion organized, she was chairperson and made the next sister to her secretary, and another sister treasurer. They put it together.

ORGANIZING THE FAMILY REUNION

How do you establish interest in the idea of a family reunion? You start with those family members who are the closest to you and, by word of mouth, feel them out to see how they receive the idea. Distant cousins -- distant, that is, in terms of miles -- will automatically be interested because of their curiosity about who their relatives are and what is happening to the other family members. All we need to do at this point is get things organized.

It may seem a little businesslike at first, but bear with me and give it a try. If a more informal way works best for your family, then adopt the parts that can be beneficial to your particular situation. It will be all right to add to the formalities that I have outlined in the next few pages. We are after success, not rigidity. Now let us look at the organization process.

To Establish The Permanent Board

The **Family Reunion Executive Board** is a permanent board that consists of at least three main members. These three main members are necessary for the very smallest families as well as the large ones. More members can be added, but the three that I will elaborate on are essential.

Chairperson, Secretary, and Treasurer are the titles of the three main members. They have the duty of making the family reunion interesting, informative, and pleasurable each year. They will be responsible for promoting a positive agenda that will encourage the entire family to attend.

Before we review the duties of our Board, let us discover who we will select for these positions.

The **Chairperson** is a very important position. Unlike the large corporation where large salaries are disbursed to the board, the **Family Reunion Executive Board** does not receive pay. In a family reunion the chairperson should be a person who is very well-liked, admired, and respected by the majority of the family tree. He/she must possess that charisma and charm that draws everyone in the family to the call of duty.

The chairperson of the **Family Reunion Executive Board** may be the central figure of the family. Since in most cultures women outlive men, there may exist a matriarch in the family that everyone looks up to and respects, a great grandmother or grand aunt who is the oldest living relative in the family. Everyone respects her and gives her his/her loyalty although she may not have the ability to pull the family together in the sense of organizing it. But, as long as the family knows that she is associated with the reunion, they will want to attend.

The magic she brings to the planning of the reunion is exciting. There is a trust factor connected with her. If the matriarch requests family members to send funds to her choice of treasurer, they will do so willingly. They are also certain that everyone will have an enjoyable time. So, if the family members elect the great-grandmother to be the chairperson for setting the foundation of having a family reunion annually, let it be done.

The **secretary** of the **Family Reunion Executive Board** is a social position on the Board. The secretary may write or call various committees or key persons in the family. He or she should feel comfortable in making recommendations to committees, key persons, and individual members of the family. The secretary carries out the direct wishes and instructions of the chairperson. The person who volunteers or is selected to be the secretary should enjoy doing his/ her duties. There are numerous letters, calls, and arrangements to be made. He/she should be of high spirit and motivation.

It should be pleasant for members of the family to be contacted by the secretary. A good secretary complements the chairperson in different ways. Whatever the chairperson lacks in ability and persuasion, the secretary compensates for and adds to the chairperson's skills.

If there is a person in the family who gets along with most of the members, who does things today and not tomorrow, who feels comfortable writing a brief letter, who enjoys verbal communication over the phone, who has his/her heart directed toward making the family grow in love for each other, we need such a person to be the secretary of the permanent family board of directors. We need this person now.

When we look at the money of the United States of America, we find imprinted on it the words, "In God We Trust." The **treasurer** of the **Family Reunion Executive Board** will have to be somebody the family **trusts** as well. A family that makes the right choice in the selection of a chairperson and secretary but fails to get a trustworthy treasurer for the **Family Reunion Executive Board** is headed for trouble.

A person of proven ability who is successful and prosperous is a good choice for treasurer. The larger the family the more money will exchange hands and the more important it is to make a careful selection. The treasurer should be a wholesome person with a good self-image.

The treasurer may be called upon to give the family a financial report on how it is doing with its savings accounts, real properties, and other financial investments. The treasurer should possess some skills in financial matters from opening a savings account to simple investment skills.

He/she should feel comfortable discussing money topics with good bankers who are interested in the survival of the unity of the family.

A stable "Rock of Gibraltar" is what we look for in this person. Restful nights and sunny skies are what we want to have after making our choice of treasurer. We need a person who will not squander, gamble, or accidentally lose the family's money. The treasurer of the **Family Reunion Executive Board** which is a permanent position must be exceptionally stable and dependable. Honesty, integrity, and good standards are necessary qualities in our treasurer.

How do we choose the **Family Reunion Executive Board?** The democratic process works best. Family members are more receptive and helpful when they are a part of the decision-making process. They feel respected and valued which is so important to all of us.

Initially, a few members of the family who are interested in getting their reunion going should act as a nominating committee and select a slate of candidates for each of the three offices of the **Family Reunion Executive Board.**

Let us think very deeply about finding a person in the family who makes everyone draw near him/her like bees to a honeycomb. The **Family Reunion Executive Board** should have a central figure with great drawing power.

After we have written down a few names for the central figure, then we should think of the family members who would work well with that person. The **Family Reunion Executive Board** should include members who function together as a team. No ego trips, power plays or head games should be a part of this group. If it is possible, seek meek, humble and enthusiastic members who want to devote all the effort necessary to make the reunion an ongoing tradition within the entire extended family.

Letters and Forms.

At this point, we use the form that has been titled "**Let Us Nominate The Members of the Family Reunion Executive Board.**" Forms should be sent to each family member. The family should be encouraged to write in candidates if they choose.

We may wish to include a short cover letter with the form. The letter should be written in a warm, friendly manner that fits our own family lifestyle. It should be made as warm and friendly as possible. We could start out with a recent event that has happened in the family which would be of interest to everyone. We might begin with a poem or quote from the Bible. The letter is an ice-breaker. Remember, the family may not have been in communication with each other for a long time. So keep it short and friendly.

The names of the nominees for the **Family Reunion Executive Board** should include the maiden names of the women. Sometimes everyone has not been informed about all of the latest marriages in the family. The maiden names will help members of the family remember who everyone is.

Let us look at a letter that we can include with the form.

Dear Family Members,

> *Let our family's hearts rejoice,*
> *Let all those near hear our voice.*
>
> *Our family will make the time to share,*
> *In a peaceful way without a big flare.*
>   *by Harry Mc Kinzie*

We are interested in getting the family reunion plans on the road.   But first, we want to avail ourselves of the democratic process and choose volunteers from all the branches of our family for members to serve on the FAMILY REUNION EXECUTIVE BOARD. This board is the permanent board that will be instrumental in making all of the plans for years to come.   The members are appointed for the duration of their lives, unless they wish to resign.

Everyone in the family tree is qualified to nominate and vote for candidates for any of the offices, and to run for any of the positions that he or she feels qualified to hold. The positions are serious positions that will require the devotion of a lot of spare time toward achieving the unity of the family.

Take a moment to nominate a person in the family that you think will be interested in the open position(s).   Also, keep in mind that if you are interested in serving in any of the positions, you may complete the form with your own name for the job desired.

Please mail the form back to us at your earliest time available.   We will send the list of all those nominated for the various positions back to you soon.   We expect to do this within two weeks.

Have a nice day and may God bless your family.

_____
Honorable Chairperson

_____*Family*_____ *Annual Family Reunion*

LET US NOMINATE THE MEMBERS OF THE
FAMILY REUNION'S EXECUTIVE BOARD

CHAIRPERSON OF THE FAMILY REUNION EXECUTIVE BOARD

```
: NAME              :          :             :
: FIRST             :MIDDLE    : (MAIDEN)    :        LAST
:                   :          :             :
:_____:_____:_____:_____
:
:MAILING ADDRESS_____
:
:CITY_____
:
:STATE_____ZIP CODE_____
:
:AREA CODE(_____)PHONE NUMBER_____
:_____
```

SECRETARY OF THE FAMILY REUNION'S EXECUTIVE BOARD

```
: NAME              :          :             :
: FIRST             :MIDDLE    : (MAIDEN)    :        LAST
:                   :          :             :
:_____:_____:_____:_____
:
:MAILING ADDRESS_____
:
:CITY_____
:
:STATE_____ZIP CODE_____
:
:AREA CODE(_____)PHONE NUMBER_____
:_____
```

TREASURER OF THE FAMILY REUNION'S EXECUTIVE BOARD

```
: NAME              :            :            :            :
: FIRST             :MIDDLE      : (MAIDEN)   :    LAST    :
:                   :            :            :            :
:_____:_____:_____:_____:
:                                                             :
:MAILING ADDRESS_____:
:                                                             :
:CITY_____:
:                                                             :
:STATE_____ZIP CODE_____:
:                                                             :
:AREA CODE(_____)PHONE NUMBER_____:
:                                                             :
```

Please take a moment out of your busy schedule to help our family by completing and mailing this form today. Thank you!

After we have received the the nomination list, we compile the names on one form called the **Nominated For The Position Form**. This form will list all of the interested candidates who have expressed a willingness to serve in the best interests of the entire family to bring about the actual family reunion.

NOMINATED FOR THE POSITION FORM

```
:         NOMINEES FOR THE CHAIRPERSON OF THE            :
:         FAMILY REUNION EXECUTIVE BOARD                 :
:                                                        :
: NAME                                  VOTE FOR ONE     :
:  FIRST/MIDDLE/(MAIDEN)/LAST           MARK 'X'         :
:                                                        :
:1._____  _____     :
:                                                        :
:2._____  _____     :
:                                                        :
:3._____  _____     :
:                                                        :
:4._____  _____     :
:                                                        :
:5._____  _____     :
:                                                        :
:_____:
```

NOMINATED FOR THE POSITION FORM

```
**********************************************************
*            NOMINEES FOR THE SECRETARY OF THE          *
*            FAMILY REUNION EXECUTIVE BOARD             *
*                                                        *
* NAME                                   VOTE FOR ONE   *
*  FIRST/MIDDLE/(MAIDEN)/LAST            MARK 'X'       *
*                                                        *
*1._____     _____    *
*                                                        *
*2._____     _____    *
*                                                        *
*3._____     _____    *
*                                                        *
*4._____     _____    *
*                                                        *
*5._____     _____    *
*                                                        *
**********************************************************


**********************************************************
*            NOMINEES FOR THE TREASURER OF THE          *
*            FAMILY REUNION EXECUTIVE BOARD             *
*                                                        *
* NAME                                   VOTE FOR ONE   *
*  FIRST/MIDDLE/(MAIDEN)/LAST            MARK 'X'       *
*                                                        *
*1._____     _____    *
*                                                        *
*2._____     _____    *
*                                                        *
*3._____     _____    *
*                                                        *
*4._____     _____    *
*                                                        *
*5._____     _____    *
*                                                        *
**********************************************************
```

Please take a moment today to vote for the members of our family who were nominated for the **Family Reunion Executive Board** and mail us the form as soon as possible. Thank you very much for your interest in making our family a better family!

We allow about two weeks for the responses to the **Nominated For The Position Form** to arrive. After we have the results of the voting, we will notify the members of the family who have received the most votes. Whoever has received the most votes for a particular office, even by a margin of one, is the winner. If your family desires to go by a 51% majority vote, or some other method, then give it a good try. As long as the method chosen is fair and impartial to all, it should meet with approval.

Now we are ready to add up all of the votes to get the results in the mail to the nominees and members of the family. We write down the names and the total votes received by each of the nominees. Then, as quickly as time will allow, notify the winning candidates for each position, and afterwards send the names of the winners to the rest of the family. It's best not to send the tabulation of the votes but only the names of the winners.

VOTING RESULTS

```
* * * * * * * * * * * * * * * * * * * * * * * * * * * * * * * * * * * * * * * * * * * * * * * * * * * * *
*              VOTES RECEIVED BY NOMINEES FOR MEMBERS OF              *
*                   FAMILY REUNION EXECUTIVE BOARD                    *
*                                                                     *
*                          CHAIRPERSON                                *
*   NAME                                          TOTAL VOTES         *
*                                                 RECEIVED            *
*                                                                     *
* 1._____    _____          *
*                                                                     *
* 2._____    _____          *
*                                                                     *
* 3._____    _____          *
*                                                                     *
* 4._____    _____          *
*                                                                     *
* 5._____    _____          *
* * * * * * * * * * * * * * * * * * * * * * * * * * * * * * * * * * * * * * * * * * * * * * * * * * * * *
```

VOTING RESULTS

```
* * * * * * * * * * * * * * * * * * * * * * * * * * * * * * * * * * * * * * * * * * * * * * * * * * * * *
*              VOTES RECEIVED BY NOMINEES FOR MEMBERS OF              *
*                   FAMILY REUNION EXECUTIVE BOARD                    *
*                                                                     *
*                           SECRETARY                                 *
*   NAME                                          TOTAL VOTES         *
*                                                 RECEIVED            *
*                                                                     *
* 1._____    _____          *
*                                                                     *
* 2._____    _____          *
*                                                                     *
* 3._____    _____          *
*                                                                     *
* 4._____    _____          *
*                                                                     *
* 5._____    _____          *
* * * * * * * * * * * * * * * * * * * * * * * * * * * * * * * * * * * * * * * * * * * * * * * * * * * * *
```

VOTING RESULTS

```
*****************************************************************
*              VOTES RECEIVED BY NOMINEES FOR MEMBERS OF        *
*                  FAMILY REUNION EXECUTIVE BOARD               *
*                                                               *
*                          TREASURER                            *
*       NAME                                    TOTAL VOTES     *
*                                               RECEIVED        *
*                                                               *
*1._____        _____      *
*                                                               *
*2._____        _____      *
*                                                               *
*3._____        _____      *
*                                                               *
*4._____        _____      *
*                                                               *
*5._____        _____      *
*                                                               *
*****************************************************************
```

Below is the form to be used to send the **final results** of the officers elected as the members of the **Family Reunion Executive Board.** This form allows some time before we mail the certificates.

```
*****************************************************************
* FINAL RESULTS OF THE OFFICERS VOTED TO BE MEMBERS OF THE      *
*                  FAMILY REUNION EXECUTIVE BOARD               *
*                                                               *
*       NAME                            POSITION                *
*                                                               *
*1._____        CHAIRPERSON              *
*                                                               *
*2._____        SECRETARY                *
*                                                               *
*3._____        TREASURER                *
*                                                               *
*****************************************************************
```

The practice of keeping something in the mail every two weeks is good. It gives our relatives a warm feeling of family unity. They start looking forward to all of the extra attention. When elderly people find a lot of mail coming to their door, they really enjoy it. It helps remind them of all their kinfolks maturing around them. It gives them a sense of fulfillment. So keep the mail flowing.

After we mail the **Final Results** form, prepare the **Certificates of Office for the Family Reunion Executive Board.** These may be typed if desired; otherwise print the names of the winners on the forms. Note that the **Chairperson's** form does **not** require a signature. The thought here is to show our respect to the chairperson from the earliest moment.

The **Certificate for the Secretary** requires the signature of the chairperson. The closeness of the relationship of the members of FREB is special. The secretary appreciates knowing that his/her certificate has the endorsement of the chairperson.

The treasurer works very closely with the chairperson and the secretary who each endorse the certificate of the treasurer. The treasurer will shine like gold when he/she starts helping the family in the wise and careful management of family funds. The treasurer especially enjoys the task of making it possible for the less fortunate to attend each family reunion.

```
*************************************************************
*                  CERTIFICATE OF OFFICE                  *
*            FAMILY REUNION EXECUTIVE BOARD               *
*                                                         *
*  TO ALL YE  WHO SHALL HEAR THESE PRESENT BLESSINGS, BE IT *
*                                                         *
*  KNOWN THAT THE _____ FAMILY BESTOWS THE HONORARY *
*                                                         *
*  TITLE AND POSITION OF:                                 *
*                                                         *
*                     CHAIRPERSON                         *
*                                                         *
*     OF THE FAMILY REUNION EXECUTIVE BOARD OF THE        *
*                                                         *
*              _____FAMILY UPON              *
*                                                         *
*         _____               *
*                        NAME                             *
*                                                         *
*                      *AMEN*                             *
*                                                         *
*************************************************************
```

```
*************************************************************
*                  CERTIFICATE OF OFFICE                  *
*            FAMILY REUNION EXECUTIVE BOARD               *
*                                                         *
*  TO ALL YE  WHO SHALL HEAR THESE PRESENT BLESSINGS, BE IT *
*                                                         *
*  KNOWN THAT THE _____ FAMILY BESTOWS THE HONORARY *
*                                                         *
*  TITLE AND POSITION OF:                                 *
*                                                         *
*                     SECRETARY                           *
*                                                         *
*     OF THE FAMILY REUNION EXECUTIVE BOARD OF THE        *
*                                                         *
*              _____FAMILY UPON              *
*                                                         *
*         _____               *
*                        NAME                             *
*                                                         *
*  DATE_____    _____      *
*                          HONORABLE CHAIRPERSON          *
*                      *AMEN*                             *
*                                                         *
*************************************************************
```

```
*******************************************************************
*                    CERTIFICATE OF OFFICE                       *
*              FAMILY REUNION EXECUTIVE BOARD                     *
*                                                                 *
*   TO ALL YE  WHO SHALL HEAR THESE PRESENT BLESSINGS, BE IT      *
*                                                                 *
*   KNOWN THAT THE _____ FAMILY BESTOWS THE HONORARY       *
*                                                                 *
*   TITLE AND POSITION OF:                                        *
*                                                                 *
*                        TREASURER                                *
*                                                                 *
*       OF THE FAMILY REUNION EXECUTIVE BOARD OF THE              *
*                                                                 *
*                    _____FAMILY UPON                 *
*                                                                 *
*              _____             *
*                            NAME                                 *
*                                                                 *
*   DATE_____        _____     *
*                                   HONORABLE CHAIRPERSON         *
*                                                                 *
*                                _____     *
*                                      SECRETARY                  *
*                                                                 *
*                         *AMEN*                                  *
*                                                                 *
*                                                                 *
*******************************************************************
```

   We have completed the first part of the organization of the family reunion. We have taken part in the democratic process of choosing the permanent board for the family. The FREB has the green light to get started on making the family reunion a reality.

   The reunion should be an occasion that everyone cherishes and makes a commitment to attend once every year. The attendance of family reunions by the entire family will be a direct reflection of how well the **Family Reunion Executive Board** plans, motivates, and encourages the cooperation of the family members. If the **Family Reunion Executive Board** is bickering and arguing among themselves, you can be sure that a low attendance will be the result.

   If the central figure is the type of person that only desires to exert his/her influence when the reunion is in his/her state, the other times will be less successful. That is the main reason for choosing a good central figure who clearly understands the need for full participation each and every year.

   Our **Family Reunion Executive Board** must promote love, respect and commitment from the family to make the reunion a must in their annual schedules.   They must be able to reach the children and the elders, the wise and the knowledgeable, the fast and the slow.   It does not take three geniuses, but people who let the love from their hearts shine for the sake of the entire family.   The love for the family must come from within.

The Board must be willing to sacrifice a lot of their time to make the family better.   The Board must have the flexibility to change for the better with the times.   They should be able to look into tomorrow to make the present brighter.   A Board with a vision is a Board with a mission: **unite the family and save the world from vanishing.**

Love of our family is the key word.   Even though mistakes will be made because we are all human, our love for our family will see us through. So, do not be afraid to let your love blossom.   Each year we can try to improve on the next family reunion. Fun and devotion are our themes.

We will have a Board that is blessed to have the foresight to organize a family reunion that will bring our family together as a harmonious and caring family.   We should emerge from each family reunion being a little better organized and having a little more love in our hearts for one another within the family and more concern for our community.

Each year our family will look at the pictures of all of the family members singing, swimming, and dancing.   We will think about all of the things that went right and learn from our mistakes and avoid them in the next reunion.   We will not be perfect, but will try to look at the moon on our way home from the family reunion and start the planning process for next year.   We want to keep having family reunions and the sooner our committees begin the planning for the next time around - like today - the better.

PLANNING

Why we should have a Family Reunion.

Planning can be as simple as saying the ABC's of the alphabet, or as complex as trying to build the Golden Gate Bridge.   Let us make our planning arrangements very simple and direct. Do not hesitate to call upon other members of the family to give a helping hand.

We want to make all of the planning, engagements and obligations as painless as possible.   This note is especially important to those families planning their first reunion: be plain, ordinary, and practical.

But first we want to think about why we want to have a

family reunion in the first place. Basically we would think that the answer would be obvious to all of us. However, the answer is not as simple as it may seem. We want to dispel the thought that it is simply a matter of getting a whole bunch of bodies with the same blood together to have a lot of fun. Yes, fun should be included but along with some real meaningful reasons.

We want to allow our children to form a close linkage with all of their other relatives that they may never have seen, only heard accounts of from different members in the immediate family. These children deserve to let their hearts find the love that sometimes hinders the parents from associating with different members of the family. We would like to believe that this would never be the case, but the newspapers often headline hideous crimes committed against the family by family members every day.

Has anyone ever thought about the damage done to a family when one of its senior members kills another family member? Or what it feels likes to be a young person in a family that had a senior member sell all of his/her portion of the family stock to the public and cause havoc to the remaining members of the family? Or what it's like when a brother set up his own brother so the police could make an arrest causing the brother to serve time in prison? Or what it's like to be the police chief's daughter who finds a burglar in her home, only to discover that the police arrested her own brother who was stealing to support a drug habit?

These are examples of some of the reasons why we might allow our children to be caught up in our own prejudice against family members. But we must have enough maturity and reason to allow our children to form links with descendants of disgraced family members and not restrict or influence these alliances.

Second, the elder members of the family can gain a sense of well-being when they are in a family where the entire family seeks ways of providing for their needs and support. We do not need the government, old folks homes, and other ways of putting the elder members of our family on the shelf to die lonely deaths. The family reunion helps reinforce this concept.

Third, many times families which have a lot of members are able to pull the family together to grow to its fullest potential. They explore in the areas of business planning, problem solving, and spiritual revival. They enjoy the opportunity to have a family reunion to reward those members who have been useful in making the family grow together as a family and prosper as a business.

Special occasions for the family reunion.

Our families are always enjoying some type of special occasion. Birthdays, weddings, baby showers, and anniversaries are good events to organize our reunions around for a happy beginning.

For example, my family planned a reunion around our parents' 50th **wedding anniversary.** My younger brother is an ordained minister. He actually gave them their vows all over again. This occasion was full of all the joy of a wedding. Everyone there was moved by the emotion and specialness of the occasion. My parents and the entire family especially enjoyed this reunion.

Then one time we planned a family reunion around a **birthday,** my father's birthday. He is in his early eighties. We gathered for his birthday celebration with all the splendor we could imagine. The thing that amused me the most at this reunion was all of the fun the children got out of the event. They just radiated with enthusiasm.

What about a **baby shower** for that newcomer whose arrival was planned just in time for the family reunion? We cannot wait to welcome the newest member to the family set. Who could resist the idea of celebrating this moment with the entire family?

Anniversaries are special to all of us, whether it is the 10th anniversary of our astronaut's walk in space, or the first anniversary of our family reunion. We can always get the family together for what we wish to be a fun-filled and special event for the entire family.

Holidays such as Thanksgiving loan us an excuse to celebrate with all of the trimmings of turkey and dressing while we share family tales at the table with the entire group. Sometimes the holiday may have too many activities itself for us to try to include in a family reunion. Christmas is a time that everyone wants to enjoy, but most people have so much to do. It is also a time when most people find themselves lonely. Now, we do not want any of our family members lonely at Christmas time. Do we?

Funerals are times that bring the family together. We can plan an impromptu family reunion around the funeral while everyone is together. This is a time to remember that the family should not wait until grieving occurs in order to unite the family.

There is a particular point to be made at the funeral. The point is for us to get together as a family, starting now. Have someone get the current phone numbers and addresses of everyone. Take pictures to share with different family groups that will be distributed to all of the family. These pictures are great conversation pieces.

Now that we have a few ideas to plan our family reunion around, let us keep moving and plan what to do next.

Committees

Establishing The Host Committee. We have already chosen the members of the **Family Reunion Executive Board,** the permanent board that will be over all the other committees each year. Next, let us choose the Host Committee.

The Host Committee is a committee that may change each year when the family chooses a different town to host its reunion and possibly even a different state. Each family, no matter how small, should strongly consider having a reunion in a different location, even a different town. Why? This keeps the family growing in its experiences, always excited about the latest family adventures.

If your family is more comfortable with having the reunion in the same place each year, and you are able to maintain the excitement and anticipation, then go right ahead with your successful plans. What makes your family happy is your first rule. Do not feel that your family has to jockey all over the town or the world to be happy. If I may make a suggestion here, though, consider just once having a reunion in a different culture, in a foreign land. Wouldn't that be great?

The Host Committee **elects** a president, secretary and treasurer that coordinate all of their activities with the **Family Reunion Executive Board.** The Board steps aside and allows the Host Committee to organize festivities in the town designated to host the reunion. Now when the Board steps aside, it is not a complete hands-off situation; the board is still involved, but not as heavily when a host commitee is installed. We are ready to mail the **Host Commlttee Choice Letter** to the members of the family to indicate their interest in participating in the actual administration of the family reunion.

LIST OF COMMITTEES

CHECK HERE	TITLE OF COMMITTEE	NOTES
	A. HOST	
	B. TRAVEL	
	1. TRANSPORTATION	
	2. HOUSING ACCOMMODATIONS	
	C. WELCOMING	
	D. ENTERTAINMENT	
	1. INDOOR ACTIVITIES	
	2. OUTDOOR ACTIVITIES	
	E. PICNIC	
	F. RAFFLE - HOST/HOSTESS	
	G. CEREMONIES	
	H. SCHOLARSHIP AND AWARDS	
	I. SPIRITUAL/CHURCH	
	J. VOTING	
	K. COMMUNICATION	
	L. NUTRITION	
	M. PLANNING AND ADVISORY	
	1. CHAIRPERSON	
	2. SECRETARY	
	3. TREASURER	

COMMITTEE LETTERS AND FORMS

CHECK HERE	TITLE OF LETTER OR FORM	NOTES
	HOST COMMITTEE LETTER	
	COMMITTEE FORMATION LETTER	

HOST COMMITTEE CHOICE LETTER

Dear Family Member:

Now that we have decided to have a family reunion, we can have fun together planning the actual event by all of us organizing to do some of the initial tasks which make every-thing run smoothly. To start, we need only three of us to inform the rest how to make our reunion a reality.

Chairperson, Secretary, and Treasurer are the positions we need volunteers for now. I am willing to be one of the volunteers to fill any of the first three positions or to serve wherever I am needed. When you reply to this letter, please express your willingness to serve on any of the above positions, wherever the need may be, or express what you would like to do in the way of providing some services for picnics, entertainment, church planning, cooking, or other activities that go along with having our family reunion.

There will be more information to follow this letter after you have returned to me, within seven days, the activity that is of interest to you.

Please complete the form by indicating your choice with a check mark in the space provided and return this portion of the letter within seven days.

_____Yes   I. We would like to have a family reunion and we are interested in serving in the following position(s):

a._____ Chairperson

b._____ Secretary

c._____ Treasurer

_____Yes   II. We would like to have a family reunion and we would like to be available for services where we are needed. Please send us more information as to what other services are available.

_____Other III. _____

_____

God love and blessing,

_____
Honorable Chairperson

_____Family _____Annual Family Reunion

COMMITTEE FORMATION LETTER

Hello Family Member(s),

We are in the planning stage of our ____ ANNUAL FAMILY REUNION and we want to know who in the family would enjoy participating on some of the various committees that need volunteers.

A list of the various committees has been included and you may place your name next to the activity that you find of interest.

Please complete the form and return it to us within seven days in the enclosed self-addressed envelope.

Very sincerely yours,

_____
Honorable Chairperson

_____*Family* _____*ANNUAL FAMILY REUNION*

One thing we should remember above everything else is to keep our organization and planning very simple. Forget about all of the forms and all of the formalities until our family is ready for it. It means more to our families for us to go from our hearts and souls and get in touch with ourselves. Keep humble and avoid the unforgiving heart. Avoid false pride and phony airs.

Our pride shall rest on how well the member with the least amount of material, financial, and personal resources benefits from the association with his/her relatives. We may be proud of all the big names, politicians, doctors, and movie stars that make up our family. But it does not mean a thing if one of our brothers is in the bread line or dying in an alley in a big city because we are ashamed of him and have allowed him to be there. Or we have written off one of our sisters as a prostitute and dope addict because of our foolish pride.

Unless we can put the lawyer next to the bums and our family can brag about them with the same amount of vigor, we have done nothing. Our focus and joy shall be on the weakest link of our family, because our family is as strong as the weakest link. We must learn to organize our efforts around our **lost sheep.** We must **communicate** with them. Let us turn to some suggestions on communications that our family will employ in its efforts.

CHAPTER II

II. COMMUNICATION

A. SENDING THE WORD

    1. Writing a Letter to Spread the Word

    2. Sending the Word in the Mail

    3. Electronic Mail

    4. Telephone

    5. Word of Mouth

B. COMMUNICATION LETTERS AND FORMS

    1. List of Letters and Forms

    2. Letters

    3. Forms

    4. Postscript

COMMUNICATION

SENDING THE WORD

Writing a Letter to Spread the Word

The letter should be warm and friendly with kind words asking family members to come together and have a few days of family fun. Make the letter short and to the point. Use words that are easy to comprehend and understand. The letter should be like a little fireside chat to come together. We need to write from a sincere heart with love. We want our family to come to a certain location for a few days once a year and we want to foster feelings of unity from the beginning.

We should make our plans so as to bring joy to our families for generations to come. We want to have pleasurable memories that should begin now. Our first letter to members of our family is easy to write. We need not worry a great deal about the punctuation and spelling. The family members that will receive our letters are happy to hear that someone in the family cares enough to bring all of the members together for fun, entertainment, and unity.

Handwriting, Printing, or Typing the Letter. The warmth of a handwritten letter is felt by all who receive the letter. It can reach the heart and say so much with so little. A down-home feeling is often conveyed in handwritten letters. A page or two asking the family to come together is clear. We do not need big words to spell out the message; keep it simple. We do not need fancy writing paper to say, "Come together." The simpler we keep the letter, the better we are in our communication.

Printing the letter by hand is probably an alternative to choose if we have trouble with handwriting that is not clear and legible to those who will be reading the letter. Printing a letter has advantages. We can give more people the opportunity to understand our letter. Of course, we can understand our own writing, but can those on the receiving end understand it too? Ask someone to read your handwriting; if they have trouble understanding any part of it, then do not hesitate to print the letter to your family members.

Typing the letter can offer the clearest form of writing for the reader. What it lacks in warmth can be compensated for by the clarity of the typed words on paper. Sometimes, if our family is small, we should think of typing a letter after the first few letters have been written or printed by our own hands. Or, if our family is more used to the personal touch we should blend typewritten letters in with handwritten letters.

There are so many different kinds of **typewriters** on the

market that offer many options in type styles, memory, and programming, that it may be difficult to choose a typewriter to use to spread the word. Keep in mind that if we do not already have a typewriter and the duty of being the secretary will shift to someone else for the next year, we should make every effort to keep all expenses at the lowest possible. The family reunion should not be a burden or a chore to anyone. It should be something we do with joy in our hearts. So, it would be far better to print or write by hand than to create a debt that we will regret in the future.

Personal computers have become more popular today. If we have the need for a personal computer, then there are several functions to obtain from the use of it. We may purchase software packages for word processing that give us the capability of writing a master letter that can be made to be very personal. The software programs have a way of inserting each person's name, address, nickname, etc. in the right place for that not so form letter or business look.

Now, if we know that we are going to be the secretary for a long time, and we cherish this duty, then, by all means, make a wise investment in the selection of a good typewriter that will be of service for years and years to come. For example, I purchased a typewriter about 15 years ago that is still as good as new. The typewriter has been of great benefit to me in school, work, and in doing the letters for my family reunions.

But, I also discovered the many advantages that my personal computer has over the use of the typewriter. The items that I had to get for the personal computer were: a monitor, printer, software packages for word processing, diskettes for storage of material and a surge protector. I do not want anyone to become discouraged by thinking that the purchase of a typewriter or all of the items for a computer is necessary. Remember, when we organize our first reunion, all we need is paper and pencil.

Whichever method we choose: whether handwriting for warmth, the personal touch, and for the early stages; or printing by hand; or typing; we need to get the ball rolling. It may be necessary to sit down and call one or more of our relatives to help us break the ice. At one time of another, many of us have had a fear of writing. We think people can see right through us and can pierce our thin tissues. We may even feel that we are ignorant and illiterate. We need not feel all of those ways that I just mentioned, because when it's our time to be on the receiving end of the letter, we're very glad to get the word of when and where the family reunion is going to be held. So, just do your very best and do not worry about whether your punctuation is correct. Do not worry about the possibility of someone thinking that we are dumb or stupid. Most of us feel a little inadequate when it comes to writing. Let us not worry about all of these fears.

Instead let us keep the mail flowing from our hearts to all of the family, and we will be guaranteed that we will reach the hearts of all the family.

Relax and let us do our best to spread the word by letter; that is all anyone can ask of us.

Sending the Word in the Mail

Whether we use a postage stamp or we obtain a postage meter depends upon the long range objectives of the family's communication committee. My family has used regular postage stamps for the envelopes.

The licking of the glue side of the stamps often discouraged me from wanting to use stamps until I discovered that a wet sponge in a small glass bowl was better for me.

We can buy stamps at the post office that convey special messages like love or peace, or have the faces of men and women who have made positive contributions to humanity. These stamps are our way of expressing support for the post office giving recognition to persons and ideas that are positive.

Postage meters. Using the postage meter has been beneficial to families that have several hundreds of letters go out to many members of their family. Meter stamps may be used to prepay reply postage on first-class letters and postcards which do not exceed 12 ounces, or single piece, special fourth-class mail.

If your family decides to use a postage meter, the meter stamps must be printed directly on the envelope, postcard, or label, and the item must bear the return address of the meter license holder.

Meter manufacturers lease meters to our families for their mailing use. The U. S. Postal Service holds the manufacturers responsible for the control, operation, maintenance, and replacement, when necessary, of meters manufactured by them. Contact the Postal Service in your community for a current list of authorized manufacturers in your area.

A license to use a postage meter must be obtained from the post office for an annual fee of about $50.00. The family must keep the license in a safe location until the meter is returned to the manufacturer who makes sure that the postage meter is properly closed out for any credit that may be due for unused postage.

Setting the meter for additional postage is done by taking the meter to the post office. The family would give the amount of money to the clerk for the amount of postage to be set in the meter for postage. When the meter gets down to $9.99, it will stop operating until more postage has been set in the meter. It is a good idea to keep about $100.00 worth of postage in the meter.

Avoiding the payment of postage through tampering with or misusing a meter is punishable by law. This is something our families do not want to inadvertently do. So, if there is a problem with the proper operation of the meter, call the service section of your manufacturer to get the proper repair and avoid any unnecessary problems with the authorities.

The advantages of a postage meter vary with the particular family needs. Some of the advantages are:

1. The family can purchase a large amount of postage at one time and save on fuel costs by not making several trips to the post office;

2. The meter has provisions for the use of an advertisement plate that could be used to convey a family logo or special family reunion message, like, **HAPPY FAMILY REUNION,** or **MC KENZIE 1ST ANNUAL FAMILY REUNION.**

3. The postage-metered mail gets priority over regular mail, if the postal service requirements are met.

4. The postage meter eliminates the need to lick a lot of stamps or have to use a wet sponge.

Keep in mind that there are some **disadvantages to the postage meter.** They are:

1. The safekeeping, maintenance, and supplies for the postage meter are an expense to the family.

2. The meter costs money, around $20.00 a month, just for the rental fee that is paid to the manufacturer who leases the postage meter to your family;

3. The annual fee (around $50.00) is paid to the post office for the license to use the postage meter.

Some general information on bulk mail. A family reunion where there will be the need to do several large mailings will probably want to consider the use of bulk mail. Here are a few of the main requirements to ponder in making your decision to use this service. I have found this service to be extremely valuable for large mailings.

Now is a good time to tell your family that all of these postal service rules and regulations seem impossible at first, but do not be dismayed, because the post offices throughout the United States offer classes during their hours of operation to help family members to learn the correct way to get the bulk mail to all of its members in an efficient manner. The classes usually last four hours.

A minimum quantity of 200 pieces or 50 pounds is required for each mailing.

Weight and size. All pieces must be identical in size and number of enclosures. The maximum weight of each piece of third- class mail is 15.99 ounces. Pieces must be rectangular and not less than 3 1/2 inches wide (high) or 5 inches long, and at least 0.007 inches thick. (Note: Mailings of non-identical pieces can be made at the regular bulk rate. The permit imprint systems can be used only on non-identical bulk rate mailings at the pound rates of postage. What have I said here? Contact the Post Office if your mailings are not identical so that they can review the rules, **otherwise, make all of the envelopes identical** -- say the same thing, look alike, and match each other.

The bulk mailing fee is $50.00 which must be paid each calendar year by any family who mails at the bulk third-class rate.

Zip codes are required to be on all bulk rate third-class mail; the bulk mail must have the **correct zip code** in the address. The post office will not accept the bulk class mail that does not have a zip code.

The sealing of third-class mail must be done so that postal inspection is possible without destroying the envelope. Usually the edge of the envelope is lightly sealed to allow convenient postal inspection. Whenever the family mails sealed articles at the third-class rates of postage, it is deemed to be with the consent of the mailer to postal inspection of the contents. The clerk will periodically open and examine a few pieces of the mail to make sure all of the enclosures are identical.

Foreign mailings at the bulk third-class rate are not available. This is a domestic privilege.

Lottery material, including Bingo, games of chance, raffles, door prizes, etc. is not permitted to be mailed. Postal law prohibits the mailing of such material. Any questionable material should be discussed with your family's community post office.

Postage payment. There are three (3) options available for payment of postage by the family who chooses to use bulk mail:

A postage meter machine is the first option. If your family does not have one, refer to the yellow pages of your telephone directory and look under "Mailing Machine & Equipment" for listings of meter manufacturers. Your family must contact the manufacturer to make arrangements for the lease or rental of the meter. Since the family has to order an ad plate/slug that reads BULK RATE for insert, this is a good time to add your family reunion logo to the insert. The marking <u>Blk</u> <u>Rte</u> must appear as a part of the meter stamp impression.

In order for a family to use a postage meter for bulk mailing the Mail Classification Office must be notified, a record of the family's meter license must be registered with the post office in the city of mailing, and the annual bulk mail fee must be paid.

Precanceled stamps or precanceled envelopes are the second option. Precanceled stamps are adhesive postage stamps that must be individually affixed to each piece. Precanceled stamps show two highly visible bars drawn through the face of the stamp. A Permit must be obtained as authorization to purchase this type of stamp. There is no fee for the permit itself; however, when mailing at discounted rates, the annual bulk mail fee must be paid.

The family must be aware of the fact that precanceled stamps are sold in coils of 500 stamps and can be purchased only at certain post offices. The correct marking "Bulk Rate" must appear on the precanceled stamps or precanceled envelopes. If the correct marking does not appear, the family may rubber stamp or have printed the words "Bulk Rate" above or below the precanceled stamp.

The family using precanceled stamps or precanceled stamped envelopes must always show a complete return address on the front of the piece. This includes the permit holder's name, physical address, city, state, and zip code.

The third option is the Permit Imprint indicia which costs the family a one-time fee of $50.00 (which is required for an application to mail material without affixing postage stamps, specifying each city where mail will be sent).

Identification. In order to avoid mailings being made by individuals or commercial enterprises which are not qualified to mail at special bulk third-class rates, the mailing pieces must bear the name and return address of the authorized permit holder in a prominent location. Bogus names of persons or organizations may not be used. If the mailing pieces bear a name and return address, it must be that of the authorized permit holder. If the mailing pieces do not bear a name and return address, the message must contain in a prominent location the name and return address of the authorized permit holder.

Your family may have its Communication Committee select a representative to visit the post office. The post office has classes, materials, and publications to help your family get started. At first, all the regulations will seem impossible, but your family will discover that it is easier after each mailing. Also, your post office may have some very **helpful** and resourceful people that really care about your family having a successful reunion.

If the prices seem staggering and too high for your family's present use, just review the various mailing options and use what is practical for your budget at this time. As more of your family members join your mailing list in future years, you may decide to use the more involved mailing procedures.

Business Reply Mail (BRM). We can use the business reply mail envelopes for our family's return mail. What we do here is mail a letter with an envelope enclosed for the family to return to the Communication Committee. The BRM envelopes can be inserted in the letter so that family members can respond to various request forms that we send them, to let us know if they are coming to the reunion and to reply to other important matters.

The thought is to shift the expenses to the various committees and away from the individual family members. It makes it pretty easy for someone to fill out a questionnaire and mail it back to us in an envelope that does not require the person to pay the postage. Let us pause for a moment to go over some of the U. S. Postal Service requirements for using the BRM.

Briefly, BRM service enables a family Communication Committee to receive first-class mail back from the members of the family by paying the postage on the mail that is returned to them. The permit holder of the Communication Committee guarantees payment of the correct first-class postage plus a handling charge per piece on all returned BRM distributed under the permit holder's permit number.

Distribution of business reply cards, envelopes, self-mailers, cartons and labels may be done by a valid BRM permit holder in any quantity for return to any post office in the United States and its territories and possessions, including military post offices overseas. Domestic BRM **must not** be sent to <u>any foreign countries.</u>

Permit application for BRM and an Annual Renewal Notice are required by the Communication Committee in order to become and remain a permit holder. The annual permit fee is $50.00, which must be submitted to the post office issuing the permit. The postmaster will provide the proper form. The postmaster will complete the permit portion of the form, assign the permit number and issue a receipt. The postmaster has various publications to provide the family with instructions on how to properly prepare the mail for BRM. Classes are also available free of charge which last about four hours.

Remember, the BRM is not required for your family re-unions. However, the use of BRM saves the individual family members money and usually results in a greater percentage of returned forms.

Permit Imprint. Permit Imprint indicia is another method for a family to use to get the word to the whole family. A one-time fee of $50.00 is required for an "Application To Mail Without Affixing Postage Stamps" in each city where mail will be deposited. The postal service will automatically set up an advance deposit trust account for the permit holder upon receipt of payment for the permit imprint application. The family must pay the application fee in addition to the annual bulk mailing fee. So there is an initial cost of $100.00 to establish the permit imprint system (indicia) for third-class bulk mailing.

The Communication Committee would have to make at least one mailing during a twelve month period; otherwise the family permit imprint number would be canceled for non-use.

The Committee must deposit funds for each mailing at the designated finance unit prior to presenting mail there. Funds may be deposited in advance to cover more than one mailing.

Permit Imprint indicia must be prepared in accordance with definite postal requirements. For example, absolutely no circles, stars, triangles, or similar forms are permitted.

Deviation from this rule may result in rejection of the entire mailing at the time of mailing. Indicia may be made by printing press, hand stamping, lithography, mimeograph, multigraph, addressograph or similar device. They may not be typewritten or hand-drawn directly on the mailing piece. Permit Imprints indicate that the postage has been paid for the items on which they appear.

Electronic Mail

With the advances made in home computers, some families may have a budget that will allow for the use of electronic mail. The family may acquire a software package that will enable it to connect up with companies that are set up to transmit letters from computers at one location to other locations. The letters can be transmitted from the family keyboards and converted to hard copy for receipt at the other end. Electronic mail can be expensive if families have to purchase equipment for this purpose. If the family has the equipment, then this would be a good idea to employ.

For example, Western Union has an electronic mailing service called **Easy-Link.** This service is used with the home computer. The family needs a computer, monitor, modem and software package. The modem allows for telephone to computer connection.   The software package is provided for $150.00 by Western Union to be used with a special coded number provided for your family.   Once you have obtained the basics, then electronic mail is ready for sending out messages, letters and memos to the entire family.

Western Union has different types of user accounts.   Generally, a charge is billed to the user each time the family logs on to the Easy-Link service, $.45 to $.75 per minute. Then there is a flat charge for sending the electronic mail.

Easy-Link has a way of sending several letters to many locations at the same time.   This way the Communication Committee could have a designated member in each state or city spread the word by telephone, local mail or personal visit. The system can be designed whereby communication is encouraged.   The more friendly and cordial the contacts between family members, usually the warmer the family reunion.

Sometimes spreading the word can foster good will and joy among members of the family.   It may have been months or even longer since some family members have communicated with each other.   We need to create avenues to help warm conversation flow between the members of the family.

Telephone

The fastest way of talking directly with members of our family is via the telephone.   Presently, many cities have phone carriers that provide for discount calling during non-busy times such as late in the evening, Saturdays and Sundays.

Competition has also introduced many long distance carriers that offer special low rates for long distance calls via some of the local telephone companies.   These rates can provide savings to families that wish to use the telephone to spread the word.

Conference calling allowing three members of the family to be connected on the same phone link to discuss the family plans can be done without using the operator.   The telephone customer has to pay extra money each month for the conference-calling feature.   Operator assistance is needed to make a conference call connecting several family members at the same time while they are in different cities or states.   One advantage of doing this is to inform key members at the same time who can then spread the word to others.

The telephone is a useful tool.   All calls can be properly noted on a long distance calling record which will give the family an idea of the expenses incurred.   Maybe one day the government will see the positive benefits of family reunions and provide legislation to allow for tax deductions for the expenses of the reunions.

By Word of Mouth

Direct communication with the families in one location by a key member of the Communication Committee is a positive achievement. For one thing, it encourages discussion and gives the members of the family the feeling of being a part. It raises members' self-esteem. Enthusiasm and unity are the main by-products of the discussion of ideas, plans and activities. At every possible level of planning, communication by word-of-mouth should be encouraged.

Whether the family uses letters or the telephone, word-of-mouth can be actively put into practice. Good results will be sure to follow this practice.

Communication is probably the easiest part of any family reunion, but is often neglected. We cannot rely solely on our letters, mailgrams, and other means of written communication; we must follow up with word-of-mouth to all the family members.

COMMUNICATION LETTERS AND FORMS.

LIST OF LETTERS AND FORMS

CHECK HERE	TITLE OF LETTER	NOTES
	INTRODUCTORY LETTER	
	MAILING LIST	
	FAMILY ADDRESS & TELEPHONE FORM	
	SENDING THE WORD TO OTHERS	
	FAMILY BIRTHDAY LIST	
	RESERVATION FORM	
	ANY PROBLEMS	
	DEADLINE	
	VACATION LEAVE REQUEST	
	RESERVATION CONFIRMATION	
	TEAM LETTER	
	"A FRIENDLY HELLO" (NAME TAGS)	

Letters

INTRODUCTORY LETTER

Dear Family member(s),

Our family is important to each one of us. By coming together once a year for a little family get-together we can share in the growth, joy and love of the little ones. We can bring comfort and companionship to the senior members. All of this we can do, plus much, much more.

We could have activities for everyone and marvelous food at our first annual family reunion. Time would be made for the kids to get reacquainted with all of their relatives. The adults could join in an old-fashioned outdoor picnic. The plans and arrangements can all be made very soon. An announcement with all the details will be mailed about twelve months prior to the reunion.

In the meantime, let us communicate with one another frequently.

Very sincerely yours,

_____
Honorable Chairperson

_____*Family* _____*Annual Family Reunion*

MAILING LIST

Dear Family Member(s),

We have inserted the most current mailing list of all of the nuclear families so we can write to each other before the next family reunion.

If there are any corrections to the Family Mailing List, print them on the enclosed form that will be used for making the updated list.

After your family has made the corrections, place the form in the self-addressed envelope which has been enclosed for your convenience and please return it within seven days; no postage is required.

Thank you in advance for your cooperation with our family request. Along with the many letters that we write, say a little prayer every chance you get for our family to be a blessed and closer family.

Very Sincerely Yours,

_____
Honorable Chairperson

_____*FAMILY* ____*ANNUAL FAMILY REUNION*

_____ FAMILY ADDRESS AND TELEPHONE LIST

Dear Family Member(s),

NAME: LAST_____FIRST_____MIDDLE_____

MAILING ADDRESS_____

CITY_____

STATE_____ZIP CODE_____

HOME ADDRESS_____

CITY_____

STATE_____ZIP CODE_____

HOME PHONE: AREA CODE_____NUMBER_____

BUSINESS ADDRESS_____

_____

CITY_____

STATE_____ZIP CODE_____

BUSINESS PHONE: AREA CODE _____NUMBER_____

This address list will provide the family historian with current addresses for the entire family. The information will be used by family members only and should be maintained in the most confidential manner by everyone. The list will be sent to the members of the family for correspondence purposes.

After your family has completed the form, place it in the self-addressed envelope which has been enclosed for your convenience and please return it within seven days; no post-age is required.

Thank you in advance for your cooperation with our family request.

Very Sincerely Yours,

Honorable Chairperson

_____FAMILY ____ANNUAL FAMILY REUNION_

SENDING THE WORD TO OTHERS

Dear Family Member,

Please help me get the word to everyone.   If you know of anyone who may desire to attend the FAMILY REUNION whose name does not appear on this mailing list, please complete the name label below.

NAME_____

STREET ADDRESS/P. O. BOX _____

CITY_____STATE_____ZIP_____

PHONE: AREA CODE_____   NUMBER_____-_____

NAME_____

STREET ADDRESS/P. O. BOX _____

CITY_____STATE_____ZIP_____

PHONE: AREA CODE_____   NUMBER_____-_____

NAME_____

STREET ADDRESS/P. O. BOX _____

CITY_____STATE_____ZIP_____

PHONE: AREA CODE_____   NUMBER_____-_____

NAME_____

STREET ADDRESS/P. O. BOX _____

CITY_____STATE_____ZIP_____

PHONE: AREA CODE_____   NUMBER_____-_____

NAME_____

STREET ADDRESS/P. O. BOX _____

CITY_____STATE_____ZIP_____

PHONE: AREA CODE_____   NUMBER_____-_____

FAMILY BIRTHDAY LIST

Dear Family Members,

Please take a moment to complete the birthday list of the members in your immediate family. This list will be compiled to obtain the birthdays in each nuclear family to be mailed to everyone in the entire family tree. The year of your birthday is optional; however it is sincerely requested that the year be included for the purpose of having a complete and accurate record for the family historian's record book. Your prompt attention to this matter will be appreciated. In advance, we thank you!

CHECK HERE:	NAME (S) LAST / FIRST / MIDDLE	BIRTHDAY: MO / DAY:	YEAR (Optional)
	FATHER/HUSBAND		
	MOTHER/WIFE		
	CHILDREN:		
	1.		
	2.		
	3.		
	4.		
	5.		
	6.		
	7.		

After your family has completed the form, please place it in the self-addressed envelope which has been enclosed for your convenience and return it within seven days; no postage is required.

Very sincerely yours,

Honorable Chairperson

_____ FAMILY ____ ANNUAL REUNION

RESERVATION FORM
MAIL TODAY

Dear Honorable Chairperson:

We plan to attend the _____*FAMILY* _____*ANNUAL FAMILY REUNION:*

PLEASE send me _____*tickets for the following members of my family (and my guests) whose names appear below.*

We have enclosed the necessary money in the form of:
_____*CHECK*
_____*MONEY ORDER*
_____*CASHIER'S CHECK*

Family Members: Please indicate your guests by placing a check mark in the "Guest" column after their names.

	NAME	:	CATEGORY :	AMOUNT :	FAMILY :	GUEST :
1.	_____	:	_____	_____	_____	_____
2.	_____	:	_____	_____	_____	_____
3.	_____	:	_____	_____	_____	_____
4.	_____	:	_____	_____	_____	_____
5.	_____	:	_____	_____	_____	_____

STREET ADDRESS_____

P.O. Box Number_____
CITY_____
STATE_____ZIP CODE_____

PHONE: AREA CODE_____   NUMBER_____-_____

Please return this stub in the self-addressed, stamped enve-lope enclosed in this letter, or mail this stub in your own envelope at your earliest convenience for the _____ *ANNUAL FAMILY REUNION, full of fun and joy for everyone. Don't wait until tomorrow, do it now, now! If you need additional time to pay or decide, please inform us.*

Very sincerely yours,

_____
Honorable Chairperson

_____*FAMILY* _____*ANNUAL REUNION*

ANY PROBLEMS LETTER

Dear Family Member,

The ____ ANNUAL _____ FAMILY REUNION is proceeding as planned, except we have recently noticed that your family reservation form has not been received. Perhaps some unexpected matter has contributed to your family having to contemplate attending our reunion.

Actually, we don't go around but once on this beautiful planet and we thought it would be nice if our children could get together with their cousins, and all the adults in our family could share in greeting one another without it being a sad occasion.

The Planning Committee will contact your family soon to provide assistance and to seek ways to help encourage your family's attendance. Our goal is to provide a family reunion which everyone finds enjoyable and to have all the members of our extended family in attendance to join in all the festivities.

If there are any problems that your family is experiencing that you feel may be alleviated by anyone else in the family, or by myself, please contact me soon.

Very truly yours,

Honorable Chairperson

_____FAMILY ____ANNUAL FAMILY REUNION

DEADLINE LETTER

Dear Family Member,

We know the pace of our modern society is hectic and perhaps your family forgot to mail the Reservation Form that was expected on _____.

If your family has not mailed the Reservation Form, please take this time to drop it in the mail in the pre-stamped, self-addressed envelope provided.

If your family will not attend this splendid event, will you please check which one(s) of the <u>reasons</u> listed below contributed to your family's decision? Or note in the space designated "Other" your reasons for not attending. Your answer will help us in planning a more successful family reunion next year when we hope you will be able to attend.

Also, if for some reason conditions change to allow your family to attend our reunion, please accept this letter as our special invitation to let your family know that we really love you and desire your presence for whatever time you have available even if you can only be with us for the closing ceremonies.

We will miss your family and wish there was something more that we could do to make it possible for you to be present. May God bless your family.

REASONS FOR NOT ATTENDING THE REUNION

```
Illness  ___              No clothes ___
No money ___              Other:
No transportation ___       1. _____
No vacation time   ___       2. _____
```

Very truly yours,

_____
Honorable Chairperson

_____*FAMILY* _____*ANNUAL FAMILY REUNION*

VACATION LEAVE REQUEST

DATE: _____

TO: Supervisor_____

FROM: _____

SUBJECT: <u>Vacation</u> <u>Leave</u> <u>Request</u>

Dear Supervisor:

In advance, I request a vacation leave to start on _____, 19__, at __:__ a.m. and to extend until _____, ____, at __:__ p.m., a total of __ hours from my accumulated time. My extended family is planning to celebrate our _____ annual family reunion which will require my immediate family and myself in attendance for this grand occasion.

I will appreciate your earliest approval of my vacation leave request prior to _____, 19__, which will allow me sufficient time to submit my reservation confirmation to my extended family.

If there appears to be any scheduling difficulties, please advise me so that I can make up the work in advance or in some other way resolve the conflict and attend this very important gathering of my family.

Thank you in advance for your kind consideration of my request.

Sincerely yours,

_____
Employee

_____ *FAMILY* _____ *ANNUAL FAMILY REUNION*

RESERVATION CONFIRMATION

Reservation confirmation is made for:

NAME _____

NAME _____

NAME _____

NAME _____

NAME _____

NAME _____

NAME _____

NAME _____

to attend the many wonderful activities of our family reunion with lots of fun and joy for everyone.

We will see your family and/or guests:

CITY _____

STATE _____

TIME _____

DATES:

From _____

To _____

We thank you for taking the time to invest in making our family a closer and better family which also helps our community, country and our world. We eagerly look forward to enjoying family festivities.

_____
Honorable Chairperson

_____FAMILY _____ANNUAL FAMILY REUNION

TEAM LETTER

Dear Family Member(s):

The team concept as applied to family reunions is a very effective technique for bringing families closer. This concept helps encourage, motivate, and initiate more communication between the members of the families. It is friendly and open in nature.

Let's examine how this concept works from the most basic point of view. Members of the families are matched up according to the following principles: First, outgoing members are paired up with shy members.

Second, members are paired up with those who are closest in age. Generally, those who are close in age are more communicative and have shared a closer relationship growing up. They share more of a common bond during the growth years that can be beneficial in bringing members of the family together in a reunion.

Third, a very motivated member is teamed up with a uninterested member. This provides a real challenge to the motivated member. Think of all the politicians, ministers, and community workers who have given up on the challenge of bringing their families together. They have written their families off as a bad investment, and off they go into the community preaching their community-love hypocrisy. There are many corporate leaders who are quite capable of organizing large conglomerates across cities, states, and national borders, yet they completely refuse to labor in their families to bring about family love, unity and pride. It's no wonder that so many of our young people are completely
confused and misguided, what with having the television as a companion, the maid as a mother, and no one as a father. Even athletic figures are disenchanting many youths who can't understand why someone who purportedly has it all discards his or her life on drugs, alcohol or other vices.

We have all forgotten the basic foundation that has made many nations great; the family must be preserved and nurtured with new meaning and vitality.

Honorable Chairperson

_____*FAMILY* _____*ANNUAL FAMILY REUNION*

Forms

A FRIENDLY HELLO
(Name Tags)

A FRIENDLY HELLO!

MY NAME IS _____

MY FAMILY NAME IS _____

CITY _____

STATE _____

HOBBY _____

A FRIENDLY HELLO!

MY NAME IS _____

MY FAMILY NAME IS _____

CITY _____

STATE _____

HOBBY _____

A FRIENDLY HELLO!

MY NAME IS _____

MY FAMILY NAME IS _____

CITY _____

STATE _____

HOBBY _____

SUPPLY LIST

CHECK HERE:	ITEM (S)	QUANTITY	NOTES
_____	Writing Paper		
_____	Paper Clips		
_____	Rubber Bands		
_____	Stamps		
_____	Envelopes		
_____	Pens		
_____	Pencils		
_____	Calculator		
_____	Erasers		
_____	3 x 5 Cards		
_____	Mailing List		
_____	Labels		
_____	File Folders		
_____	Tickets		
_____	Balloons		
_____	Scissors		
_____			
_____			
_____			
_____			

MAILING LABELS

```
:Your Name
:Your Street
:Your City, State
:   ZIP CODE
```

Postscript

When we put our pen down to reflect on the different choices in communicating with our family, we want to feel sure that we are trying our best to keep our letters, phone calls, and other ways of spreading the word very simple. **Keep it simple** will be the phrase to remember throughout our conversing.

We know we can write a letter by handwriting, printing by hand, or the use of the typewriter. The personal computer has many advantages in family reunion planning. As we continue in our quest to bring our family together, we can even blend in all of the advantages of the above choices. Use whatever is most effective for the occasion.

How do we mail our warm-hearted letters, postcards and brochures? We may want to use the plain old simple way of writing a letter and applying a stamp to the envelope at first. But as our family reunion messages make contact with our entire family tree, we will want to keep in mind additional ways of spreading the word. We can use postage meter machines after we have selected the meter from the manufacturer that we feel will give our family the best deal.

Precanceled stamps or precanceled envelopes may ease the way we efficiently get the mail out to the family. The Permit Imprint Indicia works much like precanceled stamps and envelopes in that it is an imprint indicating that postage has been prepaid.

When we have many of our family members that are waiting to receive the word of the family reunion and we have developed to the point of readiness for use of the Domestic Third-Class Matter at bulk rates we can cut our postage costs almost in half by utilizing this system of mailing. We want to remember that the Postal Service offers classes to our family members who are willing to help the family save costs.

Business Reply Mail (BRM) offers a way for the members of our family to just use the extra envelope that we enclosed inside the letter and get the reply form in the return mail. The BRM has already provided for the payment of the postage. All the family member has to do is mail the envelope back. This shifts postage and stationery costs from the family member to the Communication Committee.

Electronic mail made possible from Western Union and other carriers provides ways to key in our letters on a computer and spread the word swiftly by telegraph, telegram, or mailgram. Western Union sells a software package called "Easy-Link" which allows a family to get the word the same or next day. This method may be an easy way for the Board to connect up with various heads of committees in providing written confirmation to them. This should be available to large family reunions when the need arises.

The telephone provides that personal feeling of well-being when members hear the voices of their mothers, fathers, and other loved ones. The phone is one of the fastest ways for committees to keep in touch with one another. Various phone carriers have begun to make cheaper rates available to customers who call during discount rate times. We will want to call the telephone company that offers the most economical way with the most courteous, efficient service to our family.

Some letters for samples. We will want to use the letters found on different pages only as a guide. They are not meant to be the law. However if the letters express what we want to convey at that time, just photocopy the letter and fill in the empty blanks to customize them. There will be more letters to come to help make the committee work a little easier and more enjoyable.

If any one has a few letters of their own that he/she has found useful, then please feel free to provide me with your written consent to include them in the next book on family reunions.

Since we have overcome the task of communication and made it very easy, let us get on the road to the family reunion. After all, we may write the best letters, at the best prices, but if we do not get to the reunion, what good would it all have been? Please turn the page.

CHAPTER III

III. TRAVEL

A. TRAVEL AGENTS

1. American Society of Travel Agents (ASTA)

2. United States Tour Operators Association (USTOA)

B. TRANSPORTATION

1. Private Vehicle

2. Airplane

3. Bus

4. Train

5. Transportation Letters

C. HOUSING ACCOMMODATIONS

D. HOTEL ACCOMMODATIONS

E. CAMPING

F. CAMPING CHECKLISTS

G. DUDE RANCHES

H. TRAVEL CHECKLISTS

I. HOME INVENTORY LIST

TRAVEL

*If a rose had eyes, what do you
think it would say to each sunrise?
If a tree could travel, who do you
think it would go to greet?*

We are different from the flowers and the trees. When we get the chance, we should travel. It is a good idea to help our family develop. Having the family reunion in different locations can enrich our family experiences, whether the places change from town to town, state to state, or even from country to country. It is a big growth proposition. It is an opportunity for the family to grow and become familiar with different people, areas, environments, and settings.

We all gain something when we enlarge our horizons. We take a little from the place we are visiting, and in return, we give a little of ourselves. We meet each day on the road with exuberance and good will. What can we make of all of the experiences we gain from the places we visit? They all help us grow and prosper.

All of this is meant to be positive for our family. First, we need to think of the means of transportation we will use to get us to and from the family reunion. Will it be by air, train, or by vehicle? We want to learn about the people who specialize in providing services in relation to travel. Hotel accommodations, airplane reservations, river rafting tours, dude ranch reservations...all these and many more are considerations that come under travel. Let us examine a few of them now.

TRAVEL AGENTS

American Society of Travel Agents (ASTA)

Principles of Professional Conduct & Ethics. The American Society of Travel Agents, more commonly referred to as ASTA, is one of the watchdogs of travel agents. They are an organization that helps police the industry of travel agents in order that the degree of professionalism remains high. We are often told stories of how not to trust a travel agent. Well, many of the problems of the past caused by agents who abused the trust that the public placed in them have been eliminated. ASTA has created higher standards and money reserve requirements of its membership. Also, government legislation has had a part in making the industry more attuned to fairness in dealing with the public.

What does this mean to the family? It means that the family can make bookings in advance without all of the worries that the family had in the past. There are good people in the industry who want to help the family, and we can find them and put our trust in them. Many agents are becoming aware of the demands being made on the travel industry by families.

We need agencies like ASTA to continue doing the good job of keeping the travel industry honest and loyal to the family. We need travel agents to be concerned about the many families who need their services. ASTA has a code of conduct for its membership. Review the preamble and if your agent is not living up to the standards, drop a line to ASTA and let them know. On the other hand, be just as diligent in letting ASTA know about the agents who have gone out of their way to provide services that are above the normal call of duty. We should be just as quick to write a letter of compliment as we are to write a letter of dissatisfaction.

Principles of Professional Conduct & Ethics

Preamble

We live in a world in which travel has become increasingly important and intricate. The travel industry is now highly specialized and travelers, faced with a myriad of alternatives in transportation, accommodations and other travel services, must depend upon accredited travel agencies to guide them competently and honestly in the choices they must make. Similarly, carriers, hotels and other suppliers which appoint travel agencies to represent them depend upon the travel agency to follow the best traditions of salesmanship and ethical conduct. In recognizing the vital role of travel agencies, all ASTA travel agency members voluntarily pledge themselves to observe the spirit in all of their activities and to conduct their business in accordance with the following Principles of Professional Conduct and Ethics.

Part I: Travel Agency Relations with Consumers

1. ASTA members should attempt to ascertain and inform their customers of all pertinent facts concerning tours, transportation, accommodations or other travel services offered to consumers.

2. ASTA members should be factual and accurate when called upon to give an opinion of a service provider.

3. ASTA members should endeavor to keep their employees informed in an accurate and timely manner on domestic and international travel in order to give consumers competent travel advice and to secure for them travel services and accommodations suitable to their needs and desires.

4. ASTA members should try to protect consumers against any fraud, misrepresentation or deceptive practices in the travel

industry. Members should endeavor to eliminate any practices which could be damaging to consumers or to the dignity and integrity of the travel agency business.

5. ASTA members should   consider every transaction with a customer to be confidential unless the person authorizes disclosure or such disclosure is required by law.

6.   ASTA members should   advise their customers in writing about cancellation policies and any service charges prior to the time initial payment is made for any booking.

7.   ASTA members should avoid false and misleading statements and doubtful superlatives in their advertising.   Phrases such as "our services are free" or "it costs no more", or words of similar import should not be used unless such statements are true.

8. ASTA   members should clearly disclose to their customers their agency-principal relationship with service providers prior to the time initial payment is made.   In the event of a failure by a service provider to provide a service booked through an ASTA member, the member should assist its customers in trying to reach a satisfactory settlement of the matter with the service provider.

Part II: Travel Agency Relations With Service Providers (Carriers, Hotels and Other Industry Members)

9.   ASTA members should follow the best traditions of salesmanship and fair dealing by according fair, objective and impartial representation to all service providers which they represent.

10. ASTA members should   attempt to make themselves conversant with all applicable rules and regulations of service providers.   They should take appropriate steps so that their employees and representatives know of these rules.

11. ASTA members should not attempt in any illegal manner or through actions or means that violate the policies of a service provider to influence the employees of service providers for the purpose of securing preferential consideration in the assignment of space or for any other purpose.

12.   ASTA   members should release reserved, but unsold, space and return cancelled accommodations.   Members should refrain from suggesting or making duplicate bookings or reservations.

13. ASTA   members who undertake to recruit sales representatives or to franchise new locations should avoid misrepresentations and unrealistic promises in statements relating to such activities.

14. In the event of a complaint or grievance by a customer against a service provider, ASTA members should as a first step notify the service provider involved so that it may have an opportunity to resolve the matter.

What do we have to say about the above? Adherence to these Principles of Professional Conduct and Ethics signifies competence, fair dealing and high integrity. Failure to adhere to these principles may subject a member to disciplinary action, as set forth in ASTA's Bylaws.

Now, for the most part, travel agents take care of many of our travel needs. They specialize in trying to make the family comfortable in reaching its destination, whether it be by train, bus, or airline. They have the ability to make hotel reservations, arrange to have a vehicle at our destination, and suggest sights to see along the way that will make for a more enjoyable trip.

For example, when my boys and the rest of my family were traveling across the country, Southern California Automobile Club helped plot the trip. The travel agent that we had was very helpful in suggesting sightseeing adventures for the family. The agent had already visited some of the spots along our journey. He recommended inexpensive places to stay and affordable restaurants to dine in along the way. He made suggestions on areas to refuel for the best services available. The list grows longer of the many helpful services our agent provided.

When the family travel advisor selects a travel agent choose with great care, because a good travel agent can save the family money and help make the trip more pleasant. The size of the travel agent's company is not always significant. This I found out the hard way when I called American Express Travel Agency and was put on hold by rude and uncaring agents.

Sometimes a small travel company can best serve our family needs by assigning one agent to us who can get to know our concerns and worries and take care of them. After all, what do we need with a travel company if we have to do all the work and pay for the tickets and other accommodations anyway? The agents get their earnings from the airlines, tour operators, hotels, etc. they book for.

United States Tour Operators Association (USTOA)

Tour Operators' Code Tour operators function in the capacity of making arrangements for tours for the family that wishes to expand its horizons by including a tour in the family reunion package. For instance, the family of a friend of mine decided to have its reunion in the Bahamas. The family sought out a tour operator that would provide the most economical package for the family.

United States Tour Operators Association (USTOA) is the agency that sets standards for tour operators to operate by in their dealings with the public. A family will be delighted to know that many of the abuses that people suffered through unethical tour operators in the past have been eliminated. Let us review the tour operators guidelines for a moment.

Principles of Professional Conduct and Ethics

1. It is the responsibility of Active and Affiliated Active Tour Operator Members of the United States Tour Operators Association (USTOA) to conduct their business affairs forthrightly, with professional competence and factual accuracy.

2. Representations to the public and retailers shall be truthful, explicit, intelligible and avoid deception, and concealment or obscuring of material facts, conditions or requirements.

3. In advertising and quoting of prices for tours, the total deliverable price, including service charges and special charges, shall be stated or clearly and readily determinable; and the pendency of any known condition or contingency, such as fares subject to Conference and/or Government approval, shall be openly and noticeably disclosed.

4. Advertising and explanation of tour features shall clearly state and identify the facilities, accommodations and services included; any substitutions of features or deviation from the advertised tour shall be communicated expeditiously and the cause thereof be explained to agents and/or clients involved.

5. Each Active and Affiliated Active Tour Operator Member of USTOA shall so arrange and conduct its business as to instill retailer, consumer and public confidence in such Member's financial stability, reliability and integrity, and shall avoid any conduct or action conducive to discrediting membership in USTOA as signifying allegiance to professional and financial "Integrity in Tourism."

Do the standards make the person, or does the person make the standards? The critical concern here is for the family to realize that most tour operators take pride in providing a good service to the family. The tour operators want the family to have a good trip and to use their service again and again. They also want the family to tell other families about them so more good business will come their way. It is extremely important for the family to be on its best conduct also. It is a pleasure when hosts tell the tour operator that the family that visited their facilities was of the highest character, good-natured and pleasant to be around. This kind of respect makes everyone a winner. Let us get on the road.

TRANSPORTATION

Transportation should be planned far in advance to derive the best price discount. Try to make your arrangements with enough flexibility to take advantage of a better discount package that various airlines or other transporting carriers offer at different times. Usually, airlines have special rates available if families purchase their tickets far enough in advance. Listen to ads on the radio and TV to become aware of some of these special offers. Watch for ads in newspapers, especially the Sunday edition travel section of most papers. The travel section includes many interesting articles with good tips for the family to consider.

Go to the local or regional public library and look in the periodical section to obtain current copies of travel magazines which provide helpful information for the family travel plans. Take the entire family, but teach the children to keep any conversation to a minimum. Some libraries provide a study room which could be used to plot the trip and discuss the different plans for travel. Ask the librarian for help in finding recent articles on the places you want to visit.

My six-year-old son enjoys going to the library with me. He brings along some of his school homework to fill in the time while the research work is being done. When he gets a little older, he will have an opportunity to help his older brother with the research. Kids enjoy this type of outing. It helps teach them how to use the library. Reference librarians are on duty to help the family with difficult research questions and to explain where various magazines, books, and video cassettes are kept in the library. The library has many tools available to help the family in making their travel plans.

After the family has done its research, after it has visited libraries, travel agents, and clubs to learn about all the places the group wants to see, the family will have more assurance and confidence in making their needs and interests known to the travel agent. But our family can make the best preparations, and all will be useless unless we take care of our health.

Medical and health considerations are an important part of our early travel arrangements. For example, early September is the time my doctor gives me a flu shot to help me avoid a bad case of the flu during the winter months. The initial planning to avoid the flu is done months before the winter season approaches.

We need to see our doctor early in our family reunion planning to make a genuine effort to rid ourselves of any medical problems within human control. The doctor can make suggestions for the prevention of motion sickness and other travel problems. Getting an early start helps us to keep our health in the best condition all year long.

The health of each of our family members has a direct bearing on the overall enjoyment of the entire family. Each member of the family feels a deep closeness for other family members and no one wants to have anybody in their family experience medical illness of any kind.

Have your doctor do an electrocardiograph (E.K.G.) if you are thirty-five years of age or older. This is already a requirement for single-engine pilots to help detect certain medical defects at an early stage. Remember, the medical check-up is done early which helps reduce an expense later in the planning stage. I hope you do not consider your health a financial burden anymore than you might consider grocery bills an expense you cannot afford.

Good dental care is important to avoid having to spend an otherwise lovely family reunion at the dentist's office suffering untold pain. A toothache can be avoided if proper professional care and good dental hygiene are maintained.

Dental floss, tooth paste, toothbrushes and proper check-ups are a necessity. Proper dental care should be maintained at least twelve months prior to the reunion. We know that everyone is already doing this, making this brief reminder unnecessary.

Whatever mode of transportation is chosen, many families may not travel together for safety's sake. The wife and half the children may fly together on one airplane and be followed on the next by the husband and the rest of the children. Cases can be cited where bus, train and airplane accidents have occured and wiped out entire families. Car accidents of course are not excepted.

Private vehicle.

If you travel by auto, it is very important to have the car serviced before you go: oil change, filters, lubrication, tires rotated, and make sure your brakes are checked and you have a good spare. Sign up with a good emergency road service or auto club before you go. Take the precaution of having at least two good, dependable drivers. Get plenty of sleep before taking the trip.

Do not drink and drive! Plan to drive comfortably and safely even if it means taking more time and staying overnight at some motel while driving to or from the family reunion. Your trip will be far more pleasant, profitable, and **safe.** Sightseeing along the way makes the trip more interesting and worthwhile.

Vehicle Checkup.   We will need to do some things to prepare our vehicle for the trip.   We need to focus on the proper maintenance and care of our vehicle.   Here are a few items to consider for the preparation of our vehicle.   Check with a good mechanic for more ideas.

   Spare Tire.   A spare tire is one item that is probably taken for granted more often than any other necessity of travel on the road.   Many times we just automatically assume that the spare tire is in perfect condition just like it was when we purchased the vehicle, the last time we checked it. Do not be surprised to discover that the spare tire has lost some air pressure.   A note on rental cars: make sure you ask for the location of the spare tire and physically remove the tire for an examination of its condition.

   In my experience, a rental agency had inadvertently left the spare tire out of the car on at least one occasion and the spare was inoperative on another.   It can be disastrous to have a puncture in the middle of nowhere at midnight without having a spare tire in the vehicle.

   When our family is considering driving cross-country,   the tires are most important and must be in excellent condition for road travel with no short cuts or chances taken. Next to the brakes, the tires are on my list of most important features to check on the motor vehicle before traveling. Review the owner's manual for the recommended tire pressure. Oftentimes, adding extra weight to the car demands a different tire pressure than our ordinary day-to-day driving; generally less air pressure is suggested.

   Maintenance Checkup.   Get a major motor vehicle's road checkup prior to departing on the trip.   The maintenance check-up provides for oil and filter changes, a radiator fluid check to correspond with the weather conditions, a check of the air conditioning Freon level, and a very thorough check of the brakes.   A reputable vehicle mechanic may make recommendations for a safe trip.   Do consider his suggestions very carefully.

   Brakes.   Make sure that the brakes are in excellent condition, even if the installation of new brakes is required.   We must have this work done before our journey is started.

   A thought just occurred to me that reminded me of my cross-country driving experience when I was traveling from Camp Le Jeune to the West Coast while I was in the U.S. Marine Corps.   It was raining hard when I had to make a sudden stop after just going through a large puddle of water. The brakes were soaked.   When I applied them, the car did not stop as I expected.   The car skidded a long distance before stopping.   Fortunately, an experienced driver in the car coached me to a safe stop. This is just a thought about good brakes and the bonus of having an experienced long distance driver on the trip. Fortunately for me, drivers with considerable long distance driving experience in all types of weather were with me on the trip. They calmly told me to step on the brakes and let off the pressure, and to follow this procedure repeatedly. The car came to a safe stop without causing damage to the car ahead of us.

This story will not only emphasize the importance of having good brakes, but also provide some insight on using them in wet weather.

Emergency Road Equipment may include the following items:

1. **Illumination Flares.** At least three should be taken. Check the flares to make sure they are still functional. That is, make sure no oil, water, or other substances have caused the flares to get wet. A rigid waterproof container helps keep the flares from getting wet and from being damaged.

2. **Distress Signals.** Truckers have a triangle that is luminous when light shines on it. Some distress signals serve more than one use. An air pump for the tires, a flashlight, and the blinking amber distress signal are all included in one unit.

Some distress signals come equipped with an adapter that allows connection to the cigarette lighter in the vehicle. Others are operated by batteries. Make sure that the batteries are good. If the equipment has been stored without use for a long time, check the batteries to make sure they are functioning properly. Hardware stores have a battery check meter to determine the battery condition which may be purchased if your needs will be heavy; otherwise, see if the store clerk will check the batteries free of charge.

3. **Air Pump.** You can select hand or foot pumps or the type that works from an adapter that connects up to the cigarette lighter. The pump may be useful in the case of a flat tire when no service station is near.

4. **Battery Cables.** Good thick cables are recommended for the best results. Let us hope that we will never need to use them, but we should take some cables with us.

5. **Flashlight.** The flashlight will be a friend indeed in our travels on the open road. A flashlight on the highway at night will come in very handy. A flashlight should be kept in a spot where everyone can locate it.

6. **Empty Fuel Can.** Leave the can unsealed. A friend once told me that a sealed gas can stored in the trunk of a car is very dangerous. The heat in a trunk can get so hot that it could cause the can to explode. The explosion can be more lethal than dynamite. Recently, manufacturers have tried to alleviate this problem by making plastic gas containers instead of metal. The plastic cans usually have a safety plug that can be left unsealed when the container is empty to avoid the build-up of fumes.

Actually, if your trip is well-planned, there should be no reason to run out of fuel. But it's still a good idea to take a fuel container along to be ready for the unexpected situation on the road.

7. **Vehicle Jack, Jack Iron with Lug Wrench.** So we remembered to check our spare tire. We made sure it was secure, but we forgot to replace the jack, tire iron and lug wrench in the vehicle. We had not used the equipment since we changed the brake linings. Now here we are miles from a service station with a flat tire and no telephone anywhere.

We do not want this to happen to us on our trip to and from the reunion. We want to be prepared and have all the necessary tools with us in our vehicle.

8. A pair of **pliers** approximately six inches long will work well for most occasions.

9. **Screw Drivers.** Flat head and Phillips screw drivers are necessary. Although one flat head and one Phillips screw driver should be sufficient, it is possible to obtain a reasonably-priced set of each type for your trip.

10. **Container of Water.** Carrying a gallon-sized container is an idea which may not be necessary if you continuously check your radiator's water level at each gas stop. Even if we do plan to take all of the necessary precautions, it does no harm to have a container filled with water. The container of water may be useful in helping some-one else out.

11. **Portable Fire Extinguisher.** A small portable fire extinguisher that is Underwriter Laboratory (UL) listed is recommended for your vehicle during your trip. Actually every vehicle should be equipped with a fire extinguisher located in a safe place at all times. The fire extinguisher has different ratings which are basically for oil, grease, gasoline and live electrical fires. Some extinguishers are not effective on wood, paper or cloth. Make sure you read the label to see what ratings apply to your extinguisher. Obtain a multiple-rated extinguisher.

The **Fire Extinguisher** also has an indicator to let us know about the condition, that is, when the extinguisher is satisfactory, needs recharging, or overcharged. The indicator should be kept in the green. This shows that the unit is in the proper operational condition.

Fire Departments offer recharging facilities and information on having the extinguisher recharged by private agencies. When purchasing an extinguisher, check with the clerk for a location that is approved for recharging the extinguishers.

Follow the instructions in the Owner's Manual and on name plate of the extinguisher for the proper use, storage and installation instructions. **Make sure to keep the fire extinguisher away from children.**

12. **Portable Battery Recharger.** A small portable recharger can be carried with our family on the trip. We should consider the amount of electrical usage of the vehicle when not driving that will drain the power of the battery. This factor will help us to determine whether or not to take a recharger.

13. **Gloves.** A pair of work gloves or garden gloves proves to be essential in colder weather and very useful for certain minor vehicle repairs.

14. **The Vehicle Certificate of Registration** is needed to identify the owner of the vehicle. It should be kept in the vehicle in case a peace officer requests it. The registration should be kept current.

If the vehicle being used is a rental from a rental car agency, keep the contract in close reach to prove that the vehicle is in the lawful possession of the family.

When the vehicle is being borrowed from someone, get a current copy of the registration papers and a letter from that person granting, in clear, legible handwriting, authorization to your family to operate the vehicle. The letter should be dated, signed by all parties involved, and if desired, notarized. Generally, when a document is notarized, it is considered more authentic and official.

Insurance. Automobile insurance is required in most states. The owner of the vehicle must maintain minimum amounts of liability coverage. **Proof of insurance** is a must in many of the states in the United States. The family is required to provide the name of the insurance carrier, policy number, amount, and the classification of insurance. A photocopy of the policy is needed to show the coverage. Some insurance companies are now sending out a form to their policyholders with all of the requested information to meet the government requirements.

My practice is to photocopy the policy and keep it with me in the convenience compartment of the vehicle to display if a safety officer of the highways requests verification of insurance. Rental cars have the insurance coverage indicated on the contract. Make sure that the proper coverage for the areas that the family is driving through is provided. Therefore, check with your insurance agent to get your policy requirements adjusted for the states you plan to travel through during your trip.

Some Accessories To Consider Taking. **A toiletries bag** with the personal items that will be needed most frequently while on the road should be kept in an easy-to-reach location for quick access. Each family member should bring along his/her own individual bag.

It can be irritating and frustrating to realize that someone has packed away his/her toothbrush, mouthwash, eye drops, contact lenses, or some other hygiene neccessities. We usually need something at the most inconvenient time. To make things worse, it is usually late at night when these items are needed while driving on the road. The irritation spreads to the other members of the group when it is necessary to remove all the luggage in the trunk to obtain something that should be in a hassle-free location.

By each person bringing along an individual tote bag stored comfortably within reach, the trip will be more enjoyable.

Driving Shoes. Comfortable shoes are very desirable on long trips on the road. Soft shoes of natural materials that will allow your feet to breathe, with plenty of toe space, and loose-fitting enough to allow the blood to circulate are essential. Before you depart for your trip soak your feet in some warm water and epsom salts to help relax them for a long driving trip.

After 4 Feet Treat is a liquid feet treatment that I have found soothing to use for my feet when undertaking a long trip. Jogging shoes are comfortable to wear during long drives across country. Tennis shoes are preferred by some other drivers. The family will desire some comfortable shoes for the trip. Bring shoes that will allow the blood to circulate in the feet. Shoes that allow fresh air to flow through, making them odor-free, are desirable.

Sunglasses. Sunglasses help reduce road glare and eye fatigue, and prevent dust particles from disturbing the eyes. Choose a pair of sunglasses that allows for the best road visibility and blocks the glare from the sun. It is a good idea to purchase more than one pair of sunglasses, and have at least one pair that is light in weight to keep from irritating the nose. One pair may have a darker tint for daytime driving when the sun is brightest. Then select another pair with a lighter tint for inclement weather and early-evening driving.

Flight glasses that are light in weight with lenses that automatically adjust to the sun's brightness have been beneficial to me. Also, keep in mind that it is wise to carry an extra pair of glasses. It is not unusual to have a pair of sunglasses broken or misplaced. So, there is an extra pair of sunglasses securely packed away in a location where it will be available in a time of need to save the day.

Suntan lotion should be carried especially if your family reunion includes many outdoor activities. Keep the small children in mind early in the morning before they go out to play, especially if the sun's rays will be a major factor throughout the outdoor day activities.

Many suntan lotions have a sunscreen factor designated from 1 to 15. The higher the number, the better the protection provided from the sun. In other words, a designation of 15 provides the most protection. If your family reunion takes place during the wintertime at some ski resort, you will require maximum protection from the sun's rays.

Driving On The Road To And From The Family Reunion. Drive safely and with caution on the roads. Regardless of the name we give our highways: whether it is the beltways in Maryland, expressways in Memphis, freeways in Anaheim, throughways in Ohio or highways in Texas...use good, cautious driving techniques. The family may wish to avoid the fast lane when driving across-country if it is possible. Drive in the next lane over at a safe speed for the road conditions, which may mean driving less than the maximum speed limit.

A good rule for the family to follow is to drive at least five miles less than the flow of traffic. This will result in the observing of the speed limit and provide for a safer trip. Think of the money and time saved when our family avoids speeding. When we are not speeding, we will be happy to have a journey without a speeding violation which could prove to be very aggravating.

Other drivers may pass your family by on the road, but as long as we have given them the fast lane, it is all right. Do not block the fast lane driving five miles per hour less than the flow of traffic; move over and have a safe trip.

Some states have a signal which is the flashing of the high-beam light to request a motorist to move out of the fast lane so that the driver in the rear may pass. Even if we happen to be driving the posted speed, it is better to yield the lane to the signaling motorist. Maybe the person has an emergency. Sometimes, we have observed unmarked law enforcement vehicles signal with their upper-beam light to

motorists ahead of them to move over and let them pass. Some
motorists refuse to yield.

Perhaps the person who fails to observe the signal to
yield does not believe that other people pay taxes too and
are entitled to utilize the emergency signal. The other
person may have a valid priority for the need to pass by.
Give him/her the lane, better still, avoid the fast lane if
possible. Drive at a safe speed and be courteous to other
motorists sharing the road with your family.

Family Fun While On The Road. **Games and activities** seem to
make my children happy while traveling on the road and, at
the same time, sharpen their awareness. We participated in a
game we called **Animal Alphabet,** which is a game where
everyone in the car who wants to participate takes a turn and
names an animal that starts with the letters of the alphabet
in proper sequence, antelope for "A", buffalo for "B", cougar
for "C"...and so on goes the game until zebra is announced.
This game really gives the children a chance to participate
with their parents and other adults which helps build their
confidence and enhance their education.

Name a City Game is another. We used the alphabet method
again to name all the cities in alphabetical sequence, At-
lanta for "A", Baltimore for "B", etc. We would continue
this game until we ran out of cities we could think of for
the appropriate letter.

We used the alphabet game in many variations including
cars, states, etc. It is amazing how these games bring out
the sparkle in children. Oftentimes, it was the children who
performed the best.

Vehicle Counting Game. We would each select a certain
color of vehicle to count within a specified time limit,
let's say twenty minutes; one person would take blue cars,
another red, another white, and so on until everyone had a
color to count during the twenty minutes. Whoever had the
highest number would be declared the winner. Young children
get a chance to improve their counting skills while having
fun playing the game.

It is possible to invent games that are variations of
established games that your family particularly enjoys. In
our busy lives traveling on the road together gives children
a chance to find real pleasure in being with adults. Allow
these pleasurable, comfortable, relaxed moments to happen.
Make it your business to have fun.

Singing Songs. "Row, row, row your boat, gently down the
stream," we would take turns singing. Rounds are great fun
while on the road. You don't have to be a great singer to
have a wonderful time. One person leads out with the first
line, and at this point the second singer joins in starting

at the beginning while the first voice continues on. The third singer joins in when the second one completes his first line, and so forth, until everyone is singing and having a most harmonious time. "Are You Sleeping (Frere Jacques)" is another round.

Games from Automobile Clubs. Some clubs offer an array of games the family can enjoy while on the road. Connect the dots, memory games, imagination games, and coloring books are all wholesome forms of recreation for the family on the road to add to the joy of your magnificent trip.

Music in the Vehicle While on the Road. While it is true that there is music for every mood, it is not necessarily so that everyone wants to listen to the same kind of music at the same time. Driving across the country provides the time to hear a lot of music including rock, soul and country depending on what town or city you are near. Our family included a portable Walkman that had a battery-operated cassette deck which provided us with our own selection of musical entertainment. We would play our Walkman when we wanted a break from the local radio stations and when no stations were available because we were outside the receiving range of any transmitter.

A small stereo headset could also be used at nighttime when the driver wanted to listen to music without disturbing his sleeping companions. However, the headset was never used during the time we were playing games or storytelling.
Who would want to miss out on the time the big fish got away or the time when first place was just one, unachievable stride away. These moments are special ones dear to our hearts and souls which we will cherish for a lifetime.

Avoid Some Games While On The Road. Balloons. A driver can be distracted by the screeching of balloons. Balloons may also blow out of the window into the path of another motorist and startle him into an accident.

Balloons can block or partially obstruct the vision of the driver at a critical moment and can be a real hazard. My family likes balloons, but we play with them in an open area in the park, not in the car.

Water guns. The problem with water guns in a car is not always apparent at first. Besides getting everyone wet, water guns have been designed to look so much like real pistols that an unsuspecting motorist may be frightened by suddenly seeing a water pistol pointed at him. We can do without ruining the day of another person. Our objective is to have fun, but not at the expense of others.

Loud noises. There are times when we are driving together in the open desert, through deserted areas, or on long stretches of mostly vacant road when we all just yell and scream at the top of our lungs. This can be very therapeutic and good for the release of the tensions of driving when everyone is awake and eager to participate. We are careful not to engage in this practice in city areas, on crowded roads, or around other motorists. We don't want our family deemed a bunch of fruitcakes.

Our family may want to sit down together after being on the road for awhile and have an open-air discussion on those road games that were enjoyable and those that were frustrating to some members of the family. Our family can plan all types of recreational activities prior to departing on our trip, but discover that the fun we read or heard about another family having did not apply to our particular group. Our families are different, and they are constantly changing, and the things that appealed to us last year may need to be updated or even scrapped. Part of the joy of repeated trips together is the establishing of traditions, those things we repeat over again each year.

We need to create and encourage these memories, but give them new vigor and inspiration for today's trip as well as tomorrow's journey. Therefore, we parked our car at one of the scenic stops or rest stops, or we carry on this discussion during a snack at a coffee shop.

The communication between our family members is important. Perhaps we should visualize communication on the road as a family thermometer that we keep checking on by comparing it to the thermometers of the individual family members. It maintains a cool and comfortable temperature when the individual temperatures are consulted and corrected when they vary too much from the ideal. By changing from one activity to the next, listening to soft music and even enjoying moments of silence together, we can keep the family thermometer regulated to perfection.

You can make your trip a pleasurable one, and the joy and well-being of your loved ones will flourish like the flowers in a botanical garden. We can enjoy our experience of driving from our home town to the site of the family reunion. We will treasure these memories for a long time.

Visiting Special Attractions While On The Road. The auto club that we used to help route our trip had two representatives who had traveled part of the route that we had chosen and they were able to highlight the attractions and give a rather detailed explanation of all the special things to look for. They recommended good restaurants had friendly people providing good service as well as delicious meals along the way. Even when the auto representatives have not toured the area surrounding the route you are taking, they can highlight the special attractions on your map.

Our representative pinpointed lakes and streams where we stopped to play in the water, take pictures, and just enjoy nature for awhile. The kids really enjoyed taking a break from the road to stretch their limbs and get some exercise. The clean air of a lake area is refreshing and adds to the fun of the trip. Playing with our kids in the water are moments that children have long awaited. Oftentimes we are so busy trying to support our families that we do not stop to take time to bring about the true closeness that children, parents, relatives and friends can share while simply en route to a family reunion.

It is not only what goes on at the reunion that counts. It is all the family togetherness gained from everyone sharing the responsibility by helping in the trip preparation, having fun together while traveling on the road, and enjoying the celebration of the family reunion festivities. It is our investment of our time, love, and devotion to our family that makes our family respected by our communities and other families of the world. We can make our time on the road enjoyable by giving our imagination free rein.

Let us get our family vehicle together. When we prepare to travel on the highways to and from our family reunion, we should take good care of the vehicle that will take us. Here is a vehicle checklist to help us plan for a complete maintenance check-up. If an item is not covered on the following list, send a note to the publisher so we may include it in the next edition of our book on family reunion.

VEHICLE CHECKLIST

CHECK HERE	ITEM	QUANTITY	NOTE
	BRAKES		
	a. BRAKE FLUID		
	b. BRAKE ADJUSTMENT		
	c. EMERGENCY BRAKES		
	TIRES		
	LIGHTS:		
	a. FRONT		
	b. TAIL		
	c. STOP		
	d. SIGNAL		
	e. INTERIOR		
	f. CONVENIENCE COMPARTMT		
	g. INSTRUMENT PANEL		
	RADIATOR		
	BATTERY		
	OIL AND LUBE		
	TUNE-UP		
	SHOCKS		
	WINDSHIELD WIPERS		
	HEATER		
	AIR CONDITIONER		
	a. FREON CHARGING		
	b. OPERATION		
	SPARE TIRE		
	FUSES		

VEHICLE CHECKLIST

CHECK HERE	ITEM	QUANTITY	NOTES
_____	EMERGENCY SIGNAL	_____	_____
_____	WATER CONTAINER (1 GAL.)	_____	_____
_____	GAS CONTAINER (1 GAL.	_____	_____
_____	OIL (2) QUARTS	_____	_____
_____	AIR PUMP	_____	_____
_____	TIRE STOP LEAK	_____	_____
_____	FLASHLIGHT	_____	_____
_____	BATTERY JUMP CABLE	_____	_____
_____	WIRE PLIERS	_____	_____
_____	SCREW DRIVERS	_____	_____
_____	TIRE JACK	_____	_____
_____	TIRE LUG WRENCH	_____	_____
_____		_____	_____
_____		_____	_____
_____		_____	_____
_____		_____	_____
_____		_____	_____

Airplane

The primary advantage of traveling by airplane is the time saved enroute to and from the destination. Many of us feel that the air is unsafe due to the vast publicity air crashes gain on the news. Have little fear for if the same amount of publicity were given to the many auto accidents throughout the continent, we would be equally as cautious.

Get a current copy of a few travel magazines and check for any travel-related discounts. Travel agents are helpful in finding reduced rates and sometimes this service is provided free of charge. Some travel agencies will be especially diligent in their search for a good discount if you are making arrangements for large groups.

Many airlines offer family seating. A section of the plane is set aside for the group so that they don't have to be scattered and can sit together. Special areas are set aside in the waiting rooms for the family to sit together, and when the airplane arrives they are loaded together as a family.

Transporting The Unwilling Traveler. Fear of flying. My father swore he would never fly on an airplane, jet or rocket, because he had acrophobia or a fear of heights that was deeply ingrained in his consciousness. He always chose to travel by other means, such as auto, bus or train. I decided to ask my friends and acquaintances about their transportation preferences when taking trips over long distances, and I was indeed surprised that a considerable number of young adults have a fear of flying; it is not limited to mature adults by any means.

People have more traveling phobias than we realize. And these fears are valid ones and must be considered. I discovered that there is someone who has a <u>bona</u> <u>fide</u> fear of each different mode of transportation, some who are terrified of trains, some buses, some airplanes and even those who are afraid to travel by car.

The news media report vivid pictures of traffic fatalities of all kinds. How often has a major aviation accident occurred right before we are departing on a lengthy flight; bodies of the critically injured and the fatally wounded are strewn all over the wreckage of the plane's fuselage, visible to the world on the screens of our television sets. Then, as if this intricately detailed news coverage were not enough, we are bombarded with movies that capitalize on the poor fate of humans involved in an airline crash, a runaway train, the wreckage of a multiple highway collision, or a sinking, luxury cruise ship whose passengers descend to the large, upturned jaws of monstrous sea creatures waiting to have humans for lunch. It is no wonder that so many members of our family delay taking a trip to a family reunion.

We must recognize these fears as being real and reckon with them in a mature manner. If we think the matter will require professional therapy to get to the root of the phobia, then we should seek a qualified medical authority...a psychologist or psychiatrist to provide counseling. The sooner the needed help is provided to the member who needs it, the sooner we can begin having perfect attendance.

Be aware that some members of our family may not desire to discuss their fears about transportation with anyone. This is one very good reason why the planning and communication for the reunion begin way before the actual celebration. Every member of the family has someone that he/she tries to relate to about matters that are of a confidential nature. The person entrusted with this confidence should not violate it if at all possible, but help will have to be provided to the member who needs it.

There may be books on the subject that will be helpful if you go to the library. We may desire to contact our doctor, librarian, family guidance counselor, minister, or psychology professor for recommendations on books dealing with the areas in which your family member needs help.

The situation may not require professional help or the advice from books. The problem can be dealt with within the family as it was in the case of my father. We were able to sit down with him and tell him how others had overcome their fear of flying by various means. Since my father did not have any ailments to prevent him from taking a drink of alcohol at the appropriate time before boarding the plane, we got him on a flight, which proved most enjoyable for him, and it enabled him to attend our reunion.

There are no hard and fast rules for dealing with transportation fears. Sometimes it is best to plan well enough in advance to choose slower modes of transportation, or to spend the necessary time required to deal with the problem. Keep your faith.

Special rates. As to special group rates, some airlines
have what they call a convention rate which is available only to large, nationally publicized groups, which entitles these groups to a discount of from 20 to 30%. A large family with proven abilty to pay for this service may contact the airline of their choice to inquire about this rate. To take advantage of special rates available which offer one-half off and more from the regular fares, a far better discount than convention rates, the family must make plans at least eight months to one year in advance.

Special arrangements for the rich and famous. Representative of the airlines contacted stated that no special arrangements are made for celebrities, but they preferred to be notified in advance when a celebrity was flying with them.

Some Considerations for the Physically Disabled. One representative of an airline stated that special treatment for the physically disabled varied depending upon the type of disability. Notify the Acceptance Coordinator when making reservations on an airline for physical disabled persons so that the proper arrangements can be made. Some disabled people might require special medical needs, like oxygen. The medical needs would have to be arranged far in advance. Generally, there is a charge for the special arrangements made by the airlines.

Those individuals who are blind are not given seats near emergency exits. The representative stated that due to the lack of sight, blind persons could cause a problem in the event of an emergency. Persons requiring wheelchair assistance often complain that some airlines do not provide aisle space wide enough for a wheelchair to pass through. We need to ask many of the presidents of airlines to actually travel in their airline in a wheelchair across the country. We would see an immediate change for our family members requiring special assistance due to a physical impairment.

The expense is too great for the able-bodied executive who is only interested in making a profit. We must make our voice heard in the highest offices of government to make corrections for our disabled. The time is now.

These are just some examples of the special arrangements and precautions taken by airlines. We should contact the Acceptance Coordinator for detailed information regarding our requirements.

Children On The Airplane. Special arrangements for children flying on the airplane are becoming more prevalent now. Children under five are not allowed to travel without an adult escort if they have to change planes. Children over two must have a seat of their own. The parent must provide notice to the airline in advance of a minor traveling on an airline unescorted. Many times the airlines will arrange for flight personnel to take the child to the right gate.

Clearing of the ears is a major concern for a small child. Teach him/her to clear the ears to prevent the child from experiencing pains in the ears especially when the plane is taking off and landing. The change in altitude creates pressure on the ear drums. Swallowing air, chewing gum, holding the nose, closing the mouth and blowing air through the eustachian tube are methods used to clear the ear. Get advice from the family doctor on other methods to assist in this area.

In the Air with the Family Pet.   One pet per cabin is allowed.   Arrangements must be made when reservations are booked, but it is on a first-come, first served basis.   The person with the pet who arrives first on the day of the flight is the one who gets to have his or her pet in the cabin.   Otherwise the family would make plans for the pet to travel in a pet container with the cargo.

Foreign languages.   Airlines generally do not make special arrangements for foreign speaking passengers.   However, many terminals do have special signs in (usually) three languages, French, Spanish and English.   In addition, there are often special telephones which answer questions in different languages.   Some airlines that provide flights from country to country have flight personnel who speak the language of the destination country on their flights.   Interpreters who speak the language may also provide for the family who needs such help. Check with the airline for specific information.

Cordiality Rooms   Some airlines have special rooms for leisure and relaxation.   These rooms are provided at most of the major city airports.   The airlines charge an annual membership fee which ranges from $60.00 to $150.00.   Lifetime membership is available for a fee of from $650.00 to $950.00.   The price varies for single membership and family membership.   Usually, the airlines specify how many people constitute a family for the purposes of membership for the family.

The airlines provide their cordiality room members with a place to get away from the crowds, noise, and the hectic hustle and tussle of the airport.   Hot coffee, juice, and drinks from the bar are available.   Special telephones for each of several long distance service carriers such as AT&T are available.   The clientele maintains a well-dressed and businesslike profile.

What makes this service worth its price is the ability to check in and obtain a boarding pass in comfort without standing in long lines in the middle of the airport.

More families are deciding to use the leisure rooms for a meeting place at the airport.   Think about the service and if your family feels like giving it a try, call around and seek the warmest and friendliest service at the best price.

Flying is fun.   Whenever we decide to fly, keep a thought or two on the positive side of flying.   There are a few things we can do to make the flight more pleasurable on the ground and in the air.

Bus.

Taking the bus gives everyone in the family a chance to sit back while the driving is done by the bus driver.   Many states are doing more than ever to make sure that the roads are safer for the family. Bus drivers are being monitored more closely than ever before. Buses are being inspected more frequently. Bus companies are initiating safety programs with incentives to employees who have outstanding driving safety records.

Prices for the bus can be very inexpensive when the bus carriers have special fare promotions. A regular fare for an adult is considered the full fare. Children's rates vary according to their ages. Children four years old and under travel free when each child is accompanied by an adult paying full fare. One child per adult is the rule or the additional child pays full fare at the adult rate.

A child five years old to 11 years old pays one-half of the full fare. Again, the rule is one child per adult or the child pays full fare at the adult rate.

Greyhound has the **Ameripass** which provides a single fare for an adult, a flat rate price with unlimited mileage within a seven or fifteen day period. The seven day price is $189.00, and the fifteen $249.00 for adults, allowing travel to any area serviced by Greyhound within the time period. These prices and this promotion may be improved upon by the time our family celebrates its fifteenth annual family reunion.

Senior Citizen Discounts. A 10% discount of the standard fare is provided to senior citizens. The western half of the United States generally considers persons 55 years of age and above as qualifying for the discount, while the eastern half usually sets the qualifying age at 65.

Proof of age in some states must be provided at the time the ticket is purchased. Some states require the bus company to request a Senior Citizen Discount Card from the person as proof. Driver's license, passport, identification card with a picture, and other forms of proof may be accepted depending on the state where the ticket is purchased.

A senior citizen who is traveling from California will be given the discount at the age of 55 while someone in Tennessee will have to be 65 to qualify for the same discount. The family needs legislated help for liberal, uniform treatment throughout the country. A uniform age of 55 in all the states should be the goal.

30-Day purchase in advance is now at the all-time competitive price of $59.00, one-way fare, and $118.00 for round trip. This fare allows family members to travel across the country for this price. The fare is being promoted from March to September of 1987. It is a good chance that fares like this and better fares will be offered for families traveling in the near future.

Routing. Now how does everyone go on the bus to the re-union? It is possible for members in a family located in different cities to catch the same bus and go together to their destination. This could be made possible by meeting several different conditions.

One condition is that the same bus has to be traveling to the cities where each family group is located in order for everyone to arrive at the family reunion together on the same bus. Arrangements could be made to have different sections of the family group together at central locations along the route that the bus travels.

Another condition is that the bus has to have sufficient room on board for the members of the family to be seated. The bus company has a strict rule of **first-come, first-served.** Further, no reservations can be made with the bus company. While this idea has merit, do we really want our plans ruined by part of the family not being allowed on board and not getting to the family reunion? A few snares make this idea almost a no no.

Bus routing information can be obtained simply by asking the bus company's telephone information person whether a particular routing is possible. For example, request to know if there is a bus starting in Kansas that makes stops in Topeka, Kansas City, and Knoxville with a final stop in Memphis.

The routing would be explained to the family in detail. The information persons employed by the bus company are very cooperative in trying to help our family with our travel needs. If the family chooses the bus, then give a call to the bus company for the best fare, routing, and service available.

Luggage on the Bus Trip. The maximum amount of baggage allowed on the bus for an adult paying full fare is two pieces. The maximum weight per piece is 100 pounds. The maximum dimensions are 24 inches x 24 inches x 48 inches.

Three additional pieces are permitted for an extra charge which varies depending upon the ticket amount.

A child paying one-half of the full fare is allowed only one piece of luggage.

Carry-on luggage is limited to two pieces that can fit either in the overhead rack or underneath the feet of the passenger bringing the luggage on the bus. The luggage must not be stored in the aisle. And the luggage must not take up any more room than that allowed for it.

Considerations for Disabled Persons. **Blind persons** are allowed to take an attendant or a trained dog on the trip at no extra charge. However, the standard fare would have to be paid by the blind person. Reduced rates are not generally provided when an attendant or a trained dog accompanies the blind person.

A **physically disabled person** has the same opportunity to take an attendant at no extra charge if his/her impairment requires it.

Motorized wheelchairs are not allowed. Non-motorized wheelchairs are folded up and placed in the luggage compartment. No ramps or lifts are provided to assist the entrance or departure from the bus of physically disabled persons. Someone would have to perform the service of assisting them on and off of the bus.

Items Not Permitted on the Bus. Some items are restricted on the bus for the safety of all passengers. **Alcoholic beverages** are not permitted. A passenger who is drunk in the judgment of the bus driver can be denied from entering the bus. If somehow a passenger becomes drunk during the trip, the bus driver will remove or cause that individual to be removed from the bus.

It is possible for a passenger to consume alcoholic beverages at the different stops along the way, if alcohol is sold at the locations of the bus rest stops. A note of caution could be exercised here, by informing the members in our family who drink, to drink with moderation and take care not to offend other passengers en route to their family reunions.

Non-prescribed drugs are not permitted. Take along a note from the family doctor indicating the type of medication, the dosage strength, and the frequency of taking a prescribed medication. This note may prove to be very helpful in the event a family member loses his/her medication and needs to get a refill. A lot of time and money can be saved by having the letter from the doctor.

Firearms are not allowed on the bus. The passenger may not take any firearms in his/her luggage. Firearms are not permitted to be carried on the bus. Some places, like the Port Authority in New York, have metal detectors to check luggage for metal objects that may be harmful.

No animals are allowed on the bus, nor are there provisions for the animals to be included in the storage compartment of the bus. A trained dog for the blind is an exception to this rule.

Nor are **most chemicals** allowed on the bus. The bus

company has a book of tariffs with a complete list of prohibited items. Each state may have different rules in addition to those made by the federal government.

Smoking is prohibited on buses in some states. Other states permit smoking in the rear portion of the bus in the section designated for smoking. Otherwise, a smoker would not be able to smoke until he/she got off the bus when it stops for coffee and meals.

No pipes, cigars, or herbs (marijuana) may be smoked while aboard the bus. Even in the states where smoking is allowed, these items are not permitted.

Stop-overs and stay-overs. Sixty days are allowed to complete a total trip on one ticket. In essence, a members of the family could stop over in one of the cities along the route and do some sightseeing. The family could book a hotel and spend the night. Or, if the family members have relatives along the route, they could stay over to visit after the family reunion. Also, this is a good method for one of the members of the Communication Committee to visit everybody on the bus route to spread the word of the family reunion. It works almost like a political barnstorming campaign, but the message is to get the family together.

Some tickets **do not** allow stay-overs. With special or reduced rates, bus companies are more likely to limit the trip to the special location of the promotion. For example, let us say Continental offers a $22.00 fare from New York to Los Angeles during the the month of June. The ticket may not allow any stopovers. The conditions would depend to a large degree on who is writing the tariff and the individual state guidelines for various promotions.

Timing is everything. The bus companies have a saying that goes like this, **"You can never be too early to catch the bus, but you can be too late!"** Take heed, the family should arrive at the bus terminal approximately one hour earlier than the scheduled departure time.

Relax while waiting. Talk to the kids about some of the things we have always wanted to take the time out to discuss, but never seemed to find the time for. These spare moments are essential and make things work out for a happier family.

A little general information on the bus. **Air conditioning** in the bus is to help make the trip more comfortable. If cool air is a problem for any members of the family, then consider taking along a sweater or coat to keep warm during the evenings. A small blanket to cover up while sleeping helps family members keep warmer.

Seats recline to allow for a more relaxed ride. Before letting the seat back though, inform the person behind you.

This will give the person a chance to make adjustments, and it will help keep harmony on the bus. This courtesy is often appreciated. When someone ahead of your seat informs you that he/she will be reclining his/her seat, always express your **thanks** to the person for being so considerate.

Restrooms are provided on the bus for the passengers' convenience. Do not spend any more time than necessary in the restroom. Give priority to elderly women, young children, and to those who have physical disabilities in the use of the restroom. Keep the restroom neat and clean. Remember to use the appropriate disposable containers for their intended use.

Properly **dispose of babies' diapers** in a manner that will not be offensive to other passengers. We were all babies once, and we must be understanding to other families who have babies on the bus. We have to give and take.

Luggage is stored in a compartment located in the portion of the bus under the floor. This bay area holds all of the luggage not carried on the bus. The luggage is loaded in a priority type system. This allows for the baggage to be removed according to stops along the route. Baggage of the first stops are toward the front for removal.

Loud music is not to be played on the bus. Headsets, earphones, and keeping the volume low are the requirements for the use of small portable televisions and tape recorders.

Security of the bus. At the bus stations of large populated cities, security guards may be present. The bus companies have been spared some of the problems with terrorists and hijackers that have plagued the transportation industry.

Valuables are the responsibility of the passenger. No safe is provided by the bus company to secure valuables. A family should take the precaution of buying travelers checks instead of carrying much hard cash aboard the bus.

What do we say about the bus driver? The bus driver is in charge of the bus and the driver has the final word. Remember that the bus driver is a member of one of our families who is just trying his/her best to make the journey to our family reunion safe and pleasurable. We do not want to give the driver a hard time.

A Change of the bus driver on long trips occurs every eight hours. The bus drivers are given an eight-hour driving shift in an effort to lessen fatigue from the stress of driving on a long schedule.

Stops for meals are scheduled for three times a day on the longer trips. **Coffee breaks** are made every so often with the frequency centered around the route and the need for a break by the driver. Family members should note that food may be taken aboard the bus.

The bus driver is concerned about the safety and the general welfare of the passengers. He/she will do everything possible to make the family comfortable in an effort to encourage the group to use the service of the bus in the future for the family reunion transportation needs.

Compliments and Complaints. When we receive really good service, we do not have the time to write a little note to express our appreciation. On the other side of the fence, we do not hesitate to write a long letter to complain. Our family members must be at the forefront of correcting this injustice. What if one of our family members was the one giving the service? We would like to see good letters in our family members' personnel files. Do we agree on this point?

Let us write letters of compliment without hesitation when we receive good service. We can start an avalanche of good by doing this. We still should write the letter to complain about rude and bad service. Bad service can cause a bus company to lose business. The main office has no way of knowing what the problem is if no one writes or calls to express dissatisfaction.

We should take out a pencil right now and write a letter requesting more family-oriented service of our bus companies. Then we would see the family concerns growing more each day. We should also write about bad service. And whatever we do, we need to write with vigor about good service. We can cause a great change by using the power of the pen!

Communication. When we want to get in contact with a family member on the bus, we have to call ahead of the person to a bus terminal at which the bus will make a stop. The bus terminal manager will page the member over the loudspeaker.

No passenger manifest is maintained by the bus company. So, we would have to know the exact bus information of the family member.

Bus summary. We have had an opportunity to consider the advantages of taking the bus. We discovered some of the disadvantages as well. Now, we can make a comparison of regular bus service compared to charter bus service.

Charter Bus Service for the Family. Charter pricing strategy. We can contact the charter representative of the bus company for specific information for the family reunion. The price of the bus that we desire to use for the trip is based upon two service options. **Dropped off** and **local service** are the two basic services.

Dropped-off or release service. Release service is what the bus company refers to when the family is picked up at various locations along the way and dropped off together at the final destination. When the bus has dropped the family off at the final stop, the bus company can use the bus for another trip. The bus is released by the family. When the family has shared a wonderful family reunion for a few days, then the bus company has another bus pick them up at the bus terminal.

Local service is similar to the dropped-off service in all but one regard. The bus stays with the family. When the local service is used, the family has the bus for sightseeing tours and trips to movies, theatres and museums. The service provides transfers to the members of the family which is an ideal way of keeping an accounting of the expenses. It also allows for family members to participate in the different tours and pay on an individual basis. There are many ways of making arrangements for this local service with the bus company chosen by the family.

The **itinerary** is left up to the family, so long as the trip poses no harm or threat to the bus driver. The bus driver is still in charge of the safety of the passengers, himself, and the bus.

Time and mileage are considered in the computation of the price for the local service. The clock runs from the beginning to the end of the trip. Therefore, it would be wise for the family to have some valuable use of the bus time. Have the Entertainment Committee make out a really interesting outline of activities for the family to be involved in during the reunion. Otherwise, figure out when to release the bus until needed for the return trip. Stop the clock and save money. The family may desire to compare the cost of keeping the bus over several people renting their transportation.

Making reservations in advance is beneficial. The family has to send $100.00 to the bus company two weeks prior to the departure date. This fee is required for each bus that is reserved by the family. If the family has plans to use three buses, then $300.00 would be required in advance.

The bus company will send the family a confirmation of the trip at least one week in advance. The confirmation provides a detailed outline of the family trip. The fees charged are all listed for verification.

What if we have to cancel? The bus company has an outline of the refund policy for any cancellation that may become necessary. If the family gives eight days prior notice of cancellation, the bus company will refund all of the deposit surrendered,   four to seven days, 50% refund of the deposit,   one to three days, no refund.   If the family waits until the driver shows up at the site on the date and time of departure to cancel the trip, then the family will have to pay the bus company for the mileage and for the cost of the driver. The mileage is calculated from where the driver drove from to where he/she is due to pick up the family. Here is a little easy reference chart.

Days before cancellation	Amount of refund
8 or more	$100.
4 to 7	50.
1 to 3	0
last moment	cost of driver, plus mileage.

If cancellation should become necessary,   call the charter representative to give him/her notice.   After the telephone conversation, write a brief letter to the representative with the same notice.   This is a good idea in case for some reason the representative forgot to properly document the family call which could cause many problems.   Send the letter by certified mail with a return receipt requesting to whom, when and where delivery were made.

Payment.   The family can make payment in the form of a money order, cashier's check, or certified check.   Wire transfer of funds from a bank account or credit card are also forms of payment for the charter bus company services.

Pricing for the charter bus service.   Local service costs more than the release service.   The family has the bus from beginning to end of the trip with local service.   The release service is less expensive because the bus is used only to take the family from the various terminals of origin to the bus terminal of the town of the family reunion.   After the family reunion is over, the family catches another bus for the return trip.

The family pays for the bus.   No discounts are provided for age, whether it be for children or senior citizens.   The price is a one-seat price, with no breakdown for the per-seat cost.   The family can utilize the 43 or the 47 passenger seating design at the same cost.   Then the family can benefit by making the cost to the family members on a per-seat basis, and giving any other consideration regarding age as the family feels is reasonable and proper.

Smoking on the bus is permitted at the choice of the family that reserves the bus.   If the family chooses to smoke, the rear portion of the bus would be reserved for smoking.

Drinking of alcoholic beverages is permitted since the bus is a charter that falls under a regulation for private hire. Nevertheless, drinking is permitted with the understanding that it will be a reasonable consumption. The members of the family should not overindulge to the point of causing discomfort to other members. Perhaps, if more than one bus is going to be in use, the drinkers and smokers may wish to share the same bus.

Drugs and other chemical substances are still prohibited. The law does not allow for such use even in the private confines of the bus for charter. Drugs should be a non-permissable item for all of our family members.

The driver is still in charge of the safety considerations of the bus. The bus driver is allowed to drive about 500 miles and up to 10 hours. He/she can be on duty for 15 hours straight which takes into account waiting time. The driver is allowed to make stops along the way providing the stops are <u>en</u> <u>route</u>. A small distance off the route can be arranged with the driver within reason. These stops are to be planned at the time of making the reservation with the charter representative.

After the driver has reached his/her limit, a new driver will be available for the continued journey of the family. All of these concerns will be handled by the bus company. But it is good to know what is happening when a driver is changed so the family members can be briefed in advance and a feeling of well-being can be maintained.

Family seating arrangements. The seating capacity of the bus is for **43 passengers.** Everybody has to sit in a seat. Small babies can sit on the lap of their parents. The convenience of the parents are to be considered. If the parents elect to have the baby or other very small child ride in their laps the entire trip, then the fare of the child would not be charged. But if the parents desire to have a separate seat for the infant or small child, a one-seat fare would be charged.

The bus driver has a voice in the seating. The bus driver can object to a large child sitting in the lap of an adult. If the drivers feels that the child is too large, a separate seat would have to be obtained for the child. A bench seat at the very rear of the bus is designed for about three adults, but usually five to six small children can sit comfortably in this seat. No seating is allowed on the steps of the bus. To be sure of the seating, contact the terminal manager. The terminal manager can be very helpful.

If your family desires to have more people aboard the bus, it is possible to get a bus that seats **47 passengers.** The seats are closer together and the leg room is reduced. The price for the 47 passenger bus is the same as the price for the 43 passenger bus.

The charter bus service does not provide any additional service for the persons in a family with **physical disabilities.** The family would have to make the required arrangements for wheelchairs, trained dogs, or any other needed aids.

Who to contact. The Transportation Committee should contact the bus company that provides the most services, at the best price, with the most courteous and considerate personnel. The price should not be the main focus. If our family got the best price but the personnel were unpleasant and discourteous, then the bus company should be weighed against another company which would provide the most helpful and friendly personnel service from the charter representative to the bus driver. We should decide in favor of proper service for the family.

Train.

Pricing information. The Amtrak train has a standard fare for adults. Usually, the fare is based upon a round-trip ticket. No discounts are provided for senior citizens. Children under 12 years receive a 50% discount. For example, presently the round-trip fare for adults is $118.00. Children under 12 years would pay only $59.00.

The fare for a blind person is the same as for regular passengers. However, Amtrak will allow a blind individual to be escorted by a guide dog and have an extra seat at no extra cost.

Children under 12 must be accompanied by an adult. Children 12 years and older are allowed to travel on board a train without an adult.

Reservations made for the trip. Early booking is preferred in order to confirm a price at the amount quoted by the sales agent. For example, certain times of the year Amtrak has special discounted fares that can be reserved before price increases occur.

Baggage on the train. Let good judgment be your guide in the rush to get aboard the train in about two minutes. The sales agent recommends that passengers traveling aboard the train limit baggage to only two carry-on pieces of luggage.

A person does not have enough time to make a second trip to the waiting area to bring aboard any more than he/she can carry on the train.   Now if the passenger has help at both ends of the trip, more luggage could be brought aboard.   But keep in mind that two pieces are recommended.

The baggage is stored above the seats in the overhead compartment.   If very heavy baggage is brought aboard, then the baggage is stored on the first level.

Disabled persons.   Any family members requiring the use of a wheelchair should notify the sales agent at least two days in advance.   The sales agent prefers advance notice, two weeks for the best results.   The sales agent will make sure that ramps are provided at all of the necessary locations.
    Family members requiring wheelchairs are provided special areas in the train close to restrooms and services.   The members are not limited to these areas.   If the members desire to transfer to coach seating, they are free to do so.

Amtrak personnel are restricted from lifting or carrying any passengers aboard the train.   Therefore, family members requiring wheelchairs must provide assistants to help them in boarding and getting off the train.
.ixTrain,visually impaired family members

Blind and visually impaired family members are allowed to have a guide dog aboard the train.   The dog can take up an extra seat space at no extra cost.   No braille writing is provided to assist blind family members.   No special seating is provided.   They may request to be seated on the first level instead of the second level to avoid the stairs.   The sales agent will honor this request.

Food on the Train.   The price of breakfast and lunch averages about $5.50 per meal.   Dinner costs around $8.50.   The menu provides for a selection that will accommodate the vegetarian diet without any special requirements.   If the family members desire a salt-free diet or any other special arrangements, they should make their dining requests known at the time of making reservations.   It is possible to get special plates prepared with advance notice.

Entertainment in the lounge car.   Trains going to the West Coast have movies and bingo to offer family members.   The lounge car is open to all passengers for relaxation and entertainment.   Not all train lines have movies and bingo. Check with the sales agent to see if this feature is provided.

Family members may bring cards and other sedentary games to the lounge car.   This is the place for fun and entertainment, but be mindful not to infringe on the enjoyment of others.

Small portable televisions are permitted when used with

ear plugs. Radios used in this manner are acceptable. However, poor reception generally makes it inadvisable to take radios and televisions. The lounge car is meant to be an enjoyable spot for family fun.

Smoking aboard the train. Smoking is not permitted in certain parts of the country that prohibit smoking while trains are passing through their jurisdiction. In the areas where smoking is not restricted by legislation, only certain designated cars and areas are set aside for smoking. The rear portion of the coach car allows smoking in the seats designated for smoking.

Cigars, pipes, and cigarettes are allowed in smoking areas. No herbal substances are permitted. On train lines where sleepers are provided, smoking is permitted in the private rooms of the passengers. The door should be kept closed to keep the smoke from spreading to the other areas of the train.

Some lines may have an entire car completely designated for smoking. This is usually the case on a popular line where the sales agent has several requests from smokers for smoking areas.

Smoking areas are becoming less available due to the hazard to the health of the smokers and non-smokers sharing the same environment as the smokers. This is the time to reflect on the wisdom of not smoking. Our family members are the losers when we smoke. Let us get on a program now to reduce our smoking and finally **stop all smoking.**

Alcoholic beverages. Passengers are allowed to drink alcoholic beverages in the states that do not prohibit drinking on public transportation while it is passing through their jurisdictions. Trains have to honor the laws of the land that they are passing through.

Sleeping Arrangements. Sleepers are not always available on all lines. They are usually provided on long trips such as from the East Coast to the West Coast. There is a fare increase of $105.00 for a roomette which is for one person. A bedroom is for two persons at $200.00 extra.

For trains that do not provide sleepers, and for passengers who do not wish to pay the extra money for a sleeper, the seats in the coach car recline 30 degrees. There is plenty of leg space for the comfort of the passengers. Pillows are also provided at night.

Sleepers are available depending on the length of the trip. Short trips do not have sleepers, while some long trips do have them. Whether sleepers or reclining seats are chosen, try to relax aboard the train and get some sleep so the body will be well-rested for the family reunion.

Animals.   No animals are allowed on the train, except for the guide dogs used by family members who are blind.

Medical personnel.   The train does not provide medical personnel aboard the train.   What is done in the case of an emergency, motion sickness, or any other situation requiring medical care?   The train personnel maintain two-way communication with station personnel along the way.   A request will be made for an ambulance to meet the train in the nearest location at the soonest possible time.   The train will make a stop anywhere to assist those passengers requiring medical attention.   No long delay will be experienced.

General train information.   Phones are not provided aboard the train. Air conditioning helps provide for the comfort of the passengers.   Piped-in music is available in the sleepers. The members may choose to dress informally on the train. Wear soft and loose-fitting clothes to allow the blood to circulate.

Disorderly conduct.   The conductor is the top-ranking employee aboard the train.   He/she has assistants that report directly to him/her.   Whenever a passenger becomes disorderly and obnoxious he/she may be removed from the train by the conductor and/or his support staff.

Letters of Compliment and Complaints.   When one or more persons make your trip especially enjoyable, write a short letter to express your happiness.   Do not hesitate to bring the good news to the front office about good service, courteous treatment, and extra care given to your family. Write a letter to express dissatisfaction with poor service as well.

If the train is all right

After we have compared the advantages and disadvantages of taking the train, the committee should began work on making the necessary preparations to make the family trip a pleasant one.   Now we can write a few letters to get the wheels rolling.

Transportation Letters.

TRANSPORTATION LETTERS LIST

CHECK	TITLE OF LETTERS	NOTES
	TRANSPORTATION LETTER	
	TRANSPORTATION SURVEY	
	TRAIN LETTER WITH SURVEY	

TRANSPORTATION LETTER

Dear Family Member,

     We are taking a survey of the modes of transportation that family members will be taking from different states to get to the _____FAMILY _____ANNUAL FAMILY REUNION.

     Your answer to this survey will help our family obtain the best fare and discount rates available if the carriers have such bargains to offer. We will keep safety considerations in mind at all times.

     Will your family take a moment to complete the survey and return it to us soon? For your use the self-addressed envelope requires no postage. Some of the transportation carriers require that reservations be made eight months in advance, so please mail your completed survey to us soon.

     Thank you very much!

_____
Honorable Chairperson

_____*Family _____Annual Family Reunion*

TRANSPORTATION SURVEY

Which means of transportation does your family plan to use?

_____ *A. Airplane.*

       What is the name of the airline company?

       *ANSWER:*_____

_____ *B. Bus.*

       What is the name of the bus company?

       *ANSWER:*_____

_____ *C. Train.*

       What is the name of the train company?

       *ANSWER:*_____

_____ *D. Rental Vehicle.*

       What type of vehicle?

           _____ *Auto.*

           _____ *Van.*

           _____ *Pick-up Truck.*

           _____ *Recreation Vehicle.*

           _____ *Camper.*

           _____ *Bus.*

       2. What is the name of the rental company?

       *ANSWER:*_____

_____ *F. Private auto.*

_____ *G. Motor bike.*

_____ *H. Bicycle.*

_____ *I. Other.*

       1. _____.

       2. _____.

If your family would like to make any suggestions on transportation please mail your ideas or call us.   Maybe your family will know of some economical solution that will be beneficial to all of our family members who have to make transportation arrangements.   We all realize that the sooner these arrangements are made, the better.

Sincerely yours,

_____
Honorable Chairperson

_____*FAMILY* ____*ANNUAL FAMILY REUNION*

TRAIN LETTER

[NAME]_____

[ADDRESS]_____

[CITY]_____[STATE]_____[ZIP CODE]_____

ATTN: _____

Dear Sir/Madam,

Our family is celebrating its ____ Annual Family Re-union in _____ from _____ to __, 19__. Some of our members will be seeking the most economical, comfortable, and expedient way to depart from their home states to arrive at the family reunion safely.

Will your office please help us by furnishing some information to aid in making an intelligent decision?

We would like some information on the following:

1. Will your office furnish us with a brochure that outlines the amenities that your company offers to passengers?

2. If there is no brochure describing the amenities and services your company offers, please describe on the back of this page, or on a separate page what is available.

3. What services are provided to the physically disabled passenger?

ANSWER: _____

4. What special accommodations are provided for:

a. Children:
b. Senior citizens:

ANSWER: _____

5. Do your dining facilities allow for a diet that eliminates one or more, or even all of the following:

a. Salt
b. Sugar
c. Pork
d. Meat
e. Butter, margarine and/or
f. Grease?

ANSWER: (Please elaborate.) _____

_____

6. Does your company provide any entertainment?

ANSWER: _____

7. *If so, what is the*

    a. *Type*
    b. *Time, and*
    c. *Duration of entertainment provided?*

    ANSWER: a. _____

                    b. _____

                    c. _____

8. *May families provide their own entertainment?*

    ANSWER: _____

9. *What type of sleeping arrangements does your company provide?*

    ANSWER: _____

10. *What kind of discounts does your company offer to:*

    Individuals _____

    Family Groups _____

    Children _____

    Senior citizens? _____

11. *Will your company give any discounts when a family makes reservations in advance?*

    ANSWER: _____

12. *If so, how far in advance?*

    ANSWER: _____

13. *Does your company provide areas where a family of* _____ *(fill in with how many) family members could meet together for:*

    a. *Recreation Activities? Yes____ No____*

    b. *Group Meetings?   Yes____ No____*

14. *If so, how much do the areas provided cost?*

    ANSWER: _____

15. *If the areas are free, how far in advance would your company suggest that a family make the necessary reservations?*

    ANSWER: _____

16.   Will your company forward the necessary forms for our family to make the reservations?

17.   Will your office send us a diagram of the design of your train and its facilities with emergency exits emphasized?

18.   Will your office please enclose any other material that will be beneficial to our family that our letter may not have covered?

Thank you.

Sincerely,

Honorable Chairperson

_____FAMILY_____ANNUAL FAMILY REUNION

The letters are only meant to be a guide. Write the letter to suit your family style. Do not have a perfection complex to the point that the ink in the pen dries without your writing one letter. Written communication from time to time is necessary. Let us do our best and the recipient will understand.

HOUSING ACCOMMODATIONS

As a means of keeping the cost reasonable, we may choose to stay with relatives in the city or town of our family reunion. Perhaps we will have to make plans to have local relatives provide accommodations for out-of-towners. Sometimes we fail to consider the many hosts who feel uncomfortable about having guests in their homes they have never seen before or the many guests who feel uncomfortable staying with someone they have never met.

When homes are not available and for those who prefer public accommodations, low-cost motels and hotels must be found. We need to find the best price for our money. We must make it known that our family is going to be demanding high quality for a reasonable rate. What type of preparations should we make?

It is better to take small trips several months in advance before undertaking a long trip with our children. A small trip is good for children and especially useful when the parents allow the children to discover and make semi-independent efforts during the trip.

When we are the guests of our family members, we are to be very considerate of the privileges extended during our short stay in our family members' home. We have to be be neat, quiet, and orderly in our actions. Respect is the word, integrity is our motto, and we have to remember to bring honor to the home that we are staying in during the reunion.

It is a good idea to get an understanding early in the planning stages as to what is expected of our family. What times are good times to arrive -- whether early morning, noon or night. Find out what sleeping arrangements will be made, and whether or not it will be necessary to bring sleeping bags for the kids or adults.

Will we be expected to share in the cost of the food and utilities? Will there be a need to provide our own transportation, or will we be allowed the use of our host's vehicle? What is expected of us in the way of providing our own insurance coverage for the vehicle? If our host has a standard shift car, will we be able to drive it satisfactorily? All of these questions are important to know ahead of time. Above all, we want to keep peace with our family members. We want this peace to exist year after year.

Be courteous in the use of bathroom and kitchen. This is one area that causes significant strain on families sharing the same home. Therefore, find out in advance what times the bathroom is required for the host's use. Unless there are special circumstances, your needs, if possible, should be subordinate to those of your host.

When we do use the bathroom, we should spend the least amount of time possible and give our host first priority. If our host has not made room for the towels of our family, carry a clothes hangar to neatly hang up the towels. If it is a case where the host may have simply forgotten, ask our host where the towels should be placed. Our host is trying to think of so many things to make our family comfortable that there might be something that was overlooked. Just know that none of us are perfect. We should remain in the spirit of cooperation and help our host wherever possible to make him/her feel more at ease about the wonderful preparations already made.

One day the family reunion will be in our town, some of our family members will be our guests, and we will have a chance to return the kindness and warmth. Once we have had a chance to be the host, then we will understand exactly what is meant about the spirit of cooperation. Our host needs our support and goodwill to make all feel comfortable. We must be thoughtful and kind.

If someone in our family requires special consideration due to a physical impairment, we should make the special provisions necessary for his/her care far in advance.

Housing with the family during the reunion can be a friendly and a unique experience, one that we will always remember and cherish. If we are considerate of our host's wishes, we will be like a blessing to our host's family. Our host will invite our family back to his/her home. The kindness can be reciprocated when we have a chance to be host at one of the future family reunions.

HOTEL ACCOMMODATIONS

Some families will elect to stay in a hotel. Many hotels have group rates. If a family has a hundred people in the family group, hotels are willing to provide special rates, especially if they think more family business will be recurring. Smaller hotels and motels are often more accommodating because they are less well-known and need different ways of getting more business.

Many reunions now occur at hotels. Families who have had several reunions are finding hotel accommodations and banquets preferable to homes of family and friends and picnics in the park. The hotel then takes care of the banquet as well as the rooms.

Consider hotels close to the homes of the local family members, near the airport or train station as a second choice. These arrangements for out-of-town guests should be done as far in advance as possible after checking the alternatives for the best facilities and rates. Always take into consideration the financial position of those who are staying in the hotel so that their budget needs and their expectations are met.

If most of the family members are staying in a hotel, the host family may want to book rooms there for themselves as well to allow a maximum amount of time to be spent with the group. This is often practical when the banquet and most of the festivities are to occur at or in the vicinity of the hotel. It allows for better coordination by the family that has done most of the planning too.

Baby-sitting. Often there are teen-agers or grandparents within the extended family who are willing to care for the little ones while their parents are attending special activities. A reminder should be sent in the organizing letters asking that parents who will need sitters indicate this to the host family, along with the age, sex and special needs of the children.

Having a place to lay our heads. We have reviewed family places to stay and relax while at the family reunion. Some of our family members will be at the hotels and motels. Others will be at the homes of relatives. We will want to be considerate of our home away from home in all respects.

CAMPING

Why should we limit our imagination when it comes to the different ways to have a family reunion? There are many ideas of ways to have a family reunion. Let us look to the outdoors as one of the ways. Nature offers a family that chance to really get close and to experiment with enjoying outdoor life with its array of beautiful sunsets and equally treasured sunrises, lighting up all those places where squirrels hide their nuts, and flowers with soft, colorful petals wait for little bees to pollinate them and take their nectar from them. Watch the leaves of the trees sway, glittering with sparkling sunshine as they wake up to gentle breezes. This is what we have been missing each day amongst the concrete, noise, and pollution of city life.

Back to nature. We need to take our family back to nature, and having a family reunion outdoors is just the time to make it work for the entire family. There are many ways that those corporate planners, school teachers, and good, everyday workers can put their heads together to make it all happen. Not that we would plan a family reunion every year to be an outdoor camping event -- unless that is the desire of the family.

The recreational activities could center around what is available -- like fishing together, along with guitar play-ing, and all of the outdoor games: badminton, horseshoes, volleyball, and softball are only a few of the games that would make your reunion a wholesome delight for the whole family to remember for many years. If your family would study the Milky Way and name the constellations, and benefit from the knowledge of the family astronomy buff; all could share in the celestial experience.

Each family could have a combined potluck dining exper-ience, or individual food preparation done by each family, and then all could join together for family talks while dining under the heavenly skies. Friends of mine have a camping reunion each year of about 40 people, and they make reservations at a state park at adjoining campsites of approximately eight people each. The reunion might last a week, and each night a different campsite acts as host and prepares all the food for the group. Planning is easy, and on the other six nights, campers become carefree guests.

Camping is a very meaningful experience with nature when the entire family can dine together, talk together, and enjoy a variety of outdoor activities. Pleasant and meaningful outdoor experiences help the whole family appreciate the many small wonders that unfold every minute from sunrise until moonlight.

CAMPING CHECKLISTS

We do not want to get to the site of the family reunion that may be two thousand miles away and then realize that we forgot something important. What if we had a list to help us remember what to take with us on the trip? Here are a few aids to help us with things we might want to remember.

At the end of the list, there are spaces to add some items that are not mentioned. Actually, the list can be tailored to suit the needs of the family. If necessary, draw up your own list for the special needs of the entire family.

CAMPING CHECKLIST

CHECK HERE	Items	QUANTITY	NOTES
_____	CAMP SET (POTS,PANS,PLATES)	_____	_____
_____	FLATWARE (KNIVES,FORKS,ETC.)	_____	_____
_____	PAPER PLATES	_____	_____
_____	PAPER CUPS	_____	_____
_____	PLASTIC GLASSES	_____	_____
_____	SPATULAS	_____	_____
_____	KNIVES	_____	_____
_____	SHARPENER	_____	_____
_____	TONGS	_____	_____
_____	WOODEN SPOONS	_____	_____
_____	CAN OPENER	_____	_____
_____	ICE PICK	_____	_____
_____	CHEESE SLICER	_____	_____
_____	GRIDDLE	_____	_____
_____	PLASTIC CONTAINERS	_____	_____
_____	COFFEE POT	_____	_____
_____	HEFTY PLASTIC FOOD BAGS	_____	_____
_____	PLASTIC TRASH BAGS	_____	_____
_____	ALUMINUM FOIL	_____	_____
_____	SPICES	_____	_____
_____	CLOTHESLINE	_____	_____
_____	DISH DETERGENT	_____	_____
_____	SPONGE	_____	_____
_____	SCRAPER	_____	_____

CAMPING CHECKLIST

CHECK HERE:	ITEM	QUANTITY	NOTES
	DISH TOWELS		
	PAPER TOWELS		
	TENT		
	SUN SHELTER		
	COOLERS		
	STOVE		
	FUEL		
	TABLE		
	CAMP STOOLS		
	BEACH CHAIRS		
	COTS		
	SLEEPING BAGS		
	PADS		
	PILLOWS		
	WATER CONTAINERS		
	DISH PAN		
	BUG CANDLES		
	CLOTHESPINS		
	CAMERA EQUIPMENT		
	AX		
	LANTERN		
	KITCHEN MATCHES		
	FLASHLIGHT		

CAMPING CHECKLIST

CHECK HERE	ITEM	QUANTITY	NOTES
	PAIL		
	BROOM		
	SHOVEL		
	LANTERN FUEL		
	BATTERIES		

Dude Ranches

Why sit at home looking at sick soap operas when the whole family could be riding on the open range breathing pure, fresh air and feeling glad just to be alive.

Ride Western-style for hours and hours over beautiful countryside, help round up the cattle, learn how to rope and barrel-race. Burn off those delicious Western-style meals by square dancing the night away. And at many ranches in your spare time, you can brush up on your tennis and golf as well as seeing the range on cross-country ski trips during the winter months.

The informal outdoor life provides a warm and wonderful setting ideal for a family vacation. Contact the ranches listed below for brochures and start planning your vacation.

```
Tanque Verde Ranch              Lost Valley Ranch
Route 8, Box 66                 Route 2
Tucson, AZ 85710                Sedalia, CO 80135
Phone: (602) 296-6275           Phone:  (303) 647-2311

Rancho de los Caballeros        Eaton's Ranch
P. O. Box 1148                  Wolf, WY 82844
Wickenburg, AZ 85358            Phone:  (307) 655-9285
Phone: (602) 684-5484

The Home Ranch                  The Colorado Dude
Box 822-K                           & Guest Ranch   Assoc.
Clark, CO 80428                 Box 300
Phone:  (303) 879-1780          Tabernash, CO 80478
                                Phone:  (303) 887-3128

C Lazy U Ranch
Box 378B-W                      The Dude Ranchers' Assoc.
Granby, CO 80446                P. O. Box 471
Phone:  (303) 887-3344          LaPorte, CO 80535
                                Phone:  (303) 493-7623

              Farm & Ranch Vacations, Inc.
              36 East 57th Street
              New York, NY 10022
              Phone:  (212) 355-6334
```

Wherever we go for our reunion, we will want to take along comfortable and appropriate clothing. We will want to make sure that our favorite toiletries go along with us on the trip. Lists to help us do just that are on the following pages.

What we wear: a list to help us

The list that helps remind us of what to take is beneficial for the family to be extra sure to take what is needed.

MEN -- CLOTHING CONSIDERATIONS

CHECK HERE:	MEN:		NOTES
_____	• Shoes_____	_____	_____
_____	• Socks_____	_____	_____
_____	• Pants_____	_____	_____
_____	• Underwear_____	_____	_____
_____	• Athletic Supporter_____	_____	_____
_____	• Short Pants_____	_____	_____
_____	• Belts_____	_____	_____
_____	• Shirts_____	_____	_____
_____	• Sweaters_____	_____	_____
_____	• Coat_____	_____	_____
_____	• Neckties_____	_____	_____
_____	• Hats_____	_____	_____
_____	• Sun glasses_____	_____	_____
_____	• Pajamas_____	_____	_____
_____	• Robe_____	_____	_____
_____	• Slippers_____	_____	_____
_____	• Rain Coat_____	_____	_____
_____	• Rain Hat_____	_____	_____
_____	• Umbrella_____	_____	_____

Please let this checklist serve as a general reminder of items that family members might take along with them on their annual family reunion.

WOMEN -- CLOTHING CONSIDERATIONS

CHECK HERE: 1.	WOMEN:	:	:	NOTES
____ : ____	• Shoes_____	: _____	:	_____
____ : ____	• Stockings_____	: _____	:	_____
____ : ____	• Pants_____	: _____	:	_____
____ : ____	• Panties_____	: _____	:	_____
____ : ____	• Slips_____	: _____	:	_____
____ : ____	• Bras_____	: _____	:	_____
____ : ____	• Blouses_____	: _____	:	_____
____ : ____	• Skirts_____	: _____	:	_____
____ : ____	• Dresses_____	: _____	:	_____
____ : ____	• Shorts_____	: _____	:	_____
____ : ____	• Bathing Suits____	: _____	:	_____
____ : ____	• Nightgowns_____	: _____	:	_____
____ : ____	• Robes_____	: _____	:	_____
____ : ____	• Slippers_____	: _____	:	_____
____ : ____	• Dress Suits_____	: _____	:	_____
____ : ____	• Evening Clothes__	: _____	:	_____
____ : ____	• Coats_____	: _____	:	_____
____ : ____	• Scarves_____	: _____	:	_____
____ : ____	• Raincoat & Hat___	: _____	:	_____
____ : ____	• Umbrella_____	: _____	:	_____
____ : ____	• Boots_____	: _____	:	_____

Please let this checklist serve as a general reminder of items that family members will take along with them on their annual family reunion.

BABIES -- CLOTHING CONSIDERATIONS

CHECK HERE	:BABIES:		:QUANTITY:	NOTES
_____	_____	. Shoes_____	_____	_____
_____	_____	. Socks_____	_____	_____
_____	_____	. Pampers_____	_____	_____
_____	_____	. Diapers_____	_____	_____
_____	_____	. Safety Pins___	_____	_____
_____	_____	. Lotion_____	_____	_____
_____	_____	. Powder_____	_____	_____
_____	_____	. Oil_____	_____	_____
_____	_____	. Bibs_____	_____	_____
_____	_____	. Undershirts___	_____	_____
_____	_____	. Rubber Pants__	_____	_____
_____	_____	. Training Pants_	_____	_____
_____	_____	. Sleepers_____	_____	_____
_____	_____	. Shirts_____	_____	_____
_____	_____	. Pants_____	_____	_____
_____	_____	. Dresses_____	_____	_____
_____	_____	. Hats_____	_____	_____
_____	_____	. Coats_____	_____	_____
_____	_____	. Blankets_____	_____	_____
_____	_____	. Bottles_____	_____	_____
_____	_____	. Formula_____	_____	_____
_____	_____	. _____	_____	_____
_____	_____	. _____	_____	_____
_____	_____	. _____	_____	_____

ACCESSORIES FOR BABIES

CHECK HERE	BABIES.		QUANTITY	NOTES
_____	_____	Toys_____	_____	_____
_____	_____	Pacifiers_____	_____	_____
_____	_____	Teething materials	_____	_____
_____	_____	Books_____	_____	_____
_____	_____	Safety Stroller___	_____	_____
_____	_____	Safety Car Seat___	_____	_____
_____	_____	Safety Carrier____	_____	_____
_____	_____	_____	_____	_____
_____	_____	_____	_____	_____
_____	_____	_____	_____	_____
_____	_____	_____	_____	_____
_____	_____	_____	_____	_____
_____	_____	_____	_____	_____
_____	_____	_____	_____	_____
_____	_____	_____	_____	_____
_____	_____	_____	_____	_____
_____	_____	_____	_____	_____
_____	_____	_____	_____	_____
_____	_____	_____	_____	_____
_____	_____	_____	_____	_____
_____	_____	_____	_____	_____

MEN --TOILETRIES

CHECK HERE	MEN	ITEMS	QUANTITY	NOTES
_____	_____	Toothbrush_____	_____	_____
_____	_____	Toothpaste_____	_____	_____
_____	_____	Dental Floss_____	_____	_____
_____	_____	Denture Powder___	_____	_____
_____	_____	Denture Paste____	_____	_____
_____	_____	Mouthwash_____	_____	_____
_____	_____	Hydrogen Peroxide	_____	_____
_____	_____	Face Cleanser____	_____	_____
_____	_____	Lotion_____	_____	_____
_____	_____	Anti-perspirant__	_____	_____
_____	_____	Cologne_____	_____	_____
_____	_____	Comb_____	_____	_____
_____	_____	Hair Brush_____	_____	_____
_____	_____	Hair Shampoo_____	_____	_____
_____	_____	Hair Conditioner_	_____	_____
_____	_____	Hair Dryer_____	_____	_____
_____	_____	Shaving Cream____	_____	_____
_____	_____	Razor & Blades___	_____	_____
_____	_____	After Shave_____	_____	_____
_____	_____	Scissors_____	_____	_____
_____	_____	Nail Clippers____	_____	_____
_____	_____	Plastic Bag_____	_____	_____
_____	_____	_____	_____	_____
_____	_____	_____	_____	_____

WOMEN -- TOILETRIES

CHECK HERE	WOMEN	ITEMS	QUANTITY	NOTES
_____	_____	• Toothbrush_____	_____	_____
_____	_____	• Toothpaste_____	_____	_____
_____	_____	• Dental Floss_____	_____	_____
_____	_____	• Denture Powder___	_____	_____
_____	_____	• Denture Paste____	_____	_____
_____	_____	• Mouthwash_____	_____	_____
_____	_____	• Hydrogen Peroxide	_____	_____
_____	_____	• Face Cleanser____	_____	_____
_____	_____	• Lotion_____	_____	_____
_____	_____	• Anti-perspirant__	_____	_____
_____	_____	• Perfume_____	_____	_____
_____	_____	• Comb_____	_____	_____
_____	_____	• Scissors_____	_____	_____
_____	_____	• Nail Clippers____	_____	_____
_____	_____	• Feminine Hygiene_	_____	_____
_____	_____	• _____	_____	_____
_____	_____	• _____	_____	_____

After we have packed the necessary items to take to the family reunion we should make an inventory list for the home. With the growth and spread of family reunions, we will see a decrease in crime. Burglaries will be a thing of the past. But until then, it will be of considerable help to have an inventory of the entire family home. This list of valuables will contribute to the family serenity.

The list provides for every room and we can include all of the items that have serial numbers. Such a list will make any insurance claim for theft loss more reliable. In addition, if the family has not already started saving sales receipts, it should now begin this good habit for verification of purchase. The list should be kept in a safe deposit box in the bank in which the family does business.

HOME INVENTORY LIST

INVENTORY LIST FOR OUR HOME

FAMILY NAME   _____

STREET ADDRESS_____

CITY   _____

STATE   _____ZIP CODE_____

PHONE: AREA CODE_____NUMBER_____

Your family should take a moment to complete this inventory list now. The contents in your home are of value to all of the members of your family and care must be taken to guard against loss.

KITCHEN, LAUNDRY ROOM

No. of Items	Item	Year Purch'd	Cost / Notes

TOTAL $_____
(Record on summary page)

LIVING ROOM

No. of Items	Item	Year Purch'd	Cost / Notes
	Art objects		
	Books		
	Carpet / Padding		
	Chairs		
	Chests, and contents*		
	Clocks		
	Coffee tables		
	Couches		
	Desk, and contents*		
	End tables		
	Lamps		
	Paintings		
	Rugs		

*Where applicable, itemize contents in extra space provided.

TOTAL $ _____
(Record on summary page)

DINING ROOM

No. of Items	Item	Year Purch'd	Cost / Notes
	Carpet / Padding		
	Chairs		
	Tables		
	Buffet, and contents*		
	China		
	Crystal		
	Rugs		
	Silver		
	Curtains/Blinds/Shades		

*Where applicable, itemize contents in extra space provided.

TOTAL $ _____
(Record on summary page)

MASTER BEDROOM

No. of: Items	Item	:Year :Purch'd	: Cost / Notes
	:Bedding	:	:
	:Beds	:	:
	:Books	:	:
	:Bureaus, and contents *	:	:
	:Carpet/Carpet padding	:	:
	:Chairs	:	:
	:Chests, and contents *	:	:
	:Closet contents *	:	:
	:Curtain/Blinds/Shades	:	:
	:Desk	:	:
	:Dresser, and contents*	:	:
	:Dressing table	:	:
	:Lamps	:	:
	:Mattresses	:	:
	:Rugs	:	:
	:Sewing machine	:	:
	:Springs	:	:
	:Tables	:	:
	:Wall shelves	:	:
	:	:	:
	:	:	:
	:	:	:

*Where applicable, itemize contents in extra space provided.
TOTAL $ _____
(Record on summary page)

BEDROOM 2

No. of Items	Item	Year Purch'd	Cost / Notes
	Bedding		
	Beds		
	Books		
	Bureaus, and contents *		
	Carpet/Carpet padding		
	Chairs		
	Chests, and contents *		
	Closet contents *		
	Curtain/Blinds/Shades		
	Desk		
	Dresser, and contents*		
	Dressing table		
	Lamps		
	Mattresses		
	Rugs		
	Sewing machine		
	Springs		
	Tables		
	Wall shelves		

*Where applicable, itemize contents in extra space provided.

TOTAL $ _____
(Record on summary page)

BEDROOM 3

No. of Items	Item	Year Purch'd	Cost / Notes
	Bedding		
	Beds		
	Books		
	Bureaus, and contents *		
	Carpet/Carpet padding		
	Chairs		
	Chests, and contents *		
	Closet contents *		
	Curtain/Blinds/Shades		
	Desk		
	Dressing table		
	Lamps		
	Mattresses		
	Sewing machine		
	Springs		
	Tables		
	Wall shelves		

*Where applicable, itemize contents in extra space provided.

TOTAL $ _____
(Record on summary page)

BEDROOM 4

No. of Items	Item	Year Purch'd	Cost / Notes
	Bedding		
	Beds		
	Books		
	Bureaus, and contents *		
	Carpet/Carpet padding		
	Chairs		
	Chests, and contents *		
	Closet contents *		
	Curtain/Blinds/Shades		
	Desk		
	Dresser, and contents*		
	Dressing table		
	Lamps		
	Mattresses		
	Rugs		
	Sewing machine		
	Springs		
	Tables		
	Wall shelves		

*Where applicable, itemize contents in extra space provided.

TOTAL $_____
(Record on page___)

FAMILY ROOM, DEN, OFFICE

No. of Items	Item	Year Purch'd	Cost / Notes

TOTAL $ _____
(Record on summary page)

GARAGE

No. of Items	Item	Year Purch'd	Cost / Notes
_____	_____	_____	_____
_____	_____	_____	_____
_____	_____	_____	_____
_____	_____	_____	_____
_____	_____	_____	_____
_____	_____	_____	_____
_____	_____	_____	_____
_____	_____	_____	_____
_____	_____	_____	_____
_____	_____	_____	_____
_____	_____	_____	_____
_____	_____	_____	_____
_____	_____	_____	_____
_____	_____	_____	_____
_____	_____	_____	_____
_____	_____	_____	_____
_____	_____	_____	_____

TOTAL $ _____
(Record on summary page)

YARD, PATIO

No. of Items	Item	Year Purch'd	Cost / Notes

TOTAL $ _____
(Record on summary page)

ITEMS WITH SERIAL NUMBERS IN CASE OF THEFT

Item / Brand	Serial Number	Year Purch'd	Cost

TOTAL $ _____
(Record on summary page)

ITEMS WITH SERIAL NUMBERS IN CASE OF THEFT

Item / Brand	Serial Number	Year Purch'd	Cost

TOTAL $ _____
(Record on summary page)

SUMMARY PAGE
TOTALS

KITCHEN, LAUNDRY ROOM   _____

LIVING ROOM   _____

DINING ROOM   _____

MASTER BEDROOM   _____

BEDROOM 2   _____

BEDROOM 3   _____

BEDROOM 4   _____

FAMILY ROOM, DEN, OFFICE   _____

GARAGE   _____

YARD/PATIO   _____

ITEMS WITH SERIAL NOS. 1   _____

ITEMS WITH SERIAL NOS. 2   _____

TOTAL   _____

Leaving the home behind

We have made an inventory of our possessions and stored the list in the safe deposit box at the bank. We can do a few more things to make the chance of a misfortune less likely to take place. The way we leave the home determines the security of mind we will have on the road and at the family reunion.

CHAPTER IV

IV. NUTRITION

NUTRITION

We are very concerned about what we eat, especially for the entire family. All too often we have been too much in a hurry to prepare a decent home-cooked meal and opt for the fast-food outlets that are jumping up all over the place. We need to return to the basics, prepare our family a good hot meal and stop going to the fast-food establishments except on special or rare occasions. Three to five times a year is more than sufficient to visit the fast-food hot dog and hamburger places, and those that serve batter-prepared chicken and fish that is deep-fried in pounds and pounds of grease, salt and preservatives.

Our families are gaining weight, fat and cellulite at an unusual pace. Most of us are just lazy and uncaring about our health. We eat fast foods and feed our children potato chips, corn chips, and pork rinds. We are too busy to make a hot meal of vegetables, broiled fish, chicken and other healthy foods.

Now we will focus on the family reunion food preparation for the once-a-year feast for the entire family. We will return to the preparation that the family goes through all year long before the family reunion. We will discuss the food plans. Then we will develop a fun-filled family exercise program **gentle enough** for the entire family. And we will make up our minds to have a family nutrition program that will control our weight once we lose the excess pounds. We want to do this in this chapter because food without exercise ignores the needs of the heart, mind and body. We must reverse this family tragedy.

FOOD PREPARATION

Many families prefer to have the food preparation done by family members. This may be the most economical method and usually the cooks in the family love providing their own special dishes. It is their way of giving to the group, of expressing their love and caring for the whole family. These special dishes...Aunt Jane's chocolate pies and cousin Mary's cornbread are remembered from year to year and are musts on the menu for each successive get-together. The continuity and the traditions build up adding to the strength of the coalition.

Often special preparations must be made for particular family members, especially when many in the group are elderly. Many may be on special low-cholesterol diets for heart ailments, low-sodium diets due to high blood pressure, frequent portions of high protein, low sugar foods for diabetics. Often it is possible to plan menus which take all of these matters into consideration thus making the most number of dishes available to the most people and at the same time providing better health for everyone.   Let us examine a few ways to get the nutrition to the family at the reunion with love and good taste.

Family cooking, communal cooking, potluck, and bring your own (BYO) are a few of the ways to make it all happen.   Hotels and caterers are also considered here. Let us begin.

Food Preparation by Family Cooks.

We approach the area of nutrition with delicate care because this is the area that most of the family conversation will center upon.   If this area is overdone, that is, if the host city planners load too much cooking on the same families in that city too often, the results will be negative.   So when making plans for cooking with the families doing the food preparation, we must give much thought to dividing the cooking duties so that there are several families, if possible, doing the food preparation throughout the years to come at the reunion.

The menu may be simple and basic so that less time will be absorbed by the work of cooking and more time will be devoted to pleasurable entertainment activities.   Cooking should be shared by the men and women, young and seniors alike if physical abilities permit.

Food preparation should be planned early to allow for adequate time to purchase food items on discounts or to be purchased wholesale.   Our family bought the meat, fowl, and other items approximately three to six months in advance.   We used a deep freeze to keep the food from spoiling.   We took our time to cook the food approximately two weeks prior to the family reunion and then we stored it in the deep freeze. We made sure that the food was wrapped very well in freezer wrapping to eliminate freezer burn.

To achieve the goal of successful family cooking we may try two methods: first, communal cooking and second, alternating family cooking.

Communal cooking is when each of the families in the host city provide at least one member to be on the Nutrition Committee.   The Nutrition Committee divides the food preparation up in a fair manner.   This provides for good, home-cooked meals that are familiar to the taste buds of the entire family.   For this reason, family cooks may offer a very good choice over other means of food preparation.

We do not want to overuse this handy means of food preparation for fear that it will burn out the cooks and their families who join in the chores.   Think for a moment about the enthusiasm that the cooks have initially and do not be misled into thinking that the fatigue factor will not take a toll after a period of five or six family reunions if the same people do all of the work.

Be fair and the members who volunteer to do the food preparation will perform their duties with great care and pride.   The duties should be agreed upon and done without hesitation according to the dictates of the Nutrition Committee. A problem can arise if some of the members shrink from their responsibilities and do not perform.   The hard feelings created by this type of immaturity will do harm to the family reunion for years to come.   Family members are ofen slow in forgiving the mistakes of other family members. Avoid this by making sure the work is divided evenly and that the members accept the responsiblities without pressure.

Second, the **alternating family cooking** method provides for one family being totally responsible for the cooking one year in the host city.   Then, the next year the duty shifts to another family in the next host city.   If the host city is the same city for each consecutive year, then the duty of cooking rotates to another family.   A problem can arise when no other family volunteers to share in the cooking.

Where   there is more than one host city, the cooking should be alternated from family unit to family unit in each of the host cities until every family has had a chance to share in the cooking. If this method is to be successful, a family log should be made that gives the year that each family unit has had the honor of cooking and shows the name of the family that has the honor next.

Potluck is arranged so that each family has the joy of providing a dish needed to make the menu complete.   The Nutrition Committee consists of members of the different nuclear family units.   The members may use as a guide the **menu for a family reunions** which is included in this section. Or, they may make their own menu with different ethnic, national or regional styles of cooking.

Then   each member selects a dish to prepare for the family feast.   Another way to choose what dishes are to be prepared by the members is to draw individual menu selections from a hat. Each member agrees to the method, and the dishes to be included are selected by the Nutrition Committee.   Each item on the menu is written on a separate piece of paper.   All of the separate pieces of papers are folded individually and placed in a hat for the drawing.

POTLUCK INDIVIDUAL MENU ITEM

The item that I will prepare is:

_____

POTLUCK INDIVIDUAL MENU ITEM

The item that I will prepare is:

_____

POTLUCK INDIVIDUAL MENU ITEM

The item that I will prepare is:

_____

POTLUCK INDIVIDUAL MENU ITEM

The item that I will prepare is:

_____

POTLUCK INDIVIDUAL MENU ITEM

The item that I will prepare is:

_____

We want to do our part to make our family peaceful.

Potluck Master List. Everyone waits anxiously for a turn to draw an item from the hat. After all of the members have drawn their selections from the hat, they are responsible for the preparation of that dish for the menu. Each puts his/her name, item, address, and phone number on the potluck master list. Make sure to include the area code with the phone number and the zip code with the address. Our food preparation will help us to belong and be a part of the overall happiness of the family reunion.

Keeping a record of what everyone is responsible for preparing for the family reunion is the duty of the chairperson of the Nutrition Committee. The chairperson of the Committee will make sufficient copies to distribute to all of the members of the Committee.

For large families that are scattered across the globe, it is a good idea to have a family meeting at the first family reunion to discuss the next annual family reunion that the family will be having the following year. Be sure to take this book to the reunion to be used in making plans for the next one. The family will have a meeting to discuss the food, travel, and other plans for the next reunion. The potluck list can be made at the site. Here is a **potluck master list** to be used in writing the information necessary to keep the reunion momentum going.

```
::::::::::::::::::::::::::::::::::::::::::::::::::::::::::::::::::::
#                    POTLUCK MASTER  LIST                        #
#                                                               #
#    ITEM           | NAME        |ADDRESS          |PHONE NO.  #
#1.                 |             |                 |           #
#                   |             |                 |           #
#                   |             |                 |           #
#                   |             |                 |           #
#2.                 |             |                 |           #
#                   |             |                 |           #
#                   |             |                 |           #
#                   |             |                 |           #
#3.                 |             |                 |           #
#                   |             |                 |           #
#                   |             |                 |           #
#                   |             |                 |           #
#5.                 |             |                 |           #
#                   |             |                 |           #
#                   |             |                 |           #
#                   |             |                 |           #
#6.                 |             |                 |           #
#                   |             |                 |           #
#                   |             |                 |           #
#                   |             |                 |           #
#7.                 |             |                 |           #
#                   |             |                 |           #
#                   |             |                 |           #
#                   |             |                 |           #
#8.                 |             |                 |           #
#                   |             |                 |           #
#                   |             |                 |           #
#                   |             |                 |           #
#9.                 |             |                 |           #
#                   |             |                 |           #
#                   |             |                 |           #
#                   |             |                 |           #
#10.                |             |                 |           #
#                   |             |                 |           #
#                   |             |                 |           #
#                   |             |                 |           #
#11.                |             |                 |           #
#                   |             |                 |           #
#                   |             |                 |           #
#                   |             |                 |           #
#12.                |             |                 |           #
#                   |             |                 |           #
#                   |             |                 |           #
#                   |             |                 |           #
#14.                |             |                 |           #
#                   |             |                 |           #
#                   |             |                 |           #
#                   |             |                 |           #
::::::::::::::::::::::::::::::::::::::::::::::::::::::::::::::::::::
```

We love to share in making our family happy.

```
::::::::::::::::::::::::::::::::::::::::::::::::::::::::::::
#                  POTLUCK MASTER  LIST                  #
#                                                        #
#    ITEM         | NAME       |ADDRESS       |PHONE NO. #
#                                                        #
# MEAT/FISH/FOWL                                         #
#                                                        #
#1.               |            |              |          #
#                 |            |              |          #
#                 |            |              |          #
#                 |            |              |          #
#2.               |            |              |          #
#                 |            |              |          #
#                 |            |              |          #
#                 |            |              |          #
# HOT VEGETABLES  |            |              |          #
#                 |            |              |          #
#3.               |            |              |          #
#                 |            |              |          #
#                 |            |              |          #
#                 |            |              |          #
#5.               |            |              |          #
#                 |            |              |          #
#                 |            |              |          #
#                 |            |              |          #
#6.               |            |              |          #
#                 |            |              |          #
#                 |            |              |          #
#                 |            |              |          #
# SALADS          |            |              |          #
#                 |            |              |          #
#7.               |            |              |          #
#                 |            |              |          #
#                 |            |              |          #
#                 |            |              |          #
# BREAD           |            |              |          #
#                 |            |              |          #
#8.               |            |              |          #
#                 |            |              |          #
#                 |            |              |          #
#                 |            |              |          #
# BEVERAGES                                              #
#                                                        #
#9.               |            |              |          #
#                 |            |              |          #
#                 |            |              |          #
#                 |            |              |          #
::::::::::::::::::::::::::::::::::::::::::::::::::::::::::::
```

Do not forsake the family.

```
:::::::::::::::::::::::::::::::::::::::::::::::::::::::::::::::::
#                    POTLUCK MASTER  LIST                     #
#                                                             #
#   ITEM            | NAME           |ADDRESS        |PHONE NO. #
#                                                             #
# DESSERTS                                                    #
#                   |                |               |        #
#10.                |                |               |        #
#                   |                |               |        #
#                   |                |               |        #
#                   |                |               |        #
# PICKLES, ONIONS, RELISH, OLIVES                             #
#                                                             #
#11.                |                |               |        #
#                   |                |               |        #
#                   |                |               |        #
#                   |                |               |        #
# PEPPER, VINEGAR, CATSUP, MAYONNAISE, MUSTARD                #
#                                                             #
#12.                |                |               |        #
#                   |                |               |        #
#                   |                |               |        #
#                   |                |               |        #
#                   |                |               |        #
#                   |                |               |        #
#                   |                |               |        #
#                   |                |               |        #
:::::::::::::::::::::::::::::::::::::::::::::::::::::::::::::::::
```

We can give today for a brighter future; let us give our best now.

Miscellaneous items that no picnic or family feast is complete without include the following:

```
:::::::::::::::::::::::::::::::::::::::::::::::::::::::::::::::::::::
#                    MISCELLANEOUS  ITEMS                        #
#                                                               #
#                                                               #
#                                                               #
# ITEM             | NAME         |ADDRESS        |PHONE NO.  #
#                                                               #
# Paper towels,                                                 #
# Napkins, Spoons,                                              #
# Forks, Knives,                                                #
# Plates, Glasses,                                              #
# Toothpicks, and cups.                                         #
#                                                               #
#1.               |              |               |           #
#                 |              |               |           #
#                 |              |               |           #
#                                                               #
# INSECT REPELLENT                                              #
#                                                               #
#                                                               #
#2.               |              |               |           #
#                 |              |               |           #
#                 |              |               |           #
#                 |              |               |           #
:::::::::::::::::::::::::::::::::::::::::::::::::::::::::::::::::::::
```
Seek ways to make our family a better family for God.

A Master Menu list for the family reunion

MEAT/FISH/FOWL

____ Barbecued pork (spare ribs)
____ Barbecued beef (short ribs)
____ Barbecued hot dogs (beef, pork, chicken or turkey)
____ Barbecued hot links and sausages
____ Barbecued chicken
____ Barbecued turkey
____ Barbecued duck
____ Barbecued goose

HOT VEGETABLES

____ Boiled corn
____ String beans
____ Baked beans

____ Sweet peas
____ Sweet potatoes
____ Steamed potatoes
____ Greens (different varieties)

SALADS

____ Green salad
____ Cole slaw
____ Spinach salad
____ Potato salad

BREAD

____ Hot cornbread
____ French toast
____ Hot dinner rolls
____ Wheat bread
____ Rye or raisin cinnamon bread

BEVERAGES

____ Water
____ Iced tea
____ Lemonade
____ Soft drinks
____ Juices
____ Coffee

DESSERTS

____ Sweet potato pie
____ Coconut pie
____ Family reunion anniversary cake

____ Homemade ice-cream

____ A course of fresh fruits
____ Cheese

This menu list offers a selection to choose from to make the menu for the family. The meat section can be adapted to the needs of the family to choose either meat, fish of fowl. A family could have a menu that is light in calories, but yet fulfilling. The list may seem long but it allows families, especially smaller families to choose an item or two from each category.

Thus, we can put together a little menu for the reunion:

____ Barbecued beef
____ Barbecued chicken
____ Barbecued hot links

____ Baked beans
____ Boiled corn

____ Turnip Greens

____ Green salad
____ Potato salad

____ Family reunion cake
____ Homemade ice-cream

____ Soft drinks
____ Lemonade

Have fun and make up a menu for the family reunion with your family style in mind. When the taste buds of the family are better known, then consider some other dishes. But the first reunion should be basic. During the reunion the family could vote on a menu selection as well as who will do the food preparation for the next family reunion. Perhaps the family will try a Spanish or a French menu. A combination of kosher food may be the idea for a later reunion. The possibilities are numerous. If the family can afford it, let everybody chip in to a general fund to cater the food for the family reunion.

Why cater? After a period of time, about seven reunions down the road, the cooking members of the family will want a break. Either they will not come to the reunion and lack the courage to tell anyone the real reason, or they will make arrangements to be on some assignment for their jobs as reasons for not attending. And the reasons will grow and grow. Avoid these types of absences by catering early in the game.

Catering can be an enjoyable experience with the entire family being better rested from not having to do a lot of cooking. No pots and pans to clean up. No boxes and trays to unload from the cars, trucks, etc. Caterers bring everything and take it all away again when the party is over, so clean-up is provided for. It can be a reasonable, affordable affair.

Catering

Careful planning at least six months prior to the family reunion will offer a chance to select a good catering company. There are a number of reasonably-priced caterers available today. Look in the yellow pages under "Caterers". Check your favorite restaurants too. Many do catering, will come to your location and take care of everything: table-cloths, table settings, flowers, plates and the food.

When looking for a caterer, check with your friends for their experiences, especially friends whose tastes are similar to yours. Find out who they would recommend, and when they used that particular caterer last. Most caterers charge on a per-person basis. Do some price-comparison shopping, and then go back to the shop you prefer. Many caterers who learn that you're expecting 100 people or more are willing to give you a competitive price.

Once you find out how many people are coming it is important to prepare a budget. You must determine the amount of money at your disposal from all sources, the amounts to be spent on all non-food items such as transportation and entertainment, and the remainder is the amount you will have for food, usually the largest expense.

Basic types of caterers. Caterers' services vary from the simple to the complex, from a picnic in the park to a sit-down wedding feast. The family can choose the caterer that will supply everything to simplify the arrangements. The particulars are good to establish ahead of time to eliminate hurt feelings and disappointments.

Two basic types of service are available. The first is **buffet style** where tables of food are set up and everybody goes through a line and helps himself/herself. The food is kept hot by the caterer with heating appliances or small cans of thermo burners to insure a continuously hot meal. The caterer keeps the cold food cold by providing ice or portable refrigeration.

Within the buffet style of service, caterers' prices will vary according to whether the family wishes to pay for everything that the caterer brings out to the site or chooses the less expensive all-you-can-eat-on-site method. If the family chooses the latter method, the caterers do not mind people coming back several times for more food, but no people or doggy bags are allowed. If the family desires to pay for all of the food that the caterer brings out to the site, all the leftover food can be divided among the family members and taken home.

Some caterers may only offer one type of buffet service since they may be able to resell the unused food in their food chains or restaurants. Check with the caterer to get the specifics of how the service will be handled. Ask all of the necessary questions up front to avoid confusion later.

The second type of service is a **sit-down dinner** where the caterer serves the food that is brought out to the site. The food is set up to allow the family to dine in a dinner-table setting.

This service really offers the family a treat in that everyone is served while being seated. It will make the family want to come back to many more reunions where all of the members of the family who do all of the cooking are treated to a couple days of rest from the kitchen. This treat is a real winner with a good caterer.

Prices of caterers. The prices vary according to the service desired. The level of difficulty in obtaining the menu selections and the time of the year influence prices. If, for instance, the meat is purchased when beef is high the price may reflect this depending on the caterer. This is another reason for planning early for the food selection. The caterer will have a chance to obtain the best deals for the best price to help the family economize. The small, good caterers are usually more flexible and humane.

A minimum service charge is added on to the family bill in some cases if a certain number of persons are not reached. Some caterers state that if the family has less than forty persons attending, they will charge a $75.00 surcharge to be added to the price of the regular service. Usually these are caterers who are set up to serve only the large to super-large family reunions. We do not need these insensitive creatures if our first reunion is less than their minimum-persons charge. Who needs to throw away money?

Avoid caterers that are strictly commercial and are not warm, humane, and reasonable in their pricing. The attitude of the caterer at the time of the early negotiations should be observed very closely, because the same attitude will be the one brought to the family reunion. Find a caterer that is not into it just for the money, no matter how large or good the caterer may be. The family deserves a service that is concerned about the family happiness and enjoyment.

Oftentimes the small mom and pop caterer will do the best job for the family. That does not mean all large caterers are bad. Take your time and try to find a good, concerned caterer at least six months before the family reunion.

Special dietary considerations. Low sodium to no sodium diets should be made known to the caterer early. Sometimes it is our desire to have everybody do as we do in life. If we do not like salt, then we expect everybody else to refrain from salt. However, when we are preparing for several of our family members, we must be reasonable in our approach to other people's needs. If some people want pork, salt, and other items that we are not in agreement with, we need to find the middle road to make everybody as happy as possible.

No sugar in the food other than raw sugar, honey, or one of the safe sweeteners may be important to the family. Sometimes caterers are not geared to change their method of food preparation. If the caterer is inflexible in this area, take a poll of the family leaders and get a majority vote.

A vegetarian plate can often be made available by most caterers. Some members of the family do not want to eat meat of any kind. Pork, beef, or lamb are not for them. Then ask the caterer to provide a selection, for the vegetarians of the family. Some semi-vegetarians will eat chicken, turkey, duck, or fish. Honor their wishes or seek ways to provide for their needs.

Spicy foods are more of an individual choice that can be provided for by having a spicy dish or two or providing spicy seasoning to be added at the table by the members of the family who desire hot foods.

In some families everybody seems to like hot, spicy food. The family members have eaten only highly-seasoned food all their lives. Then we have a different situation. The caterer should be notified from the beginning of the family seasoning preference so that the menu can be prepared accordingly. In such a situation, a few bland meals can be prepared for those who cannot tolerate the highly-seasoned food.

Thirst Quenchers. Soft drinks with flavors like orange, root beer, cola, and lemon lime are what all of the little children usually prefer with their special meals. Nutrition-conscious families will not serve these drinks on a regular basis, but most picnics are not complete without these soft drinks.

Lemonade is a supplement that goes well with the food. Ice-cold lemonade makes the day a little brighter and the fun of drawing Mr. and Ms. Frost on a chilled glass of cold lemonade delights the little ones.

Iced Tea is still in the running as a thirst quencher. A lemon or a lime can be added to make the flavor a bit more interesting if desired.   A mild mint-flavored iced tea may also be considered.   Make a hot, strong mint-flavored tea, then chill it and add ice for a flavor that is hard to beat.

Ice water is sometimes easy to forget when the family has thought of all the other thirst quenchers.   But do not forget water. Nothing really takes the place of it.

Juices that are full of natural fruit flavors like combinations of cranberry and apple, cranberry and raspberry, and cranberry and grape are all delicious for a family reunion.   Orange, apple, and grapefruit juices are good and really make healthy drinks.

Now what do we do about those adults who want something strong to drink?   Let us examine this area with care.

Hot coffee and tea may be included. Decaffeinated coffee and tea are available for those who desire it.   Provide both kinds if necessary, and mark them clearly.   The reunion is not the time to start an overnight salvation crusade.

Alcoholic beverages   are a concern for many families, especially those families that are very religious.   This is topic of delicate consideration.   If the family is primarily of a religious persuasion that prohibits the use of alcohol, then the majority rules.   No alcohol should be provided during the reunion at the site where all of the members gather, none at all.   The members of the family who drink should get together during a break and go off somewhere away from any of the non-drinking members and indulge in a cold beer or a good glass of wine to refresh themselves.

Be careful to take along some breath mints to eliminate the alcohol odor from the breath.   This solution and consideration makes for the best blend of the two worlds. The family unit as a whole will not be compromised by the few in this case.   Why?   Actually we know the answer.   Most families did not get religious overnight so all are aware of the family's religious feelings.   The family reunion is not the place for the religious members to force change on the non-religious ones and vice-versa.   Keep harmony and show a little respect.   It will go a long way and encourage several more years of happy family reunions.   Do not underestimate the harm that can be done if the alcohol issue is not handled with care.

Some families have achieved a mutual respect between the drinkers and the non-drinkers.   These families will often have tables at the picnic site where alcohol is served.   Then the non-drinkers have their tables with punch.   The coexistence is a better road if the family is at the level of mutual love and respect for all of the family to permit it.

This approach eliminates the air of the drinkers being judged and condemned by the non-drinkers.

If the family can set up tables for the drinkers where the non-drinkers are not offended, then the middle road is the happy solution for the family that wants to stay together as a family. Leave judgment to the Almighty.

Serving times. Make absolutely sure in writing of the times the family desires to be served. A good caterer will always arrive at least 45 minutes to an hour earlier to have the food ready to be served without a moment's delay at the exact time the family designated to be served. Let us face the truth here. When the family is hungry, people are ready to eat right then and there without delay. Little children are told the time to be ready for meals and they are going to be on time for some good food to give them more fuel to continue having a good time.

The serving time should be set so that out-of-town visitors do not have to eat breakfast or dinner that day at a restaurant or the homes of relatives. Usually around one o'clock in the afternoon is the best time. Inform the members of the family to arrive at the park at 11:00 a.m. or 12:00 noon for the picnic and games. The caterer will arrive at about 12:15 p.m. to have the meal completely ready for service at 1:00 p.m.

Remember some of the family would have gone sightseeing or slept in late. So, 1:00 p.m. is a good time for all appetites to be ready for a delicious meal.

Table setup. The caterer may include table setup in the charge. Make sure it is clear whether or not the caterer will provide for the table setup. **Tablecloths** are not always provided in the setup arrangements. If the family desires to purchase its own cloth, plastic or paper tablecloths the members who are responsible for this duty should make early plans.

Flatware, spoons, knives, and forks, are usually included by the caterer if the family desires plastic flat-ware. Otherwise check with the caterer about providing metal flatware, or have members of the family bring it. Provide enough for the specific number of people who will attend, and add a few extra place settings for last-minute arrivals.

Picnics

Having a picnic seems like the ideal starting place for the feast of the first family reunion. A very basic picnic provides for less pressure and expense. It also provides the added advantage of informality -- no one has to get dressed up to attend or spend a lot of money on something suitable to wear.

The family reunion planned during the summer season usually provides for plenty of sunlight. But occasionally it rains, and provisions should be made for inclement weather.

A shelter house is often located in parks, for rent by the hour, day, or week. The prices are reasonable: approximately $5.00 for half a day, $11.00 for a whole day, and $62.00 for a week. The shelter house normally has rest rooms that are well-maintained. Electrical outlets are available for plugging in 110v appliances for re-heating food, running stereos, and video camera recorders.

A roof over family heads is the added attraction to a shelter house in that it can be used even if it rains. A shelter house may have a barbecue grill under its roof or one may be near by. The family can bring a portable barbecue grill along and barbecue the meat, fish, or fowl over mesquite wood or the like.

Tables and sinks. Picnic tables are usually provided with bench seats. Families may bring lawn chairs for additional seating and resting if desired. A large sink is available for washing up any cooking appliances, tables, and other items that need it. These added conveniences make the shelter house very appealing for a family reunion.

Reservations for the Shelter House. The entire area where the shelter house is located is on a reservation-only basis. Many families are able to reserve a shelter one year in advance. The more popular parks may demand an advance reservation of up to one year to insure the availability of the site. So give a call to the park of your family's choice and make the necessary reservation today.

All of the various catering services, potluck, and family alternating cooking plans will fit quite well into the shelter house scheme.

Open parks. A pass which will allow the family to come and go during visiting hours is available in some counties, states and national parks. If your city or town has a tourist bureau, give them a call and get information on the correct agency to write for an annual pass. Take your immediate family out to the park more often. During the family reunion, the entire family will find the trip back to nature well worth the time and small charge levied by some of these parks. Some parks do not have an entry fee. Ideally, all should be free to family reunions and family picnics. The government should give some benefits to the family to encourage more of the positive contributions families can make.

The open park is still very nice even if the family cannot

get a shelter house.   The family can bring blankets, outdoor lawn sets, and other conveniences for the comfort of the children and mature adults.   The open park is more popular in regions where the weather is predictable, where hot weather and no rain are the forecast during summer months.   If this is descriptive of the area for the family reunion, then by all means give it a try.   The thing to remember is most of these events must be planned several months in advance with no more accurate prediction of the weather available than the **Farmer's Almanac.**

Restaurants

Many families eliminate a lot of confusion and planning over who is going to cook what and who will pay for this and that by deciding to have their meals out in a family-style restaurant.   Usually the family patronizes a restaurant that provides an array of hot, healthy vegetables with meat, fish, and fowl.   The family picks a place that has a warm and friendly atmosphere for all people, regardless of their nationality, race or creed.

Prices.   These family-oriented restaurants may provide a good meal for a price less than it would cost the family to do their own cooking.   One of the advantages to this system is that each nuclear family pays its own individual bills. No record keeping, cooking or work are required.

The menu selections can be distributed to the entire family early after the Nutrition Committee first contacts the restaurant for a copy of the menu.   Most restaurants will be glad to provide the family with a free copy of the menu once their intentions are made known to the manager of the restaurant.   The chairperson of the Nutrition Committee will be responsible for providing each leader of each nuclear family with a copy of the menu with prices.

Many restaurants require large groups to agree on one or two entrees for the entire group so that all can easily be served together.   When this is the case the Nutrition Committee will have to choose the entrees based on their knowledge of the group, and each nuclear family will have to pay a predetermined amount depending on the number in their group attending.   It helps to get the money for these outings far in advance to satisfy the prepaid reservation charges of the restaurant and to firm up the intentions of family members.   Most of us have a more enjoyable time anyway when we have paid for something far in advance; it makes the actual event seem almost free.

The time and place for the appearance of the entire family will be sent to the members of the family by the chairperson of the Nutrition Committee of the family reunion.

Hotel food services for the family.   Many hotels provide for buffet-style service at a flat price.   The family can be entertained while dining at the hotels.   The family can arrange to rent an entire ballroom and have the food delivered, with the added convenience of having the food served to the family by the hotel waiters and waitresses. The food which needs to be served hot is hot and the cold food is served cold.   The elegance and beauty of most hotels adds to the relaxation and enjoyment of the family.

Hotel food prices may be as reasonable as the family could wish, from $10.00 per person upward to $40.00 per person.   When a family is planning the first reunion, it is better to stick to the very basic price which is affordable to all of the members of the family.   The prices should always be gauged for the family with the least amount of financial resources.   To deviate from this rule requires the entire extended family to consider contributing to the families with very limited resources.

The $10.00 food service price includes a basic balanced menu.   The meat selection will be chicken prepared as the family desires.   Hot vegetables, potatoes, salads, desserts, and beverages are included in the basic price.   Actually, the basic food service is sufficient to provide the entire family with a balanced diet for a reasonable price.

If your family has arrived at the point where the family with the least financial ability can afford the deluxe menu so much the better.   The mid-range price up to $40.00 per person includes such items on the menu as lobster, shrimp, champagne, and even caviar.   The service, table setting, and decor are more elaborate with this menu.

The family may elect either buffet-style or a sit-down dinner. Usually, the sit-down dinner costs more.

The family may choose a hotel that has a pool near the dining facilities where the price includes the use of the pool, jacuzzi, and hydrotherapy pool, and the family may even want to do a little sun tanning depending on the time of day and season selected for the reunion.

The price of the food service may be less if the family has reserved rooms at the hotel.   Then the hotel will generally provide banquet rooms, meeting rooms, and ballrooms free.   This in itself is a real savings because an average price for a meeting room in a good hotel is $1500.00 a day.

The more rooms rented, the more nights reserved, the better negotiating power the family has.   Do negotiate because the hotel is more flexible with rates for groups than individual rates.   The family can look forward to having a grand time at a reasonable price.   Swimming, tanning, dining and dancing can be combined for an experience all will remember for years, from the little ones on up to the seniors.

Reservations for Hotel Dining.   Some reservations can be made as far as five years in advance at some hotels.   The prices quoted may include a 10% price increase provision due to probable inflation.   But the earlier the reservation is made the better.

Most families should make their reservations nine months to one year in advance.   If the reunion is still in the organizational stage, then try to make the reservations no later than three months in advance.   If your family needs more time, call the hotel catering manager and make your requests for the dates needed.   It is quite possible a time slot is open that fits perfectly into the hotel schedule. Give it a try.

The Nutrition Committee will delight the family by making early plans to accommodate the entire group.

Hotel menu selection influences the price.   From chicken to lobster will make a difference.   Another idea a family may want to consider is the selection of a hotel that includes a banquet room with a kitchen.   This way the family can save money by having a ballroom for shows and dancing while the family is doing the cooking in the same area.   Some ballrooms have stages, kitchens, seating for large groups, no host bars and patios that lead to the pool area.

The Nutrition Committee may give thought to a variety of different plans to derive the best service from the hotel at the best price.   Nutrition can be provided at a reasonable price, whether it be from the family cooks or the executive chefs of fine hotels.   Whether picnics or fine hotel cuisine, a delicious nutritional feast can leave its lasting impression on everyone from the young in years to the young in spirit.

LETTERS

RESTAURANT LETTER

Dear Restaurant Manager/Owner,

My family plans to celebrate its _____ Annual Family Reunion in _____ next year on _____, 19__.

We are interested in seeking an affordable caterer that will provide a well-balanced picnic menu to be completely served by the caterer in _____ Park for approximately 50 people on Saturday and Sunday at lunch time, 1:30 p.m. exactly.

Our menu specifications are as follows:

--Barbecued Chicken and
--Barbecued Beef Ribs prepared without salt.
--Fresh Garden Salad with very fresh vegetables.

--Fresh Boiled Corn	*--Fresh Green Beans*
--Sweet Potatoes	*--Baked Beans*
--Rolls	*--Cornbread*
--Cake	*--Pie*
. Coconut	*. Sweet Potato*
	. Coconut

We will bring our own beverage.

Please provide us with the following information pertaining to your company:

1.   Who is the owner?

2.   What is the owner's address?

3.   Is your company bonded, licensed and insured for the services you provide?

4. With what insurance carrier are you insured?

a. Name of Company

b. Representative

c. Mailing Address

d. Phone: Area code___Number_____

e. Amount of coverage?

5. *Do you guarantee that all cooked food will be hot and fresh and prepared without salt or meat tenderizers?*

6. *Will you provide a price rate-schedule for the menu we desire?*

7. *What is your regular menu and price schedule?*

8. *How much advance notice does your company require?*

9. *How much money will be required in advance for the menu, if any?*

10. *What is your cancellation policy regarding refunds?*

11. *Will your staff remain at our picnic site to serve my family, or will they leave after they deliver and set the table?*

12. *Does your staff provide picnic tablecloths, eating utensils, place settings, etc.? If so, is there an extra charge?*

We wish to thank you in advance for supplying us with this information.

Very sincerely yours,

_____

Honorable Chairperson
_____ *FAMILY* _____ *ANNUAL FAMILY REUNION*

SPECIAL NUTRITIONAL NEEDS

Dear Family Member,

 We have written letters to several restaurants, caterers, and food preparers to obtain the best service, with the most economical prices, to provide a very nutritious and well-balanced menu of food choices that we believe will satisfy everyone's appetite.

 We have enclosed the menu, prices, and set-up advice of the company that we have chosen. If your family requires a selection not provided for on the menu, please use the space provided below or use the back of this page to inform us of your specific requests.

 We will do our best to make all happy and satisfied.

(COMMENTS SPACE:)

 Sincerely yours,

_____
Honorable Chairperson

  _____ FAMILY _____ANNUAL FAMILY REUNION

FAMILY-FUN EXERCISE PROGRAM

The Annual Program

The Annual Program for the immediate family should include an outline of a physical fitness program that involves every member of the immediate family. Why work first with the immediate family? If each nuclear family starts an exercise program, we will have the beginning of a healthier, extended family. With this revolution of family physical fitness spreading throughout the towns, cities, and counties, we will soon have healthier states. Within a reasonable amount of time we will have our country joining other countries in a similar family fitness explosion.

What is the benefit to the world? The positive programs developed by all the families will result in better government. The world will experience a more peaceful atmosphere. Government leaders in all of the world governments will have a healthier approach to their jobs and their families.

The exercise program generated by the family should include programs for babies, children and adults. Children are growing up in a society where physical fitness is at a very low point. Obesity among children is increasing. Why? With the lack of recreational facilities comes another problem: there is a lack of safe recreational facilities where facilities exist. So the parents feel uncomfortable sending their children to parks and recreational facilities out of fear for the safety of their children.

We need to establish a home fitness program with an annual plan. The program should include light to moderate exercises leading gradually to good fitness. A program should be started that will make everyone happy to be a participant. Make the program full of fun. Do not equate the family fitness program with a military physical training program. The family fitness program must be steady, continuous and full of fun to be successful.

The annual family fitness program needs to have objectives. For example, the program may start off with a workout schedule like this one:

Indoor Exercise Activities

```
Sit-ups..................... 3 per day
Leg lifts................... 3 per day
Stretching exercises....... 5 minutes per day
```

Outdoor Activities

```
Family Slow Walk ------- 50 meters or 5 minutes
Family Swift Walk ------ 25 meters or 2 minutes
Walking in the water --- Across the  pool and back
                        four times
```

There are physical fitness audio and videocassette tapes that emphasize the proper way to do various exercises. Many books offer illustrations on the way to avoid injury while exercising. Take it easy, start off slowly, and make the family exercise program a pleasure.

After the annual fitness program has been outlined with some basic starting goals, the family should have some year-end objectives to be accomplished. These objectives should be very reasonable. Here are what the year-end objectives will be like:

Indoor Year-end Objectives

```
Sit-ups ---------------- 12 each day.
Leg-lifts -------------- 12 each day.
Stretching ------------- 20 minutes each day.
```

Outdoor Year-end Objectives

```
Family Slow walk ------- 200 meters or 20 minutes
                        per day.
Swift Walk ------------- 100 meters or 8 minutes
                        per day.
Walking in the water --- Across the pool and back
                        16 times.
```

In the year-end objectives, the family needs to include attendance charts for the entire year. These charts can be obtained from most stationery stores. The exercise program should be done at least three times a week. Therefore, at the end of the year the chart should have a total of 156 days of fitness records on it.

We must realize that three hours a week is a small investment for our health and the health of our family. Many times we have spent more time than that just arguing, fussing, and fighting. Now, would it not be better to replace the negative forces within the family with a positive program? Forever?

When a family inaugurates a fitness program, it has made one of the most rewarding investments for the future it can make. There are gains and profits to be realized   by the entire family: better attitudes, more love, and better health for the entire family unit. The gains will begin to be realized within the first week of the program.

Hypertension, heart conditions, and other stress-related ailments will be decreased. It may even be possible to eradicate most illnesses completely. Our family members will begin to maintain a weight program which will lead to self-discipline and control over all aspects of our lives and destinies. We do not have to feel helpless and out-of-control anymore.

Charts

FAMILY PHYSICAL FITNESS SCHEDULE

	JAN	FEB	MAR	APR	MAY	JUN	JUL	AUG	SEP	OCT	NOV	DEC
1												
2												
3												
4												
5												
6												
7												
8												
9												
10												
11												
12												
13												
14												
15												
16												
17												
18												
19												
20												
21												
22												
23												
24												
25												
26												
27												
28												
29												
30												
31												

This is the family chart to make everything all right in the family again. We must get our family together to do the exercise at least trice a week.

Shade the area for the day that the family did the family-fun exercise program. This program will bring so much joy to all of the little ones and to all of the adults who participate in it that it will be hard to ever stop. We want our family to enjoy the major part of their health program.

WEEKLY FAMILY-FUN EXERCISE CHART

D A Y	SIT-UPS	STRETCHING	WALKING OUTDOORS	WALKING IN THE POOL
SUN				
MON				
TUE				
WED				
THU				
FRI				
SAT				

Totals from the above family-fun exercise program.

_____number of sit-ups.

_____minutes of stretching.

_____minutes or meters of outdoor walking.

_____minutes of walking in the water.

With a family-fun exercise schedule of at least three times a week, we can make a start toward eliminating many of the stress-related ailments and diseases that are associated with lack of physical fitness.

Comments:_____

_____

_____

_____

MONTHLY FAMILY-FUN EXERCISE CHART

D A Y	SIT-UPS	STRETCHING	OUTDOOR WALKING	WALKING IN THE POOL
1				
2				
3				
4				
5				
6				
7				
8				
9				
10				
11				
12				
13				
14				
15				
16				
17				
18				
19				
20				
21				
22				
23				
24				
25				
26				
27				
28				
29				
30				
31				

Totals from the above family fun exercise program.

_____number of sit-ups.
_____minutes of stretching.
_____minutes or meters of outdoor walking.
_____minutes of walking in the water.

We can use this chart to make a beginning to make the family lively and healthy again. Indicate the number of sit-ups, or the time involved in doing the various family-fun exercises.

Feel free to make notes about how much fun the members had in doing the exercises or how the various challenges were made more fun.

Comments:_____
_____

To be serious about a family's fitness program, the family will want to make notes of its progress.   The annual chart provides a monthly breakdown of what days the family has been making a contribution to its exercise program.   The objective is to have as many days shaded as possible.

What are we really doing here?   How does exercise fit into the family reunion?   First, when a family cares enough about the immediate family to promote exercise and the reduction of illness, the more likely the family will be able to attend the annual reunion.   The more diligently the nuclear family attends to the exercise program, the better the chances of having good health, longevity and prosperity.   They go together.   When a family takes its exercise program seriously, they are expressing concern and love for one another.

Exercise is an important aspect of the nutrition program.   Too much good food is ruined by too little exercise. Even the best of diet programs may be void if exercise is omitted.

The Weekly Chart summarizes the exercise of the nuclear family during the week.   Each nuclear family may want to contact another within the extended family for mutual moral support.   Share the fun and progress with a little friendly competition.   Cousins could converse with their cousins in another town to let them know that they did all three days of their program for that week.   Don't underestimate the value of having a buddy to contact, to provide that "we're in this thing together feeling."   All kinds of diet programs and behavior modification programs advocate this technique; they have you call your buddy everyday to discuss progress, problems, those uncontrollable urges, those struggles to meet goals.   It works for exercise programs too.

The program is meant to be easy and painless.   If members of the family do not feel like exercising during a particular week, then they can make up for the exercise missed by working out more days or by extending the exercises a little the following week.   But try to be consistent and experience the fun and accomplishment of exercise each week.

Make the Family Fitness Program a regular part of the family appointment schedule for at least three times a week. Doing the exercises are a real joy.   They can become habit-forming, a good habit that the family does not want to break.

Also included are blank monthly, weekly and daily schedules for the family to devise their own programs.   This is to help foster the real spirit of getting an exciting program for your family into action.   Stop talking about getting in shape and get the entire family into **fitness action.**

Walking Organizations

Several non-profit organizations exist that are dedicated to teaching people how to walk safely and enjoyably, and sponsoring special walking events. Contact one in your area for its support and help with your family walking exercise. Write or call for further information.

Event:	San Francisco Hill Stride
Contact:	City Sports magazine
Phone No.:	(212) 627-7040 (New York)
	(415) 546-6150 (San Francisco)
Note:	7-mile walk

Event:	StrideBoston
Contact:	Sportscade magazine
Phone No:	(617) 277-3823
Note:	7-mile walk

Event:	March of Dimes Walkamerica
Contact:	March of Dimes
Phone No:	Local March of Dimes
Note:	Annual April event

Event:	Crop Walk
Contact:	Church World Service
Address:	Box 968
	Elkhart, IN 46515

Event:	"Just Say No" Walk Against Drugs
Contact:	1777 North California Blvd., Suite 200
	Walnut Creek, CA 94596
Note:	May 10-16 is National Walk Week for the "Just Say No" Clubs.

Event: Walk plus window shop -- "Mall Hiking."

Contact: Your local   mall manager to plan an organized
walk.

Event: City Leg-stretchers for architecture and art
              buffs.

Contact: The Chicago Architecture Foundation
Phone No: (312) 326-1393

Contact: The Los Angeles Conservancy
Phone No: (213) 623-CITY

Contact: The 92nd Street Y -- New York City

Contact: The Walkways Center
              733 15th Street, N.W., Suite 427
              Washington, D.C. 20005

Note: Annual Walking Almanac
              Newsletter (How/Where)

WASTE-AWAY FAT WEIGHT CONTROL PROGRAM

The Regular Program

This weight control program will be instrumental in helping those of us in the family who have gotten fat. There is no pretty way of saying it but the truth. We have gotten fat! Let us do something about it now.

The weekly eating control chart is one that I use along with exercises for at least four days a week to lose on an average of four pounds a week without fail.

BREAKFAST

1 grapefruit
1 banana
2 pears
1 one-a-day vitamin
1 glass of milk

LUNCH

1   8 oz serving pasta
1   4 oz serving steamed potatoes
2   8 oz glasses of juice
1   4 oz serving broiled chicken
1   8 oz serving fresh steamed string beans

DINNER

4 oz green peas
4 oz broccoli
2 servings fresh fruit
       plum/peach
Salads of lettuce and spinach

If we ask ourselves why we are using this Waste-away Fat Weight Control Program, the answer is very simple: it is very important to our family's well-being.   Our children should not have to see their parents die younger than parents should due to laziness.   Many a spouse should not have to suffer losing his/her mate to heart seizures in sports contests only because the spouse was too fat to participate in exercising.

Selfishness is another reason to lose all of that fat.   I know this to be true because when I had allowed myself to tilt the scale at 247 pounds on a 5' 10" frame, I was full of selfishness.   We must not allow ourselves to get this way. Let's shame ourselves into a good fitness program.   It will be a good idea to get a doctor's opinion on our progress. But the real doctor is each one us and God.

Not coming to the family reunion because of being fat is behind a lot of the excuses that obese family members give, whether consciously and out loud or unconsciously and hidden even from themselves, for not attending.   This is taking it much too far.   Go to the reunion this year and do as I did when I was fat; surprise the family next year with a loss of 57 pounds over that reasonable period of time.

Check with your family doctor before going on this or any weight-loss program.   Be sure to take a good multi-vitamin and mineral supplement for additional protection.

The Modified Program

After being on the **Waste-away Fat Diet Plan** for about four months, I was able to implement the modified **Waste-away Fat Diet** that allows me to eat everything I want to and maintain my weight between 190 and 195 lbs., which is where it should be for my body frame.   This is what makes this diet so neat; we control the weight with a modified plan.

The Modified Waste-away Fat Weight Control Program employs a few good health tricks.   For example, we have eliminated sodium from our foods.   Fried, deep fried, and heavily greasy foods are no longer a daily or weekly menu item.   We do not dare buy meals at the fast food take-out places that provide hamburger, chicken and hot dogs that are full of fat and/or deep-fried.

A very few fast food chains offer a healthy, non-fattening menu for the family.   I know of only two that offer broiled chicken instead of deep fried chicken, none that offer hot vegetables and fresh salads as well.   Fast food chains have made a very irresponsible contribution to the world.   Many of the chains are spreading fat and ill-health all over the world. Some of them even brag about how many hamburgers they have contributed to the overweight problems of the world. They are not heard or seen when it comes to fattening up the starved and deprived nations.   The buck is their only concern.   They may as well consider their products comparable to a nuclear bomb.

But let us get back to the weight control plan.   We stated that we eliminated sodium, grease, and fast food chains.   Now we structure our eating habits to fit a better system of digesting the food by eating our meals at **earlier times**, breakfast in the early morning, lunch near noon, and dinner before seven in the evening.   Eating dinner early keeps the food from sitting in our stomachs when our system is shut down and fat creeps up on us.   Late evenings and nights do havoc to our system if we eat meals then.

Lunch is a heavy meal on purpose.   It affords me a chance to utilize most of the nutrients and burn off the fat.   In addition, the more I eat at lunch the less I need to eat at dinner.

This diet program is a real winner with me.   I discovered it by gathering ideas from several persons who had their weight under control, trying different diet plans of theirs and putting one together that worked for me with the greatest amount of flexibility.   I did not want to become a servant to any diet plan.   The Waste-away **Fat Weight Control Programs** allowed me and friends of mine who sincerely tried it to reduce their weight with great joy.   We need to be the masters of our lives.   We do not need fat, ill health, and a poor exercise regimen.

We will help our families control and eliminate fat by utilizing a program that puts us at the helm of our ship. The pains, agony, and suffering of most diet plans are not for us. We have our family weight control programs at our disposal.

Over-concern about weight is a growing problem among many of the nation's teen-agers. When a person is within the weight advised for his/her height and frame, there is no need to fret about weight. This excessive worrying where some people want to be extremely skinny is unhealthy, indeed, deadly. Anorexia is the official term for this problem, and bulimia is a related food-abuse sickness in which the person purposely throws up all the food he/she consumes until the system can no longer keep anything down. Many teen-agers are in hospitals throughout the country for treatment of these illnesses. They worry themselves sick at the slightest amount of weight gain, and eventually their bodies become too thin to sustain life.

Our families do not need this over-concern about weight gain. We are sure to balance this struggle between being fat and being skinny with a healthy middle-of-the-road approach. Let us not get too fat nor cause ourselves to get too skinny.

After reviewing the whole program of weight control, let us find a relative to be our weight discipline partner. Write a short letter, or adapt the letter included here for a family weight control pal. Let us entitle it the Waste-away-fat Letter. A buddy is especially important in helping us maintain the self-discipline necessary to lose weight.

WASTE-AWAY FAT WEIGHT CONTROL PROGRAM LETTER

Dear relative,

After looking in the mirror, weighing myself on the scales, and looking at how my clothes no longer fit because of this excess fat I have gained, I am writing to you because I need your help. Presently, I have reviewed the Waste-away Weight Control Program outlined in the book FAMILY REUNION: HOW TO PLAN YOURS.

This book has suggested that after consulting with the physician for the family a weight control program should be undertaken. The Program allows me to blend in my own nutrition habits and food preferences with it in a way that will really be successful if I just give it a sincere try.

We are of the same fat persuasion, so let us begin to encourage each other to find the middle weight control program. Each month I will send to you my progress chart. In return, you may send me yours.

I appreciate your becoming my weight control pal.

Sincerely,

_____

Honorable Chairperson

_____*FAMILY* _____*ANNUAL FAMILY REUNION*

DAILY PROGRESS CHART

Date:_____

Weight Today:

_____ Morning

_____ Noon

_____ Night

Measurements:

_____ Chest

_____ Waist

_____ Hips

Other Measurements:

_____

_____

_____

_____

_____

Emotional contentment are the words Bruce Lee whispered into the ear of a young martial arts student.   Even today those same words are essential in every good nutrition and diet program.

Emotional contentment is the missing link in our weight control program.

We must conquer our emotions and control ourselves.   We must not eat whenever we are angry, sad, frustrated or tired. We must not eat to force ourselves to work when we are too tired; instead, we must re-train ourselves to take a nap. When we are sad, we must give ourselves up to tears until we feel better.   If we are to be successful we must control our feelings and emotions by satisfying them in these direct, positive ways.   Once we develop this control our weight control program will be successful beyond our fondest dreams.

MC KINZIE LAW OF PHYSICAL DECADENCE

Man is doomed to die.   As each generation of humankind passes, human life expectancy decreases.

Explanation: It is said that during the time of the early prophets, men lived to be more than 300 years of age.   Now, man is seldom reported living much past 100 years of age.

Human life expectancy has gotten shorter and shorter each passing generation.   This is true despite the inaccurately based actuarial tables that present a different picture. This decadence is directly attributed to the curse God caused to fall upon man and woman for eating the forbidden fruit of the Garden of Eden.   God said man shall surely die for disobeying the word of God.

From the dust man came and to the dust man shall surely return.   Within the words of the previous sentence lies some insight into the way in which to have a longer and healthier life during the ever-diminishing overall lifespan of humankind.

There is an order to the benefits that can be obtained from the food products of the earth.   Let us examine the priority of the values, starting with the best in value and proceeding to the least in value.

Any food products that come directly from beneath the earth have the highest value.   For example, carrots, potatoes, garlic, etc. are food products that grow directly beneath the earth.

Those food products that grow above the earth, but still are naturally close to the earth, come next in value.   Corn, beans, peas, lettuce, cabbage, etc. are examples.   These food products are still from the earth, but they grow on top of the soil and they are second in value.

Next we have those food products that grow from the earth by means of   trees; these are third in value.   Oranges, apples, pears, lemons, etc. are examples of the third value. While they are good for man and their value is high, it is not as high as those food products that grow beneath the earth and close to the earth.   One would think that the food products that absorb more sunlight would have a higher food value.   This would be true if humankind were made from the sun. Instead, humankind was made from dirt.

Let us look at the way another food product enters into this picture that we are painting. Next, we have values for the animals that are consumed by humankind. Fourth, those animals that eat a food source that comes directly from the earth have a value higher than animals which eat secondary food sources.

Briefly, it is necessary to explain what is meant by a secondary food source. If an animal eats another animal or mammal for food, it is eating a secondary food source. According to this law of decadence, the food products that come directly from the earth are a primary food product. We may look on any animal that thrives on food sources containing blood as eating secondary food sources. Primary food products come directly from the earth. Secondary food sources are the eating of the food source that eats the primary food products.

An example may help to clarify things. Grass in the open meadows is a primary food product because it comes directly from the earth. Cows eat the grass. The cows are secondary food sources. Since cows eat the primary food products, they are considered secondary food sources, while the grass is considered a primary food product. The phrases "food product" and "food source" could actually be used in each other's place. But for my discussion, I have used "product" to refer to vegetables, grains, and fruit and "source" to refer to animals.

Returning to the discussion, we have a higher value for the animal that eats primary food products over the animal that eats secondary food sources. A cow would have a higher food value than a tiger. A tiger eats other animals. The more one looks at the McKinzie Law of Physical Decadence, the more one can actually see a trend in violence.

Examine briefly the amount of violence one can expect from any animal that thrives upon secondary food sources. They are generally violent. The same tendency toward violent behavior for the same reason is manifest in human beings. If doctors, scientists and other professionals would make a study of the diet pattern of a human from the time of his/her beginnings in the womb to the time of the violent behavior of the human being, the evidence would show that the person was not on a primary-food product diet. The person was mainly on a secondary food-source diet. The study should go back a few generations, if possible, to make a finding that will be most conclusive. The result will prove that the diet of an individual contributes to the behavior pattern.

Actually, all animals that mainly eat secondary food sources are violent. Take the tiger compared to the giraffe. The giraffe is taller, larger and heavier than a lion, but it is nowhere near as violent as the tiger. Again we find the diet of the giraffe to consist of primary food products, while the tiger eats secondary food sources.

We can compare an elephant to a panther. We have a similar trend. The panther eats secondary food sources, while the elephant eats primary food sources. The panther is violent and the elephant is docile.

We have another category of food products that has been called "Junk foods." Junk food receive the lowest value. Candy, potato chips, etc. are food products falling into this area. Poor results are realized if members of a family make a diet of junk foods. The cause of hyperactivity in many children has been traced directly to the over-consumption of junk foods.

What does all of this tell us? We can alter the violence expressed by human beings by changing their diets. We need to eat more primary foods of the highest value.

A point-value table for the family can be made from the earlier discussion of the food order:

Category	Points
Food products from beneath the earth .... 50 pts.
Food products from above, but close to the earth ... 40 pts.
Food products from above, but not close to the earth 30 pts.
Food sources that eat primary foods .... 20 pts.
Food sources that eat secondary foods .... 10 pts.
Food sources that are called "Junk Foods" 0   pts.
Food sources that comes from chemicals ....-10 pts.

The family can benefit from this chart in several ways. By changing the diet of the family, the family can add many more years to the life expectancy of its members. Also, there is a reduced likelihood of violence and crime in a family that eats primary foods. Emphasis is placed on eating primary foods because some families may buy primary foods but not eat them. The food is all for show.

A young man told me that he came from a good background where there was always plenty of the primary foods to eat. His father was raised on a farm in Arkansas and was taught to eat primary foods. But his mother was raised in the city and had a life of eating mostly secondary foods or junk foods. He mentioned that his father insisted the family eat primary foods.

However, the father would have to go on military manuevers

and foreign duty and leave the children in the care of the mother. Every time the mother would go to the store and stock up on candies, corn chips and potato chips which the children and the mother would eat while the father was gone. The young man related this story to me to illustrate that sometimes a family can know and buy the right kind of food, but for one reason or another, the family will not eat it. What good is derived from such a practice?

Examples of food products and food sources that fit into the above categories are listed below:

<u>**Category**</u>   <u>**Example**</u>

```
Food products from beneath the earth ............ carrots.
Food products from above, but close to the earth ...lettuce.
Food products from above, but not close to the earth.apples.

Food sources that eats primary foods .............  cows.
Food sources that eats secondary foods ...... sharks/tigers.
Food products that are called "Junk Foods" .......... candy.
Food products that comes from chemicals  ...........cocaine.
```

The nutrition program for the family is serious business and deserves a few serious moments out of our busy schedules. Adults and children are in need of controlling our diet, exercise and emotional content for a stronger healthier family tomorrow. Note: Do not eat tigers and the like.

CHAPTER V

V. ENTERTAINMENT

A. ACTIVITIES

    1. Indoor Activities

    2. Outdoor Activities

    3. Outings to Amusement Parks, Museums, etc.

B. ACTIVITIES LETTERS

C. LIVE ENTERTAINMENT

D. CEREMONIES

E. CEREMONIES LETTERS

ENTERTAINMENT

We need fun and laughter at our family reunions. Whether we are at a picnic in the park, a hotel banquet or on a dude ranch, we need to have safe outlets to release tension. The entertainment events may be the most memorable events of the reunion, so let us adventure on the fun track.

Everyone from children to the senior members want to enjoy themselves. Sometimes we think of the middle ages of the spectrum and we overlook the senior members and children. While the amusement park offers loads of fun for little tots and young adults, games like Scrabble, Uno, and Bridge break the ice for senior adults. Let us be creative, imaginative and adventurous in bringing interesting activities to everyone attending the family reunion.

Fun is the essential focal point of most activities -- whether outdoors, indoors, or on the moon -- we all want to have more fun in whatever we do for pleasure and relaxation. Games provide us with an outlet to have fun with other members of the family. There are all types of games for different age groups -- some originating from other countries -- while many games are born in the United States of America. Let's examine some of the games to include in our family reunion.

Ice-breaker games are a must at the beginning of the festivities. For example, the family could play the game of the four favorites: color, leisure activity, city, and television or movie personality. These favorites could be varied, of course, to fit the particular congregation. Mix and mingle games with four questions, no more than that, start things out. Then the guests mingle until they find someone who has the same answers to the questions. After the game is over, those with similar favorites are likely to get together again for more conversation and a new friendship.

ACTIVITIES

First, there are activities that take place before or after the picnic or banquet while the reunion is going on. When planning activities, keep in mind three separate age groups: children, active adults and mature adults.

Physical activities for mature adults might include croquet, horseshoes, or shuffleboard. The more active adults and older children could participate in a game of volleyball, softball or baseball. Many kinds of races, tag games, miniature golf matches, etc. are suitable for young children but require a supervising adult or teen-ager to make them work. Some special games work for the entire company, such as a three-legged race pairing the youngest child with the youngest adult, the oldest child with the oldest adult and pairing the rest of the group accordingly.

Sedentary games are appropriate too. Board games like Monopoly and card games work well, especially those that do not require a lot of concentration since their main purpose is to encourage intermingling and conversation between family members.

When the banquet or picnic is not in progress, let us consider other activities. Sightseeing is always important to those visiting the host city for the first time. Arrangements for sightseeing activities should be made far in advance. It is important to concentrate on those sightseeing events that interest the majority of the family.

Some families prefer amusement parks while others are more interested in concerts, galleries and museums. Many amusement parks have discount tickets and special group discounts which are available through work places or employee unions. Get a sufficient number of these passes in advance, and determine an order of priority among the parks and entertainment centers.

In Los Angeles, the movie industry may be more popular, whereas, in Washington, D.C. those sites that relate to the federal government are important. In New York the family will enjoy plays and musicals. Each city or town has something of interest; find and enjoy it.

For concert and play goers, it is imperative that the family obtain tickets and seating far in advance. Those who want to attend these activities may send checks before the tickets are purchased. Check the galleries and museums for special exhibits offered during the reunion.

For a reunion in the old home town, many returning members may want to spend a portion of their time visiting old friends.

Indoor Activities.

Password. My nieces and nephews enjoyed playing their uncles and aunts the game called Password (T.M.) which allows for a test of wits and promotes team play. Password is a game where four players divide up into two teams, two family members on each team. Each team takes turns giving his or her team member a chance to make a guess at the word on the card. If one team is unable to guess the word from the clue given, the other team is allowed an opportunity to guess at the same word with a different clue from his or her own teammate. The fewer turns taken to figure out the clue the more points are awarded to the successful team that guesses the mystery word.   At the end of the game, the team with the highest number of points is the winner.

Cards.   Card playing can be as involved as Bridge and Pinochle or as exciting as Bid Whiz and Hearts.   Poker chips with a maximum limit of fifty cents for the highest raise and a five-cent ante will provide three to four hours of matching wits.   The game should be played with the idea of having fun, not breaking anybody's budget; limit everyone's losses to about ten dollars.   There should be extra money to spare. This card playing should never take on the tone of gambling. It would be better to use play money only, with no one losing a cent.   Playing cards is a good way for many family members to have a delightful time during the family reunion's evening of entertainment.

Uno.   Generally, it is best to select games in which more people are included such as Uno (T.M.).   Uno has brought heaps of fun to our family reunion.   All ages from seven to adult have participated with as many as eight players at one time.   The game is exciting because the outcome of each hand is entirely unpredictable.   The method of scoring is prearranged at the beginning of the game and either the player with the most points, say 200 or 500 points, or, the player with the lowest number of points after a specified number of rounds, perhaps five or eight hands, is the winner.

Chess is a more secluded game played between two persons in which mental strategy is used to capture the opponent's pieces and place his or her king in checkmate.   The game is very dynamic and mentally intriguing, although I think that the participants of the chess game should probably select a time for this game when their absence will not interfere with the overall fun and togetherness of the family gathering.

Bingo.   This is the game of chance that can be arranged where everyone has fun.   Toys, games, and household items can be awarded to the winners throughout an evening of Bingo. Senior adults have loads of fun with Bingo as do young adults.   The time passes so fast and the excitement builds up as everyone is hoping to become a winner.

The photo album can be filled with pictures of the winners, surprise pictures with the winner bursting with laughter and enthusiasm.   Have some fun with Bingo at the family reunion.

Bible Trivia, which comes in adult and children's versions, is a scholastic test that really allows the Bible readers in the family to gleam.   The version for children will probably be more rewarding for the adults playing for the first time. It is a good idea to let many of the non-Bible scholars play and gain knowledge of the Bible.   The young, the wise, the competitive -- all enjoy this game.

Beauty and talent pageants of the family can be very rewarding. Everyone who participates in the pageant should be awarded a certificate of appreciation. If trophies are awarded, then the same kind of trophy is awarded to each contestant. The family reunion should not give first, second, and third place awards in the area of beauty pageantry. The harm will be realized later. Everyone in the family is beautiful. Everyone who participates in the display of talent and beauty is a winner. The interior beauty of each member of the extended family must be exalted, elevated above any mere exterior beauty. An image with no substance is promoted by praising the flesh only.

Talent shows can call on the creativity of family members and result in gales of laughter for all. Contestants can plan their skits and performances in advance, practice together and perfect their entries. It is great fun when all age groups participate. First, second and third place trophies can be awarded to these participants, because the rating of a single performance is far less threatening than a ranking of natural beauty.

Moral judgments should be left out of this contest!
The contest judges the entrants on this day of beauty and talent, not on past experiences. Bury the mistakes of the past and cultivate new, prosperous growth.

Our goal is to have a family beauty contest that will become an international event. Families from every corner of the world will come together in a forever peaceful pageant. It will be free of the political turmoil that has plagued the Olympics.

Pin-the-Tail on the Donkey. Here's a game that has survived the test of time, a game in which a picture of a donkey is placed on the wall and the players take turns seeing who comes the closest to pinning the tail in the right place, after being blindfolded and spun around. The winner is given a prize.

It is also possible to give some type of treat to the ones who came in second and third place. Do not forget to blindfold each player right before it is his or her time to play. It is possible to have three divisions of contestants, children, young adults, and older adults. Spark the interest of senior adults by creating a fourth division and enter all those seniors before the other three divisions play.

After winners have been declared in each division, one grand prize is awarded to the grand master. The grand master is the player who comes the closest to pinning the tail on the right spot out of the finalists in each of the four divisions. This game would be fun to video.

Outdoor Activities

Outdoor activities bring us close to nature. The smell of fresh flowers, the smooth wind and the wonderful vitamin D that we get from all of the sunlight are uplifting in themselves. We will have an opportunity to consider many outdoor activities and choose some which will be appropriate for our family.

Hide and Go Seek. Ever wonder why all of these games were so much fun when we adults were children? What happened to all of the fun we used to have? Why not get out there and enjoy ourselves again? Children while away the evenings trying to find each other's hiding place. One person is "it", he or she has to close his/her eyes and count to an agreed-upon number, like 10. While the "it" person is counting, all of the others go and hide.

Now, this is where the excitement begins. The "it" person has completed counting and now has to find each player's hiding place and run like a super person to beat that player to the counting place to make that person "it". One could almost get as many variations of this game as there are countries in the world. But, the basic principle is to avoid being "it", if possible. It may be fun for adults to have their own game of Hide and Go Seek. Bring back those fond memories that made life so much fun to be a child.

Horseshoes. Four poles are placed in the ground. Put two poles side by side about 3 meters apart. Then place the other two poles 15 meters directly in front of the poles already in the ground. Give each player a chance to toss four horseshoes at each of the poles. The one who gets the closest to the poles gets a point.

The number of points necessary to win is determined at the beginning of the game. Teams can compete in this game also. The rules are the same for a team for an individual match. Do not be surprised to see the senior adults win at this game.

Durable solid plastic shoes are available, or the traditional horseshoes. Mark a safety area around the horseshoe area. Do not locate the game near children or the physically disabled because the roll or flight of a horseshoe is unpredictable. Avoid serious injuries by taking safety precautions first.

Horseshoe players immerse themselves in deep concentration. This is an excellent game to have available at the reunion picnic site.

Sack Racing. Our family was delighted to give the first place prize to a senior member of our family who was over 70 years of age. He won over the children and young adults in this race.

We gave each person a large burlap sack that would normally hold about 100 pounds of potatoes. A distance of 20 meters or more was marked off. The starting line and the finish line are outlined in white lime, flour, or powdered chalk. A rope could be placed on the ground at both ends also.

All of the players line up side by side at the starting line. "On your mark, get set, go!" are the magic words that set the family members off on the race while both legs are in the sack. Holding the bag above the knees near the waist, everyone is hopping like a kangaroo to the finish line.

Video, take pictures, and congratulate the winner. A ribbon is given to the first, second, and third place players. The family photo album will be full of pictures of all of the players just hopping up and down, in anticipation of winning the family sack race.

Swings, a sand box, and the sliding board are the right ingredients for the little ones, who can enjoy an entire afternoon in the park riding on the **see saw** and the little **merry-go-round.**

Gymnastics by the members of the family who have such agility and poise are a treat to watch. The whole family will enjoy being entertained by those who have devoted their energies and practiced long hours for the day when the family can be entertained by watching so special a performance.

It really means something to the gymnast in the family to have the family appreciate the performance. No higher praise exists than the love and admiration expressed by an audience filled with members of the family. There is no grander trophy than the families' warm and prayerful hearts for the young gymnasts who excel in this endeavor.

Track and Field. Family track and field events can be filled with giggles on how slow Uncle Harry was and how far Aunt Mary could jump. Relay races, jumping, and sprints can be coordinated to let everyone enter who is willing and able to do so. Most trophy stores have ribbons and small and large trophies that can be awarded to the contestants. Certificates of appreciation can be issued to everyone who enters and participates in the events. All the members of the family who have organized the activities should also receive a certificate of appreciation.

Softball in the park will keep the family trying to go home. A home run is the dream of all of the adults, while the kids want to catch a high fly to get Aunt Eleanor out. Keep in mind that "T" Ball is a good adaptation for the little ones.

Hardball is played if the family is very experienced in the activity; otherwise a good old game of softball will make the time pass before anyone knows what happened. Remember to coach family members ahead of time about laying the bat down on the ground instead of slinging it.

We do not want any injuries. Injuries can be avoided with the observations of softball safety rules. To enforce the rules, anyone who slings the bat causes the team an automatic out. No matter how far the ball was hit, the person is out. Before the family knows it, softball will be an activity that family members will want to share during each family reunion.

Soccer is an international sport becoming more and more popular in the United States. Soccer keeps the players using the feet and on some occasions the head. No hands are used except by the goalie when he tosses the ball back into play. Perhaps everybody will not be a player, but the joy of watching the fast pace of soccer will get the spectators involved.

Touch, Tag, or Flag Football may offer too much contact for the women, but the young men will have a day of trying to be great All-American passers.

Rope jumping brings everyone from tiny tots to robust adults into action. Single rope jumping, double rope jumping, and fast rope jumping keep the rope swinging. We adults can picture ourselves on the video being children all over again while watching who lasts the longest (usually the children).

Adults wonder how in the world the children get so much energy and stamina. We grown-ups envy all of this wonderful youthfulness that seems wasted on the young ones who appear not to appreciate it. At the same time the kids are hoping they stay young always and wonder why they ever wanted to be adults in the first place after they have watched the adults jump rope.

All of the above activities can be engaged in at the park on the day of the picnic. But for the other days your family is together, you may want to enjoy additional activities that take more time and/or involve travel to different locations.

Horseback Riding. From ponies for the kids to palominos for the adults, horseback riding will bring zest and excitement. Observe the safety rules and proper care of the horses, and enjoy the different styles of riding.

Starting early in the morning, around 6:00 a.m., will provide the coolest time to ride a horse in the summer months. Fresher horses, less time spent in long lines, and more genuine riding fun will reward the early risers. Warm feelings of camaraderie and shared experience come from riding together on the trail.

Hayrides. Young children always enjoy an old-fashioned hayride on a farm with a horse-drawn buggy. They will have fun telling stories about how they entered the school spelling bee contest, or how they worked so hard in algebra and missed getting an "A" by a few points. The outdoor air and the open spaces of the ranch provide an exhilarating experience and an evening that the kids will always remember.

Snow-Person contests can be enjoyed outdoors when the family reunion is held during the winter time. Making a snow man, snow woman, and snow children will keep the family busy for an entire day.

Make sure all the family is properly dressed for this occasion. Avoid runny noses, coughs, or infected ears in the cold weather. Find some indoor activities for those who cannot make it outdoors. The idea is to have fun without anyone getting overexposed to the winter weather.

Sledding and tobogganing can provide a lot of outdoor fun in the winter snow for the entire family. Lots of energy is expended in these very vigorous sports.

Bowling is for everyone. My little son got the record for the most misses. He and my little nephew did not let that stop them from having fun with gales of laughter at every miss, but special excitement for each pin that fell when the ball stayed in the lane. The little ones had their own competition going, while the adults tried to become professional bowlers overnight. The family reunion was where my son got his first lesson. Perhaps he will remember how he almost tied with his cousins.

For fun galore, bring along the family camcorder and capture all of the strikes, splits and spares of the evening. The next day at the shelter house play the video for even more laughs. This provides a splendid hour when all the bowlers and spectators see themselves on television as the video camera recorder rolls recalls the great family bowling hour.

Reservations for the bowling alley can be arranged so that it is possible for an extended family to rent the entire place for an evening. All the lanes can be filled, from east to west, with family bowlers, and the dining room and arcade as well. Most bowling alleys offer soft drinks for the kids and hard drinks for the adults. Be present for this event even if you do not bowl. Go along for the fun and get a shot at being on video while the family bowls the night away.

Tennis is still an attractive family sport. Two or more players on asphalt or clay courts enjoy set after set until the family tennis match has come to a wonderful end. Tennis has a little cousin called paddle tennis. Paddle tennis rules are similar, but the court is smaller and the small paddle is made out of wood or other hard material. Both regular tennis and paddle tennis can fill the activity hours with lots of fun.

Racquetball is usually an indoor sport which is limited to two to four players per court. Some spas have four or more courts that can be rented by the half hour. Gloves, the proper shoes and eye goggles are suggested, the goggles to protect the eyes from injury. Gloves provide a better grip on the racket and protect the hands from blisters. High -top tennis shoes, racquetball or basketball sneakers may be worn to provide better protection for the ankles.

Men and women, young and mature, enjoy racquetball. This swift moving activity develops quickness on the feet and fast reflexes in the hands. Right or left-handed players are in a never ending match, it seems.

Walk-a-thons are for the whole family. Physically-limited members may lead the way around the track at a nice comfortable pace. Visually impaired can be led around the track to join the family in a walk for family pride. Real family pride is the key issue here. The walk-a-thon can be coordinated with other extended families. The families could seek a sponsor or could raise money for a family-oriented charity. The money raised could also go to the family members who need financial aid in getting to the reunion.

Keep the walk-a-thon plain and simple. Glamour is not necessary. Let the walk come from the heart and spirit. Walk for a healthy family. Walk to rid the family of negative forces. Walk so that families all over the world will live in peace, love and harmony. We need this walk in our family. We need this walk today.

Roller Skating at the rink or at the beach is a complete form of exercise. Skating backwards, sideways and turning around doing the spread eagle may be a little advanced for some family members; a slow pace around the rink to some music will suffice for most of us. Give it a try, get on out there on the floor. If one member falls, help him or her up and let the fun keep on rolling.

Beach Activities are full of outdoor sunshine. Beach games from volleyball to building sand castles will provide plenty of entertainment. Make sure the entire family is properly protected with suntan lotion. Have a couple of good swimmers join with the children who desire to venture into the ocean. For water fun, locate the family near a lifeguard tower. Extra eyes and professional know-how are always helpful.

Flotation vests should be worn by the little ones and those who are inexperienced in the surf. Riding the surf on surfboards is not for a beginner. Surfing is a water activity that requires a lot of time to perfect. If there are experienced surfers in the family, then let everyone be entertained watching how something so difficult can seem so easy.

Body surfing on the other hand can be a hit and miss operation. Time the incoming waves just right and ride them to shore without a surfboard; just using the body is lots of fun. Being tumbled in the waves and rolled over so many different ways will be like a ride in the amusement park.

Exploring the tidepools is another wonderful beach activity. Sea life teems in the rocky shore areas exposed at low tide. Look at mussels, tiny starfish, brittlefish and baby octopi. Dig up a handful of wet sand and see the clams underneath. Giggle over the silly, side-scuttling land crabs. All this life fascinates the young mind. Seaweed breaks away and drifts to shore. Looking at a real kelp plant is like watching a plant spring with rigidity and flexibility at the same moment. Many tidepool areas are protected, and removing anything from them or upsetting their tender balance in any way is prohibited. Watch for signs, and always be mindful of preserving these delicate eco-systems.

Water skiing is a great sport involving a motor boat or ski boat, flotation vest, tow rope, skipper, flag man, skier, and, of course, skis. Beginners start by learning to get up on two skis, usually quite easy for the young ones from about age seven on. Adult beginners find these rudiments a lot more difficult. But after mastering the fundamentals they'll want to graduate to the showier, more graceful and responsive single ski. The real pros are even doing it barefoot these days.

Scuba diving opens up more forms of sea life. Divers uncover a spiny sea urchin, a lobster or a school of fish. Being suspended in the depths of the sea is like being in another world. Slowly doing somersaults, standing on your head looking at sea life upside down, or chasing a small octopus into a crevice in a rock will never cease to amaze those members of the family who have the proper training to set out on these expeditions.

The whole family could rent a yacht and let time sail by at the rate of a snail crawling up a tree. Underwater photography will provide everyone topside with pictures of what the divers in the family saw below. Old shipwrecks are still lying on the ocean bottom waiting to be explored.

Everyone will enjoy looking at the brilliant constellations in the skies, undimmed by city lights and smog, if the family makes an overnight outing of the ocean experience. The smell of the ocean breeze is an added premium of the trip. Scuba diving, snorkeling, and sea treasure hunts will make the open ocean outing a treasure to measure.

Para-sailing combines a parachute with a high speed boat to provide a thrilling adventure. If the family has selected a hotel on the beach that offers this land/water activity, be sure to sign up. Para-sailing is smooth and full of magic. A harness is strapped to the participant standing on the beach. A boat is waiting for the signal to lift the chute by racing out to sea and then in a circular course. No special abilities or previous training are required for this experience.

When the signal is given, the parachute which is attached to the back of the sailor is lifted into action by the burst of wind filling up the canopy from the boat zipping through the water. Soon airborne, the sailor looks at all the small trees from about three hundred feet up in the air. Once up, no one wants to come down. There is a marvelous away-from-it-all feeling up in the air and one will say, "Why come back to earth?" Enjoy the feel of a carefree airborne sail.

The boat and land operators usually arrange to slow the boat down in the right spot to allow the para-sailor to end up in the spot that he/she started from without one drop of water ever getting on the person. A flotation vest is worn just in case a sudden burst of the wind alters the planned course. Operators are on the land to provide for a safe start and end to the para-sailing trip. Give this activity a try if the chance occurs. Try taking a photo from the air for the fun of it.

Canoeing makes a person appreciate the motorboat. Two family members at a time rent the canoe. Canoers should be good swimmers who feel comfortable in the water even if their boat is capsized. Then it is time to venture into the lake, up the stream or even out into a calm ocean. Get a good partner if one is weak. Pair a strong rower with a weak one for fairness in a competition and for comfort and enjoyment in any event. Go out there and get some exercise you will remember. It is almost impossible to forget a canoeing adventure.

One can take up a class in canoeing while gaining experience at the same time. Why not take up a class? The entire family will learn to gain respect for teamwork, because the two persons in a canoe must work in unison for the best result. Like I said, it will be difficult to forget going to the lake to canoe.

Sailing is a way some families with seasoned sailors among them see the Caribbean. They rent a boat and set their sails for one island after the next. They are wise to have a person who is knowledgeable about ocean navigation and radio operation aboard. Sailing from port to port while sun bathing, swimming, windsurfing and snorkeling during the moments at anchor -- what a vacation!

The family can visit the resorts along the way at its own leisurely pace. Make sure the boat does not stray into unfriendly territory. This will be an experience the family will want to avoid. Otherwise smooth waters are ahead.

Motorboating. Many are more comfortable leaving their fate to a motor rather than a sail. Rent a motorboat from the harbor and go out to sea after a few safety lessons, tips, and directions. If the area is complicated, ask for a small craft chart from the concession operator before getting lost. Better to be safe and sure than to waste time and run out of fuel looking for the way back. The family can have safe fun while boating by observing the rules of the sea.

Flying. Single-engine pilots, sea pilots, and twin-engine pilots in the family can take the willing and daring adventure seekers for a little flying fun.

If safety rules are adhered to, family members will enjoy flying to predesignated airports for lunch. Aerial sight-seeing in a small airplane is a novel experience for most of us. It is a good idea to hire a local flight instructor to give the family a guided aerial tour. All the family pilots could tune in on a preselected communication channel to listen to the lead plane which will carry the flight instructor serving as a tour guide.

The entire family could plan lunch at a small convenient airport to watch all of the family pilots land. The pilots could do a few touch-and-go exercises, but avoid being show-offs. Do not invite trouble. Play it safe.

Then, once all the pilots have landed and met the rest of the family, all can join together for lunch.

The activities that the family could do are endless. Let us have some safe flying and enjoy an aviation treat.

Parachuting is less risky than sky diving because the static line is attached to a cable in the airplane in parachuting. The other end removes the sack holding the parachute so that it deploys automatically. One can almost go to sleep parachuting in comparison to sky diving.

Sky diving is far more demanding and requires absolute alertness for everything from checking the equipment to pulling the rip cord. Your life is seconds away from one

heart beat more if close attention to details are not
followed. All of this does not mean that there may not be
some family members who would like to try this daring
activity. Go to the drop zone as a family and observe other
jumpers try this sport if no one in the family cares for it.

How fast one will appreciate life after making a few
jumps, or watching someone else do it. Near many smaller
airports, air shows are given with a variety of air events,
all types of airborne feats. The blue angels of the U.S.
Navy may be showing how the sound barrier can be broken in
style. Parachutists, sky divers, and aircraft from stunt
planes to high speed jets are performing at some of the air
shows. If a member of the family is a part of the show, give
due respect and have fun while being entertained by people
who are putting their lives on the line for the family.

Snow skiing from the snow-plow position to paralleling is
enjoyable. Many families rent large condos near the slopes
for an exhilarating week of skiing and playing together. Go
down the slopes with Uncle Rod. Ride the lift up to the top
with Aunt Clemencia. Take the gondola to lunch at the top
while watching other skiers 'eat the snow.' Enjoy the
beautiful outdoors in its winter dress. Get reacquainted
again by the fire in the evenings after each day's outing.
Play or sing Christmas carols and holiday music all the way
home after enjoying a week on the hill. Monday through
Friday offers the least busy time. No long lines and long
waits are necessary to get back up to the top.

Each person should ski at his/her own ability. Match up
the beginners with beginners, and let the intermediates form
their own family group. The advanced skiers can go right on
to the top while the rest of us take it slow and easy on the
little baby hills. Believe it or not, suntan lotion is
advisable for snow skiing to keep from getting sunburned. At
night, jump into the outdoor jacuzzi and watch the steam rise
to the clear skies. The air is so fresh and the Milky Way so
close that no one will ever want to go down the mountain
after the fun is over.

Make reservations early. Try to get a deal that includes
lift tickets, room, and added attractions at a bargain rate
early in the season. Join different ski clubs that are able
to get special discounts and passes. The membership fee can
be recouped in discounts in a short time. Snow skiing is a
family affair to make winter a little friendlier. Give snow
skiing a try for one of your reunions.

Hang gliding looks as if the soaring human body has replaced
the fuselage. A class in this outdoor activity that looks
so effortless is essential. Small beginnings on sandy
beaches over small cliffs are an ideal way to start. High
peaks in curvaceous mountains are no place for a beginner.
The family can send a few scouts to check out the activity

first; then, after a favorable report, the ones in the family that are up to this adventure can join the birds in the air.

Outings to Amusement Parks, Museums, etc.

Sight-seeing can provide the family with a tour of the host city. Visit with one another while touring the special attractions of the city. Visit the town hall, the court rooms, both civil and criminal. Go to a government function in city hall. Educate the young ones on the responsibility of the citizen and the duties of government. Visit the libraries and museums, the arboretums and botanic gardens.

Amusement Parks. "Wow! Ah!", the kids and adults will go when they take a ride on the roller coaster. Up and down, around and around the family goes on the merry-go-round. Wham! Bam! Bang! as they dodge cars knocking up against each other. If not for the first family reunion, the family should plan to have a trip to an amusement park on one of their reunions.

Discount tickets for most amusement parks are available at many large corporations and government employees' unions. The Entertainment Committee in the host city can have the discount coupons ahead of time to provide the family with financial savings. Discount coupons may also be obtained from hotels, department stores, and travel agencies. Every dollar saved on the discounts is a dollar donated to more rides, popcorn, and peanuts.

Disneyland has a special tour and provides families with 50 or more members attending the park with discounts, guided tours, and family attractions.

Singing attractions, historical shows and studies of the galaxies can all be seen at the larger amusement parks. The small ones are adventurous with go-cart racing which can provide safe entertainment when the rules are obeyed. Whether it be seen by day or evening, the amusement park will not let the family down.

Check with the park to see if the family will be allowed to bring its own picnic, box lunches, and beverages. If so, a lot of money can be saved. In addition, the family can regulate the nutrition and control for special diets, eliminating sodium, grease or sugar.

Make your day at the amusement park an event to remember, with fun and discount savings for everyone. The family will cherish all the snapshots taken while having fun at the park.

Rodeos thrill everyone with all the roping, riding and tossing. No wonder the wild west has retained this event. Kids, young adults, and grown-ups all love this exhilarating sport. Steers, horses, and bulls are all involved in so much competition. Seconds must be shaved in order to break a new record. If the family can time the reunion around a rodeo event, the whole family can join spectators from all over sharing in the festivities. Let the whole family get into the spirit with western outfits and hats like Pecos Bill's. Go all out to enjoy this evening, but, as always, observe safety precautions.

Zoo. A trip to the zoo for the family will be a way to take pictures of all of the favorite animals that children read about in school. If the family has chosen an animal to be part of the family crest, then the zoo trip will be a splendid place to show all the little ones the animal selected. The children must be told ahead of time, as well as at the site, to obey the safety rules posted near the animal cages. They should be warned against teasing the animals, and avoid extending their arms or any part of their bodies inside the cages.

Teach them to be enthusiastic but respectful of the adults. No running, loud noises, or horseplay should be tolerated. They can have a lot of fun and the children can still be well-mannered. Appropriate, quick, firm discipline should be administered promptly for violations, and the entire day will go splendidly. The zoo offers knowledge to help educate children about the development of animals over the years. Pictures of large reptiles are next to the sites of the modern-day version of the same species.

Refreshments like roasted peanuts, fresh popcorn, and beverages are available. Again, it may be possible to tote a small picnic for the family in the zoo. If so, leave the area clean of paper, cans, and other litter from the family picnic. Let us make the zoo officials proud of family reunions. We do not have to be like the wild high school or college athletic team that makes havoc of an area. A good example could be set by every family reunion visiting the zoo.

Museums. Many will not want to miss the museums of the host city. They will want to check for special exhibitions that coincide with their visit. .ixTelevision game shows

Television game shows provide tickets to live recordings. Some shows even allow a member of the family to win prizes to take to the reunion to be shared with the others.

Watching movies stars on location of a filming of one of the family's favorite shows is intriguing.

Miniature Golf. All the dreams of a hole-in-one capture the imagination as the family lines up to play miniature golf. The courses have developed into a unique adventure in a challenging little world.

Water Slides. Although the name changes from one location to the next, if the family feels like getting wet, this activity will thrill the little ones and send the adults back to gather thoughts of younger years. In some states, an entire amusement park is devoted to water activities; the parks offer water slides at different levels of challenge. First, let the brave pioneers in the family try the water slides; then, map out the gentle courses for the little ones.

Check the age, height, and water knowledge required for participation in this water adventure. Plan on spending at least a half-day involved in water fun.

End of the Day. Add up all of the points, arrange for the first-place players, and bring the second and third-place winners together for Olympic-style pictures. The grand finale of the festivities brings all of the participants together to share in the ceremonies.

Get the cameras ready, the camcorders rolling and let the lights shine. This is an occasion worth remembering. Family reunion games and activities are good. We deserve the best family fun available. And we can make that fun a reality.

ACTIVITIES LETTERS

CHAMBER OF COMMERCE

Dear Manager:

On _____ and __ , 19 __ , our family plans to have its ___ Annual Family Reunion in (City), (State) Presently, we are trying to compile information on all the avail-ble activities in the (City) area.

We are wondering whether your office will be of service to us by providing us with all the information you may have on:

. Parks;
. Sightseeing tours;
. Discount tickets;
. Activities scheduled for the dates we will be
*   in the city;*
. Recreational facilities;
. Movies;
. Plays; and
. Other activities of interest to adults and
*   children and appropriate for family gatherings.*
. Hotel discounts
. Restaurant discounts

Will your office please notify us soon so we can make plans for some of the many events that your wonderful city offers?

Very sincerely yours,

_____
Honorable Chairperson

_____ FAMILY _____ ANNUAL FAMILY REUNION

SELECT AN ENTERTAINMENT ACTIVITY

Dear Family member(s),

LIST:

OUTDOOR:

BOAT PEDDLING	*BADMINTON*
HORSEBACK RIDING	*VOLLEYBALL*
SACK RACES	*SOFTBALL*
HORSESHOE TOSSING	*TRACK EVENTS*
SWIMMING	*STORY TELLING*

INDOOR:

PASSWORD	*CHECKERS*
MONOPOLY	*BILLIARDS*
BIBLE TRIVIA	*DANCING*
CHESS	*PING PONG*
BACKGAMMON	*STORY TELLING*
UNO (CARD GAMES)	*RAFFLE (WORTH MORE THAN $100.00)*

This list of activities planned for the _____ Annual Family Reunion is for the specific purpose of providing enough games, activities, tables, and materials for this most joyous occasion and the fun and enjoyment of everyone.

Please place your name next to the game(s) in which you would like to participate.

A schedule of events will be provided notifying participants of their choices and challengers.

Thank you.

Very sincerely yours,

_____
Honorable Chairperson

_____ *FAMILY* ____ *ANNUAL FAMILY REUNION*

LIVE ENTERTAINMENT

Band.   Live entertainment from a jazz band or a large symphonic band is within reach of a medium-sized family reunion of 200 to 300 people.   A small donation from the nuclear families, together with the interest from the family bank account will cover the fee, or include the cost of the band in the invitation fee charged to each member of the family in attendance at the reunion.

The waltz, fox-trot, and cha-cha can be elegantly danced in the moonlight.   Calypso, Reggae and slow dancing can follow the beat of the band.   The evening serenade will kindle romance in every heart and make us wish the moment could last forever.
Individual performers, whether instrumentalists, vocalists or comedians are available to delight the family.

Where to find.   Start with the yellow pages of the telephone directory, look under some of these headings:

>   *Agent
>   *Agency
>   *Entertainer
>   *Entertainment
>   *Musician Union.

A Church choir of the host city may offer talent that will be suitable for the entertainment.   After all, there are several famous persons in the music field who got their start in church.   It is possible to secure a person who will combine spiritual with other kinds of music such as country and western, soul music, ballads, and classical.

Elks lodges have a wide range of membership which may include a wide array of musical talents.

The local musician's union is an excellent place to seek singers, musicians, and other talented performers who are members of the musician's union.   First, the union is very helpful in making the difficult seem easy in finding someone to satisfy the family.   They deal with the business end of hiring an entertainer.   Let us review some of the business considerations the musician's union can help the family arrange in an efficient manner.

Contracts are made between the family and the entertainer. It is a commitment informing both parties exactly what to expect. Everything from the price to the address is put in writing.   There are so many duties to be taken care of that it is important to spell out who is responsible for what.
Hire a known quantity, that is, know the work of an

entertainer and hire that person to perform at the family reunion. This is important. The Entertainment Committee has an entertainer that the family is already familiar with. For example, the family would know what to expect if it hired Whitney Houston or Frank Sinatra to perform at the reunion. Of course, these two are out of the price range of most family reunion Entertainment Committees. But if a family does not know an entertainer that the members enjoy, it is usually possible to go to places where the prospective musicians perform and get a good idea of what to expect.

Prices. The price charged to the family should be clear, specific and all-inclusive. These charges should be submitted in writing at the time the entertainer is booked. An exact, firm quotation of how much the performer will charge is necessary. The agreement with the musician should leave no room for question or error. Such a clear understanding will promote a positive relationship between the family and the entertainment industry.

If the family goes through the musician's union be honest with them. Tell the officials that the family is trying to save money.

Electrical outlets for the performer's equipment must be the right type. Three-pronged plugs are necessary for grounding purposes. Some older buildings are not wired for the three-pronged plugs generally required by the equipment. A family could miss a whole evening of entertainment due to having an incorrect outlet.

Ask the performer what type of outlet is needed and make sure the necessary repairs are done by the hall, if you are renting the location. Or, if the facility is family-owned, contact a good electrician to take out the electrical permits and do the replacement of the outlets in a safe manner.

Lighting is a primary concern of most musicians. They are used to being in the spotlight. If they are using music, they must be able to see it very clearly. Some musicians may have their own lighting equipment, or they may recommend a place to rent or purchase the proper lighting.

A stage or platform helps to designate the area upon which the musician performs and makes him more visible to the audience. In commercial locations, a stage is generally on the premises. In the home, the family may provide a stage or platform. Make sure the platform is safe and structurally sound. Not all musicians require a stage.

A microphone is a must for most musicians. They want their music to be heard as it is intended. A solo player usually needs a microphone. A small combo wants to emphasize different instruments at different times using the microphone. A band may need a microphone only to announce what is to be played.   Provide a system with a good hum-free amplifier.

If the musicians provide their own system, provide adequate space for them to set it up.

In a park, hotel or commercial location, the amplification system generally does not disturb the neighbors.   In a home, we have to be considerate of them.   Contact the neighbors to inform them about the possibility of loud music.   Let them know that the music will be for a reasonable duration of time.   Also, let them know that the family will do everything possible to keep the music from being excessively loud.

Liability for any accidents at the location which may occur to the musicians is a question for the family attorney.   But there is some general information that may be of interest to the family.

First, the local union has a clause in their contract about liability.   Most unions state that if the family and the musician agree to request the musicians to provide insurance for their own liability, it is acceptable.   If the liability clause is to be deleted completely, it is possible   providing both parties agree to the deletion in writing.

Second, hotels and other commercial places may provide for liability insurance for musicians who perform on their premises.   Verify this with the hotel to make sure that the hotel and not the family is responsible for the liability coverage.   Get it in writing.   At least take notes of the conversation: date, time, person spoken to, their title and position and telephone number.

Musicians have been giving performances for years without any accidents.   Very seldom is there need to worry.   They are good-natured people who like to entertain.   They like to avoid hassles, but most of all, they love to entertain.

Remember that the family and the musicians can mutually exclude the liability clause from the contract.   Consult the family attorney for specific legal advice on the liability issue to eliminate doubt.

Will the family provide help to the entertainer in setting up the equipment?   Most entertainers, women included, will provide their own crew to set up the equipment.   Generally, some of the equipment is so expensive and requires such delicate care that they prefer to do the set-up themselves.

During the contract negotiation, ask the entertainer if he/she expects help from the family in setting up the equipment.   If the entertainer needs help, perhaps the family should make it clear who on the Entertainment Committee will be responsible for this duty.   Whoever is chosen should be at the curb ready to assist the entertainer at precisely the requested time. A very responsible member of the committee should be in charge. Treat the equipment with gentle care. We do not wish to ruin expensive musical instruments and equipment and the evening's entertainment in the process.

At the conclusion of the entertainment session, remember to help the musician take down the equipment and carry it back to his/her vehicle. The performer will have a good experience and want to do other family reunions if we are kind, courteous and respectful.

Provide directions to the musician as to where to set up. Show where the outlets and other needed accessories are located. Have a member of the Entertainment Committee stay with the musician to help with any needs that may come up. This person will be the family's ambassador.

The ambassador to the musician has an enjoyable mission. He/she seeks to help the musician relax. Try to get a biography and photo of the musician. The Communication Committee could work with the Entertainment Committee to release the biography and pictures to the entire extended family. This will give the family a chance to warm up to the entertainer.

The entertainer needs all the help he/she can get. Be courteous and helpful. Everyone may not like the entertainer or enjoy the music. Even though the musician will try to win everyone's heart 100%, the musician still needs everyone's encouragement. Smile, be friendly and warm up to the entertainer. Avoid being jealous; all of us have had a secret fantasy to be performing with Elvis Presley or Dionne Warwick.

The musician is trying his/her very best to appeal to the entire family. An extended family has an age span from small children to senior adults, so this is a tall assignment. The musician tries to keep the interest of the adults while not losing the attention of the children.

Dress. Musicians usually have a varied wardrobe in terms of color and style to choose from. Let the musician know the family color. The musician may even try to wear an outfit that fits into the family color theme. Let the musician know how conservatively the family would like him/her to dress.

If the family is dealing with an agent for the entertainer, the agent should specify the dress code to the entertainer. The family should let the agent know exactly what its expectations are. The musician does not want to be over-dressed or under-dressed for the engagement.

A changing room for the entertainer for make-up and changes between performances is a must. A special room for privacy is a consideration that the entertainer needs. No one should be allowed in the dressing room unless the entertainer requests assistance.

Sometimes a special room for dressing will be used for other purposes before the entertainer arrives. Let the caterers or other users know what time to have the shared room completely clear for the entertainer. Notify the entertainer in advance of the time schedule. The family should allow the entertainer to have at least one hour of preparation before the performance. The entertainer will greatly appreciate the family providing a dressing room for privacy.

Timing for the performance is crucial. After dinner is usually the best time for an audience to gain the most from a performance. Feed the family first, then entertain.

The entertainer needs to know in writing the exact time to perform, whether overtime is allowed, and if it is all right to do an encore.

Timing is everything, so feed the family and bring out the entertainer.

What kind of music to provide the family is a concern of the entertainer. Some entertainers are able to sing music from around the world. The songs are sung in the language of each country. This provides for a variety of songs.

However, there is a consideration needed here. Some families may be offended if a song is sung in a language that represents a sad memory. Find out if the family rejects any language. If so, avoid offending the family and stick to the music that brings cheer to the reunion.

Religious versus non-religious music is often a question that can be settled by majority vote. Many religious families are entirely devoted to spiritual music. Perhaps if the family is evenly divided, one-half of the session can be spiritual music and the other secular music. The members of the family can attend the session of their choice.

The music is arranged to make the evening delightful for the family. One way of pleasing the chairperson and Host Committee's leaders is to play at least two selections that are favorites of the head of the family reunion.

Our family will cherish the hour of entertainment for many months to come.

Ethnic jokes are forbidden. No family should be laughing at the expense of other families. If the family employs a comedian, make sure to instruct him/her to eliminate ethnic jokes. It seems that some comedians would not have a job if it were not for the pain they bring to other people to make a few people laugh. They lack the intellect to bring about laughter without the lowest form of profanity and the exploitaton of ethnicity.

Rules regarding cancellation are clearly stated in the contract if the entertainer is from the local union. If the family has to cancel, it should give the union and entertainer notice as early as possible. If the notice is given in less than 48 hours, a kill fee is charged. This fee is like a penalty for not giving the entertainer enough time to make other arrangements for the evening.

Even after making an early notice of cancellation to the entertainer, we should write and explain why it was necessary to cancel. A brief note of apology will suffice.

If the entertainer has to cancel, the union will try to find a substitute that is agreeable to the family. Agency and union usually are able to find a performer who does similar work. This is a good reason for dealing with an agency or a union when we hire an entertainer.

Being late is an unforgivable sin for the entertainer. Unless the entertainer has a justifiable reason, like an accident or serious illness, the union will take disciplinary action. We should learn how dependable the entertainer is in the early selection stages. Our family wants an entertainer we can depend on to be on time.

Breaks for the entertainer depend on the duration of the performance. If the entertainer plans one set which lasts about 45 minutes, the musician may perform straight through without a break. Otherwise, a break will come between the sets.

Feeding the entertainer is a good gesture on the family's behalf. A solo performer appreciates the courtesy of being invited to have something to eat, but as a rule the solo entertainer graciously declines the offer.

Members of a band are delighted to be invited to eat and they will generally dine with the family.

Live entertainment is a real pleasure for the family to treasure and we will want to take pictures of the occasion. It can really make the difference between an outstanding and a so-so day.

CEREMONIES

At every reunion, recognition is given to particular members: the birthday of the oldest member, the special anniversary of a particular couple, graduations from high school and college, job promotions, a member who has attended every reunion, etc. The Entertainment Committee coordinates honoring these special occasions so that no omissions occur.

Now, let us describe a large family reunion which took place in Washington, D.C. The participants arrived on Friday night at the inn which had been entirely reserved for the group. Friday was a free night for the individuals to do whatever they wanted. On Saturday they toured Washington, D. C., Virginia and Maryland, and the whole day was taken up by the tour. The children had special entertainment which was separate from the adults.

At night, they had a big banquet which included a fashion show, a party and the honoring of the oldest member of the family with awards. The food was catered. Besides the fashion show they had entertainers, singers, a fine band and dancing.

In addition, they had a special session called "This is Your Family," based on the television program "This is Your Life." They were honoring the matriarch of the family -- she was brought up first. They told the family history in a narrative form, and when someone's name was mentioned, they had to come up. It took about an hour and a half, and the whole family was involved.

This part of the program was done professionally as well as the rest. They had comedians and jokes, and they even had rehearsed parts. The script went something like: "Remember the time in the 1920's when jazz was very much a part of the scene..." The band would play a jazz tune and someone would dance the Apple or the Charleston, and they would be wearing the actual dress of the times. Then the script would say, "Well, Martha, do you remember how John was doing the Charleston?"

It would alternate between gaiety or a reflective, reminiscent mood depending on what was going on in the history of the family at that moment. To go on, "In 1932, the great Depression hit the country. Martha lost her mother then..." Then they would discuss her death and the funeral, and the mood would become very somber. It was done by a professional in the movie industry who was a member of the family. They were lucky to have someone with the talent who was also intimately involved with the family.

It was all rehearsed and well-planned in advance. But the family could have hired a good professional of this kind who could do the homework on the family, write an appropriate script, and direct the amateur performers. This kind of entertainment is a common thing in many families.

In the lobby of the banquet, all the beautiful dresses, gowns, furnishings and artifacts of the family were on display. The family members were able to purchase insignias and other artifacts from the family treasury.

The children attended the banquet. It was part of the history of the family, and they stayed up until about 9:00 or 10:00 p. m. While "This is Your Family" was going on, the meal was served. The young people stayed and danced until about 1:00 or 2:00 a.m. and just had a good time. An exception was made to allow the children to stay up late on that very special occasion.

A committee in the host city handled all the financial arrangements for the inn, banquet and ballroom. They put their own cooks in the kitchen and provided their own food. They did have to sign a waiver to remove the hotel from any liability resulting from the hotel not having control over the kitchen situation. They simply rented the facility. The waiters and waitresses were members of the family. The members of the family who needed to earn extra money may choose to work for hire in some of the hotel staff's functions at the banquet. There is nothing like the warmth of seeing family members help do the chores. I have always volunteered to do chores in the needed areas.

Now I would like to describe another family situation. This family had planned their reunion to occur in August and sent out a letter describing the arrangements and saying there would be a no-host bar. One member was coming from Puerto Rico and wrote back immediately that he would not attend if alcohol was to be served...more on the subject of alcohol later.

Some families who returned to the original home site have as part of the traditional ceremony the cleaning of the graves of their ancestors. Rather than do this on Memorial Day, they do it together as a family, cleaning the graves, planting and providing flowers.

Entertainment possibilities in rural environments may be limited. But these areas provide the best background for truly reuniting families without distractions.

Still families may desire to go out to do something together, especially in the evening when the mature adults are still reminiscing over the past and the younger ones are getting restless from never having shared these experiences, and just because that is the way of the younger ones. They may want to go out to a movie together, or to a club to dance. These desires are planned for in advance.

CEREMONIES LETTERS

MAYOR'S OFFICE

Mayor of the City of _____
          Office of the Mayor
Adress _____
City _____ *State* _____ *Zip Code* _____

Dear Mayor:

    On _____ *, 19__, our family will be in the midst of its _____ Annual Family Reunion in the wonderful, historically colorful City of* _____ *.*

    We would like to know if your office would be willing to present our family with a city resolution or similar form of recognition honoring our _____ Annual Family Reunion?

    We would like a member of your staff to present the resolution on Sunday at our family reunion. The ceremony should require no more than 30 minutes. However, your representative would be welcome to stay and join in the festivities of the afternoon which will include food, games and other wholesome family activities.

    We sincerely appreciate your earliest reply to our letter, and we thank your office in advance for its kind consideration of our request.

    Very sincerely yours,

_____
Honorable Chairperson

_____ *FAMILY* _____ *ANNUAL FAMILY REUNION*

CEREMONIES LETTER

Dear Family Member,

Ceremonies have been around on the earth in some shape, form or fashion since the times that tribesmen celebrated the birth of a child or the naming of the baby.

Our family desires to have ceremonies that will be in keeping with our family traditions. We have chosen your name to be placed on the Ceremonies Committee. Within a few days we will be sending you more information and material to start the ball rolling. Maybe now is a good time for reflective thinking on ideas that may be helpful to the Ceremonies Committee.

Very sincerely yours,

_____

Honorable Chairperson

_____ FAMILY ____ ANNUAL FAMILY REUNION

CHAPTER VI

III. SPIRITUAL CONCERNS

A. FAMILY ROLES

    1. The Role of the Father.

    2. The Role of the Mother.

    3. Brother to Brother.

B. ENEMIES OF FAMILY REUNIONS

    1. Chemical Dependency.

    2. Homosexuality.

    3. Recent Government Programs.

SPIRITUAL CONCERNS

Many families want to set aside time to attend church, synagogue, or temple together as a group. The pastor, priest or rabbi may dedicate a special portion of the service to the family or plan a sermon revolving around the importance of family and reunion.

Some families do not have unanimity in the kind of religious service they attend. For example, I attended a reunion in Kansas where two different churches were involved, the Baptist and the Church of God in Christ. Everyone attended one church or the other.

It might be beneficial to try to persuade such a group to unite together at one church or temple, especially if the family is going to be honored there on that day with special recognition and a special sermon. Many pastors are very willing to accommodate such a group with recognition, and when the collection plate is passed they will be well-rewarded for their graciousness.

FAMILY ROLES

Family Unity is the single most important element in world peace, and if we fail to insure today for peace tomorrow, there will be no peace, only terror and hate. Current executive leaders have advised making the courts tougher and less humane, a solution to solving the problem of crime that is a potential time bomb. To make matters worse, this idea is echoed throughout the land in the U.S. by many politicians, clergymen, and leaders. But it is like putting a Band-Aid on a cancer. We must start now curing the cancer by going to the heart of the problem and performing surgery on the direct part that is affecting and threatening the very existence of the entire body. We must begin with examining the roles played by the members of the family.

The traditional family structure as we have known it in the past has evolved. Many textbooks do not want to recognize that the home structure has been undergoing a change; this needs to be acknowledged. The framework of the family includes couples who are married and have children, couples who have decided to avoid marriage completely and yet have children, and divorced couples who started their families prior to getting a divorce. (I do not mean to say that childless couples do not constitute families, but for the purposes of this discussion I am concentrating on the interactions of families with children.) The situations may vary, but the basic structures are similar to the three mentioned.

Let us review the different forms of family relationships that vary from the traditional one that we have found acceptable. We must seek to heal the wounds of our fragmented families and brings our nations to peace. With some degree of variation, three basic types of family relationships exist: married, divorced, and single. Even in the case where the man and woman are no longer living together, the family still exists because of the existence of the child. When a person associates shame and guilt over the conception of a child out of wedlock and refuses to recognize the family as an entity, we have a problem to resolve. We must identify the roles and the duties of each segment of the family.

The Role of the Father

The role of the father is the primary place to start because the weakening of the father's role either by the fathers themselves or by society has had a disastrous effect upon the family. There are many of us fathers who have done far less than our fair share and we have allowed our families to go astray and to face the violent storms of disunity, economic havoc, and social unrest. We have refused to accept our responsibilities, yet we call ourselves men while our families are in orbit hurtling toward complete ruin. We do not want to confront our big fragile egos which we feel we must protect and we dare not hear the truth which would all but crush us to death. We are truly afraid to be gentle and kind to our children, loving and caring to our wives. We do not want to be like guiding stars in the universe, pillars or cornerstones in our communities, Sunday school teachers in our churches, fertilizer to our crop.

The father's role is to guide the family through life from one point to the next. We must not raise the white flag of defeat in our attack on the forefront of the problems of our families. Why should we give up? If we listen to our hearts, if we take the time to mend the wounds caused by society's many assaults on the very core of manhood, we must conquer the evils that strike at the heart of the family -- we will be on the course to curing the very cancer itself. We must guide our children and give love and direction to the mothers of our children. We must return to the home and become active ingredients of family happiness; this we must do without any further delay. We must search the streets for our prodigal child, and replace all our former tyranny and strict punishment with love, affection, and gentle direction.

Our children have diluted their frustrations with dope, prostitution, and lawbreaking. The jails, prisons, and reform schools are not the solution, as many ill-willed politicians would have us believe. We do not need more sick judges to fill our courtrooms. We need the father to bring his children home and guide them in the right path, and we need decent judges to help stabilize the family and make the community a home for everybody.

We fathers need to stop putting our jobs ahead of our families. I recently had the pleasure of conversing with a father who was an engineer with a large construction company. He told me that he put his family first; he had had a disastrous childhood himself in which he was unable to get along with his own father. He stated that his father was a workaholic who never had time to spend with him. The engineer said he had grown distant from and cold toward his father and he did not want the same thing to happen to his children. He wanted to be there when his children needed him, so if his son or daughter had any event that was truly important and required his presence, he would take the necessary time off from his job to be in attendance. He told me that he has learned to always put his family first.

We must take time to play sports with our children, yes, our sons <u>and</u> our daughters. The daughters want the love and affection that shines through participating in sports activities together just like the sons. We need to toss the ball, jog on the track, swim in the pool, and play billiards with our children of both sexes. The old practice of not allowing girls to be athletic is now antique and needs to be replaced with a new respect and understanding. These are the things that our children need. If we start taking time out to participate in sports with our children when they are young, they won't have to be in the streets seeking love, attention, and a sense of satisfaction.

We must love and respect the mothers of our children whether we are still married, never married, or unmarried. It may seem like pure foolishness to love someone who has been taking us to the courts, has taken more than we consider just and fair, and made off with our assets. How in the world can we love and respect someone like that?   Well, we must find a way to come to a respectful solution.

After all, we at some time or another saw fit to marry these women that we called our wives, and we went a step further to have children by them. Then somewhere down the line something went wrong; it was not our fault, it was the fault of the women. Oh no, it was definitely not our fault. Now why on earth would anyone ask us to love and respect these women?

The answer is one that truly separates the fathers who sincerely desire to make the earth a better place from those who do not care how safe our communities are going to be for our families. Our answer is that we owe it to our grandchildren to have a safe and loving environment, and it all begins with our children. Actually it begins with those women with whom we had our children. The time has come to find a way to communicate with them about these matters and bring about a genuine friendship.

One of the most pleasant divorced couples that I ever had a chance to meet was a couple that was under audit for both claiming the same dependent when I was working with the Internal Revenue Service as a field agent.   Instead of the bickering that most couples engage in when questioned for this violation, this couple met with me and explained why each one believed that he or she was entitled to the deduction.   After all the facts were revealed, the logic of each had some merit.   After I explained to them the law in this situation, they had lunch together and worked out a solution between them that was equitable for both but allowed the one who would receive the best tax advantage to claim the deduction.   Then they met with me in my office to disclose their decision and see if it was acceptable within the confines of the Internal Revenue Code.   After their audit was concluded, I congratulated the couple on how pleasant, enjoyable, and wise they were to still work together as a family unit even though they were divorced.   They saved the government a lot of time and worked for the betterment of family and country.

The father's relationship with his son is the building block of generations to come, and must be viewed as what it is, an important contribution to the family.   Often we fathers feel we must remain aloof, stern, and distant   from our sons because we want them to be men.   As fathers, we find ourselves denying our sons the love and affection they so desperately need; just as our daughters need to be involved in sports with their fathers, our sons need to be hugged and caressed, and to be told that they are loved and cared for by their fathers.

Our sons will be better citizens, husbands, and fathers of their children (our grandchildren) when they not only get sports training and development but start receiving love and affection from their fathers.   For too long now we have allowed a myth to survive that sons do not need love and affection. I remember the time a man who was a computer salesman told me and my younger son about how upset he was when his mother discarded his stuffed animal when he was a small boy   because she felt the time had come for him to be rid of his stuffed animals, especially since he was   a boy. Let us just call him "John" for the sake of   the story.   John said he became so upset by the removal of his stuffed animals that his mother soon bought him replacements.   John was a perfectly normal and well-adjusted man   who was not afraid to speak up for the right of a son to display warmth and tenderness.

The more love and affection that a son receives from his own father, the less need he will have to search the streets for love and tenderness.   We will see a dramatic decline in homosexual behavior in the future when fathers return home and provide a decent and loving role model for our sons by giving them love, teaching them sports and guiding them in the right direction.

Fathers who have daughters must know that their daughters need a father's input and guidance in order to develop into good mothers, wives, and lovers of their future husbands. A mean and strict father usually succeeds in causing much sorrow and grief in his family by trying to dictate to his daughter her every move. He often restricts her social life, makes her feel guilty about sex, and punishes her for every minor flaw. He often replaces patience with intolerance. A better way exists.

While in Hongkong, I had the opportunity to discuss the family with a young lady, "Ricky," who stated that her father would have the entire family join together in an hour of exercise which actually followed the moves of Kung Fu training. Ricky said that her father was gentle and patient in teaching the exercises. She in return enjoyed the mental discipline she acquired from the family's exercise program which also helped her to become more secure about herself. She was more able to be gentle and understanding to her future husband from the direction, patience, and love that her father gave her and her family. She mentioned that the entire family enjoyed the exercises which provided for mental calmness, peace, and togetherness within the family.

The father with the mother of his children is always reminded of the value of a good relationship with this woman, whether it be his wife, ex-wife, or girlfriend. The term "wife" will be used to signify all three for ease of expression. A good wife is to be desired above all the many riches and honors that a man could ever achieve within his lifetime. One thing to realize now is that at the time we married we thought our wife was going to be a good wife, and we were ever so wise to do the right things to win her favor for her love, companionship, and devotion to us and our children. She would be the right one above all of the rest; our wisdom and judgment was impeccable, and we hadn't the slightest doubt that we might be anything but absolutely right. Then somewhere between the wedding vows and the divorce papers something went wrong. The woman, of course, was at fault.

Very few of us are willing to undergo the pain and suffering a big strong man would have to endure to analyze what we did wrong to make the woman we onced loved so dearly become our mortal enemy. We fret with agony over how she ripped us off and how she did this and that wrong, and it was all her fault, we say to our friends and to all who will lend an ear.

But someday we must face the truth and set blame, fault,

and guilt behind us. We must raise the anchor and let our ship sail into smooth and calm seas. I know this will be hard for us to do. However hard, we must set sail as friends with our ex-wives following a parallel course where our children are concerned, even if we are unable to do so as man and wife. Actually, here again is an example of how the father, or in this case, the husband is the key force in the family; he can shape or break the good family, enhance or lessen the strength of family unity, and institute love or hatred as the family agenda. The choice started a long time ago when the man was pursuing the right woman to be his wife and the mother of his children. If for some reason everything does not work as wonderfully as he planned it to, he must stop looking for fault and blame and start all over anew and seal the cracks in the framework. He must do the right thing to make our streets empty of crime, prostitution, and dope. All of these problems started with the family and now the fathers, mothers, and the government must help bring the family together in a realistic manner. The family needs incentives that the father can provide by setting family goals, goals that are practical, morally just, and possible to achieve.

The father will be a dinosaur if fathers do not act now to save the family unit. It is all left up to a father to be loving and kind, to calm the winds to tranquil breezes, and the raging waters to glassy seas for our ships to float on in the tranquility of love and happy days. We cannot wait until tomorrow to bring about a change, for today is the only time we have to do our work on this mass problem. We fathers must accept our responsibilities. We must stop jumping ship, running from our problems. We need more love and good will in the home and more guidance and direction for our sons and daughters. The power is in our hands to help change our government to provide incentives and positive directions to fathers. The time is now to perfect a better future by investing in our children today and being the fathers that we know that we can most completely be by trying our very best. Nothing short of success will be acceptable.

The Role of the Mother

The role of the mother is the breath of the earth; without a mother, the world as we know it today would not exist. The mother's place in the home is like the heart to the body; she warms up the home and gives birth to the future. She stands by her man and provides the fuel for the growth of the family unit. The way a mother feels about her overall treatment by the father of her children will often reflect in the way the children are raised. If the mother could find a way not to allow the ill treatment of an inconsiderate man to have any effect upon her teaching the children and loving them, we would see an immediate improvement in the outlook of the family.

The ideal situation is one with the mother and father having true loving and caring hearts toward each other and the children feeling this love and affection to the point where they become warm and caring persons sharing the same love with their own children.   This will cause a chain reaction of love and admiration, and to create and sustain this chain reaction is a duty owed to society which starts early in the courtship process.

We must learn to control our passions and hot desires and to postpone our marriages and child conception to a time when we are more mature and can take on the responsibilities and serious commitment required of the man and woman who decide to bring a child into this world to start a new generation. We've got to stop dreaming of the perfect couple and accept reality; we must get to know the person completely that might be the parent of our children before we make a commitment. If at least the woman could accept the importance of this concept, there would be fewer broken homes and more happy families.

The decision regarding the right man to become the father of our children has a lot to do with the type of children we have, the way the children will be as parents when they grow up, and the quality of family life that will grow within our communities.   Women must not choose men that are the true opposite of a good father prospect.   Often women will say they do not want a man who is nothing but a dog, when in reality the dog-type of man is exactly the type most women find themselves attracted to and eventually marrying.   The wrong message is being sent out to society by the inconsistency between what women say and what they do.   The truth in what women say they want as a husband must match the reality of actually choosing a good man to be the father of their children.   The fault process is not what is being focused upon here because the determination of who to blame will not heal our torn and damaged home environments.   Let us begin now by making the best of whatever situation we have, lay aside our hostilities, and take the bold action of forgiving; let us turn around the bad tide that is taking our children out to stormy seas.

Most women want a good family life for their children and seek desperately to find the right man, and they want the type of man that will make a good father. A healthy relationship between the man and woman is a prerequisite to good parenting.   We are now facing an age when the family will take on greater importance, and mothers and fathers will give serious thought to being good parents.   They will teach their children to realize the positive environment of a good family life is a must if future generations are to flourish and prosper in a world of peace.   This change will occur in all the countries, nations, and continents of this earth, for if the realities spoken here spread like waters from a much needed rain to every village and city, there will be an awakening of the good family life. Mothers can make this a true reality by taking time out to make a better choice, a choice of wisdom instead of passion.

The mother's role with the father creates the beginning of the learning pattern for the children of the family. The mother has already selected the man that she wishes to follow and receive direction from on the way the family should develop and grow. She is willing to provide the moral support to the father of her children to help encourage him to be successful and an achiever. She will be loving and understanding with her man, for without her love and devotion the man will not be the pillar of the family and community nor make the decisions that will foster harmony. The mother should be as a soothing harp to the ears of a good father. Her touch is to be preferred over the finest linen, and her lead should always be understood as a rudder helping the family adhere to the course that the father of her children has chosen.

The mother's role with her son is important to the future mothers of the generations to come. The son perceives his mother to be the most beautiful woman in the world and he generally wants his wife to be like his mother in many respects. The son's domestic relations are deeply influenced by his mother in many ways. For example, how a son keeps his room will be very much the way he keeps his home or apartment if he does not find a good wife. The mother should instruct her son in the art of good nutrition and how to prepare food just as she would teach her daughter, for if he is to be a healthy man and bring about healthy children, he must be taught how to cook and what foods are required to make a sound body frame. The mother should teach her son how to clean up his room from a early age, and he should be taught to help clean the house when he becomes an adolescent. She should not allow him to let his clothes lie around filthy making a mess of the place and waiting for her to clean up. If problems arise in this area, the mother should call on the father of the child to help discuss the reasons for having a good outlook on cleanliness.

The views of the woman should be taught to the son at an early age with the mother teaching the child how to relate to women including the dictates of courteous behavior, which he practices toward his own mother, like opening the doors, giving his mother flowers, and helping lift objects that are perhaps too heavy for the mother, but not too heavy for him. She teaches him all the manners she desires the son to carry over to the treatment of his future mate. Many mothers fail to teach their sons social graces when they are very small. The mother cries about the disastrous results of her neglect when the child gets too large for her to be effective with anymore, especially in cases where the home is divided with no father on the scene to help correct things.

This is where all the juvenile delinquency starts, right in the home early in the life of the children, but many politicians refuse to recognize this problem primarily because they are at fault themselves. The politicians do not want the public to look at their family life because they are trying to tell the mothers that more prisons will solve everything, and this view has won a lot of support from many a mother who is neglectful in raising her son with the type of guidance to make him a responsible adult, and has made a bad selection in choosing the father of her children. Now the mother may have lost the passion for her mate. She lacks good judgment which contributes to the influx of her children into the violent territories of dope and crime.

These mothers want to have the same irresponsible politicians pass laws to stop the sale of books and magazines containing nude pictures in places that their sons might visit. The duty lies in the home. The mother must teach her son not to purchase these so-called obscene materials if she feels strongly that they will have a negative effect on his development. A mother has the duty to train her son at an early age to be obedient to her wishes in the present and in the future. If the son is given the proper type of discipline, which may mean applying a paddle on certain occasions, for the purpose of discipline and not the release of personal frustration, we will find a wholesome family.

We must realize that the journey we speak of here is a long one which we must begin today. Many mothers have borne an awfully heavy burden trying to be the head of household, both parents to their children, and still have some semblance of a social life for themselves. This is a most difficult task which requires a lot of faith in and prayers to God.

A mother's role with her daughter brings music to poetry, with the mother being aware of every growing moment of her daughter. The mother can fulfill all of her childhood fantasies through her daughter by making sure she gets a chance to do and have all of those things that are important to a girl, such as pretty teeth, elegance, and grace. The mother can truly relate to her daughter's early years like no one else in the entire world. She can truly relate to every stage of her daughter's development.

The daughter is taught the art of cooking, child rearing, and domestic caring starting at an early age. She learns social graces and becomes acquainted with the business aspects of family rearing: paying the bills, managing a budget, and purchasing household necessities without placing the family finances in a stressful position. The type of woman that the daughter becomes will be greatly influenced by the mother's training, teaching, and disciplining at this early stage.

When we stop to think about it for a moment, we wonder why some daughters constantly get into trouble as adults and always find themselves on the wrong side of the law. After giving the matter some thought, we think back to the sweet little innocent baby that came into the world without the blemishes of sin. Somewhere between home and school our daughters are going astray. It is our duty to start trying to correct this matter and provide all the love and attention that we can to our children. We cannot be perfect, but we can give it all we've got, because there is a solution to the problem.

A daughter needs a lot of attention and direction that starts at home with guidance and understanding. We want to be firm enough in the early years, so that gentle persuasion will be the major tool needed during the period of adolescence. Being too strict during the later stages of adolescence, trying to do what should have been done during the earlier stages of the child's growth, will have a backlash against the mother, with the child rebelling and hurrying off to dope, robbery, and prostitution. She will go for adventure, revenge, and to destroy the establishment. This can happen in families at all income levels.

However, we should note that the system that penalizes a poor daughter and places her in the prisons, reform schools, or in the half-way houses is a different system than the one that allows a wealthy daughter to go to ballet classes, join fine colleges, and become a debutante. The mothers of low income families face malnutrition, social prejudice, and deplorable living standards that echo upon deaf politicians' ears.

We must not allow rich daughters to escape the prosecution of their crimes while poor daughters suffer all kinds of evil, persecution, and prosecution without help or guidance. Why? Because mothers who made the right choice of marrying a good mate, living in a good neighborhood, and bringing their daughters up in a good environment had the opportunities to expose their daughters to a better choice of life.

Our poor daughters can only live in the fantasy life of today's soap operas that so dominate our television sets and their daily existence, dreaming of houses full of pretty furniture, big fancy cars, and the other trappings of wealth. The poor daughters are in constant search for fantasyland dreams and mistakenly think that it is the money and possessions that they are lacking in their lives.

Reality for the rich daughter is the expensive home that she lives in, the good sororities that she can associate with, and all of the lavishness of possessions, social life, and travel that she can extract from life. With the rich mother having time to spend with her daughter and often a husband who can afford to take more time giving his daughter the attention needed to make her mentally healthy, we have an ideal situation. I do not doubt for one moment that there are many mothers who have the right ingredients to make the best homes and family lives for their daughters.

It is the direct responsibility and duty of the mother who has a good family environment for her daughter to make it possible for another daughter to also have a good family life. Yes, she must take it upon herself to get out there and find a daughter from an extremely impoverished family background and improve her entire life, especially her home and social environment. She must make a sincere effort to do this duty and she must start today.

We must change the prison system to be a more habitable and human place for our daughters. There must be a sincere and dedicated effort to bring about the actual rehabilitation of our daughters. Ways have to be found to integrate our daughters back into the world of good jobs, education, and stable, loving homes. What need is there for us to continue to punish our daughters who are lost because of their need for a caring environment?

Dr. Martin L. King, Jr. gave his life so that we could find love for members of our family and those who despise us. This is the love that our daughters need, and it is not too late to give it to them. We should start a campaign to bring people into office who are trying to improve family life throughout the world: politicians, judges, and ministers who have devoted some time to making their own families be examples of reform and dedication to love. It is not necessary that these men and women be perfect or without sin, but they should have a high regard for the continuing growth of their families and other families. They should care about rehabilitating our daughters and want to change the entire unjust system that makes it possible for a rich daughter to become a debutante and a poor girl to become an inmate.

These injustices can be changed if the politicians put themselves in the homes of the poor mothers' families and take on the responsibility of taking those families that have the worst possible conditions and making those situations right. Don't tell us that the politicians are doing the best they can do when they refuse to take the challenge of gathering their own families' lost sheep. And if they happen to have perfect families, they should use their political influence to make this possible for all families.

Mothers need politicians that will sponsor legislation at every level of government to improve family life, including welfare reform that will bring the father back into the home and encourage the family to stay together and stand respectfully on its feet. Politicians must sponsor legislation to change the prison system so that it truly rehabilitates daughters who are incarcerated. These daughters need to have the opportunity to leave the prisons for each annual family reunion in order to spend time with their mothers in dignity. They should be allowed to visit the family reunion in a respectful way to appreciate their families but not be made to feel all the shame and humiliation that accompany an inmate. Let them go home in a positive manner. We need these changes soon.

If each member of every governing body including the mayors, governors, presidents, and their respective legislative bodies including the city councils, assemblies, senates, and the Congress would accept the joy of the challenge to take low-income families and rehabilitate those families as if they were their own daughters' families, we would see positive results that would make our heads go in circles. Mothers need this help, not all the legislation to make more prisons and tougher laws to continue to punish the prodigal daughters.

Not one of those senators and presidents would choose prison over the pardons they are accustomed to receiving for their own sins; they all expect to receive and usually get another chance. How many of us would prefer hell over heaven, or choose to have our daughters constantly punished, embarrassed, and ridiculed? They have been punished enough by our being poor parents, not giving them the best guidance that is available because we did not have the education ourselves, or the financial resources to make a better home, school, and social environment.

Some will try to deceive mothers by saying that more money and better schools to improve communities are not necessary, but ask any one of them to move into a poor community and, if they would be so bold as to undertake such a challenge for three years, ask them again how they liked staying in a poor community like Harlem or Watts compared to staying in a rich one. If the point is made, why don't mothers band together to work together in the poor communities to make those mothers have a safe and better environment in which to raise their daughters? The time necessary to achieve such a goal is endless. We should make it our duty to spend the rest of our lives devoted to such a task, and pass our work down from generation to generation. Then we will see the growth of good communities and take pride in all the beautiful daughters which our success has wrought.

We have had enough noise for more jails. We have accepted too long the dogma that there is not enough money to provide the resources and tools necessary for our poor communities. We must attack evil with positive action to eradicate crime in the only true way to remove the cancer of our poor communities: with the force of good courageous people, instead of lying politicians who only want to insulate themselves in their rich neighborhoods full of opulence, prejudice, and foolish pride.

Brother to Brother

When brothers grow up together, there is a great opportunity for them to form an everlasting bond of brotherhood and closeness. The family can foster and the brothers can achieve a oneness of purpose that will last them a lifetime as they grow toward friendship and a bond of peace between themselves.

A better world is realized when brothers maintain a genuine concern and love for each other. This is where the concept of brotherhood starts. For the most part, nothing should be taken for granted, or taken too lightly. The practice of exchanging gifts throughout the years of childhood and continuing into the adult years is a good one. My brother and I have sent birthday cards to each other for several years now. We have become closer over the years and have cherished the carefully chosen cards that we have received.

One benefit that has grown out of the closeness between my brother and I is that now the birthday cards are coming from our offspring. His children started to send me a birthday card and I reciprocated by having my children send him a card too. Now, we receive at least two birthday cards. The spirit of family love and unity is extended and reinforced.

With respect to women. My brother and I have been able to share with our younger brothers the lessons of life regarding the understanding and respectful treatment of the women in their lives.

We have shared a few experiences that we have learned from our own relationships with women who were in our lives during our youth. We have agreed that women are very delicate, even today when they are searching for an identity and following a quest to be equal to men. They still are fragile and gentle. Much of their coldness and false external hard shell is nothing more than an illusion brought about by the organizations of the women's movement such as the National Organization for Women.

The primary reason why these organizations have made such an impression on so many women is due largely to the fact that few male writers have written any works to challenge the motives behind the women's movement. Women are screaming out loud for attention; they want to be treated fairly in tbe work place, marketplace, and in the home. But they still want to be loved and caressed by the man they love and care for in their lives.

Therefore, little brother, when you meet a woman go after her mind, and her body will surely follow if she is truly interested. The secret to a woman's heart is to capture and captivate her mind and delicately treat her with affection and care. A woman cares about the man who seeks out her mind and talents. Discuss her hobbies, academic pursuits, and family plans.

Today, more so than ever before, women want to be married and raise a family. They want to be nourished with thoughts of family unity and positive home planning. These are some of the most important topics for a woman to discuss with her man. The sexual revolution has only served to solidify the woman's desire for a stable relationship with a man.

More emphasis should be placed on family planning early in the relationship with a woman. It does not mean that one must be committed initially to marriage, but at least each person would get a better idea of what to expect if marriage should follow. Less thought should be given to sex during the first stages of dating. Brother, we have had too much running after a sexually-oriented relationship and not enough thought given to what it is all about. The family has suffered because many young people have sought to satisfy their sexual desires without any regard for the outcome of their folly.

Sex education in the schools should have family planning and responsibility as a focal point of the classroom training. When children are taught at an early age about sex and family duties, our families will strengthen. Sexual and family education should be viewed as healthy and necessary.

Education concerning the family as a unit and the proper roles of family members is lacking in our society. Our children are growing up without the slightest inclination of what to expect when they become adults. The schools have rarely included this kind of training, and any study of the family has been purely from a sociological standpoint. It is no surprise that the world has lost the concept of a good family structure.

What are the results of not teaching our children about the family? We have had many examples of what happens when family education is lacking. The music industry has seen an onslaught of negative lyrics attracting younger and younger audiences. We have seen many mothers do the wrong thing by trying to censor the records written and performed by musicians who are themselves victims of the loss of positive family images.

The way to succeed in the war against negative family lyrics is to attack the matter in our homes and schools with positive education. Censorship will only serve to strenghen the devil's grip on our young children. Brother, we must take control of our homes and teach our children about good lyrics that further the goals of goodness in the family. We must direct our children to listen to selected musical entertainment. The parents who insist that more legislation and censorship are necessary use this argument as a scapegoat for their failure to properly raise and discipline their children. Instead, they have abandoned their duties as parents.

My memory goes back a few years when my mother would have us listen to good music. She also restricted what we purchased from the record stores. It is not too late for us to be good parents by instructing our kids to leave the trash outdoors, eliminate negative music totally, and grow with positive family music.

ENEMIES OF FAMILY REUNIONS

Chemical Dependency

But why are so many young people becoming dependent on chemicals as an escape? We can attempt to answer that question with a straightforward look at the myths taught to our young people from infancy to adulthood. We have given them the dream of fantasyland and have told them about the good guys wearing white hats and the bad guys wearing black hats when we know the truth is often simpler to tell.

Good guys may wear either color of hat and the same is true for bad guys.

We have filled our young peoples' minds with delusions of grandeur, dreams of becoming the richest, most powerful and best looking people in the whole world. We have told them that all they have to do to be successful is to work hard every day and get along with their bosses and co-workers.

We have made our young people think that money grows on trees, and all they have to do is go out in the orchard and pick their fortunes from the trees and everything will be all right.

What happened was we kept trying to give our kids bigger toys than our neighbors, friends, and relatives only to find ourselves under tremendous pressure at Christmas time to keep the game going.

The pressure grew and grew for our children to out-perform their friends in everything they had to do: school, band, football; the list is endless. It made our children very competitive.

One word keeps popping up every time we cite an example, and pressure is the word. More pressure is placed on kids today than ever before, and this converts to stress. The truly dirty word of all time is stress.

Alcohol does not kill. Excessive drinking is one of the worst assaults on the spirit and body of family members that we can think of on the earth. Drinking death is the drinking of alcohol to the extent that it is an abomination to the body and to the family. The entire family suffers when one of its members is stricken with the incapacitation of alcohol and the inevitable fatal liver disease which follows, caused by a person's refusal to control the bottle. Tell me why we have this suicidal death wish within ourselves? Why do we keep pouring this poison into our bodies to the extent that our livers just cannot take it anymore? Will we stop bringing all of this unnecessary grief and sorrow upon our families? Will we ever learn that someone truly loves us and cares about our bad habits? What are we waiting for -- a special invitation to attend our own funeral? Or maybe we want to be the pallbearers of our own corpse?

We refuse to believe the foolishness of over-indulgence, bottle after bottle, day after day, and drink every chance we get and to every occasion we can think of even though our behavior is damnation to our own spirit. We will change now for the better and seek help if necessary from a qualified source, like a hospital or approved institution for the helping of individuals like us who need all the expertise we can get to provide us with freedom from the bottle.

Children, spouses, and friends really are the ones who suffer the most from an alcoholic. They are the ones with the sensibility to feel the pain and suffering that an alcoholic ought to feel to give him the determination to seek help and rid the body and mind of this terrible disease in the family. We must not hesitate to pound into our thick heads the urgent message that alcohol is a menace which does not discriminate against age, race, or sex. The young and the old are dying each year from excessive drinking, white and black people fall prey, not to mention the pretty women and young men that are allowed to become inhabitants of the graveyards each day from the sin of excessive drinking.

Drinking and the road don't mix. It is not enough to

cause destruction to one's own body, but to take drinking on the road is to invite disaster involving many innocent family members who didn't do anything to us. It is unthinkable that we can be so selfish as to take the life of a poor child who has never harmed anyone. Here is a family driving on the same road that we are driving on and without any knowledge that some darn fool is trying to kill and destroy his/her own spirit and body, and will in the process take the lives of other families. Whatever we do to ourselves, we must not allow our deranged, sick minds to harm and destroy other people. Keep the drinking off of the roads.

Recommendations to make our journey and those of others safer follow. **First,** we should at least take along someone with us who does not drink and allow that person to drive our vehicles if we just have to drink. **Second,** we definitely should remember to follow the example of the single-engine pilot's rule of **"eight hours between bottle and throttle,"** which translates to **allow our bodies a minimum of eight hours between the time we drink our last drink and the time we put our foot on the gas pedal** for the sake of our lives and the lives of other families who are on the same roads that we are. Stevie Wonder sang the song "Don't Drive Drunk," good lyrics for those of us who every day just keep taking chances with our lives by drinking and trying to drive.

Legal consequences are a real nightmare. If we do not know what the words humiliation and shame represent, we should become acquainted with a most horrible moment and one that we will want to forget for the rest of our lives. I mean we will want to have amnesia about ever being thrown in jail for driving under the influence. Most countries over the entire world have become very serious with the drunk drivers who have in their hands a vehicle capable of crippling and destroying others. Do we ever stop and wonder that there is a lot of trust placed in the hands of motorists each hour they are on the roads? Have we ever given thought to the possibility that only a painted line separates us lunatics from the people who are sane drivers who do not experiment with alcohol and the lives of their families? They care. Why don't we?

Eat a good meal before and after drinking. Food absorbs some of the alcohol in our stomachs. Drink milk, or take an alkaline liquid or tablet to coat the stomach against the alcohol that eats away the stomach lining.

Don't drink and drive is the message that we must get into our foolish heads. If we cannot follow this rule, we must quit drinking now, before it is too late. Loving, caring, and considerate family persons like ourselves will find the strength to heed these lessons for the sake of our families and those around us. **DO NOT DRINK AND DRIVE!**

Homosexuality

Homosexuals can be helped. Homexuality can be stopped and completely cured. Homosexuals can return to a healthy heterosexual relationship like alcholics can return to a normal sober state and remain so. Homosexuality is caused by the absence of the father from the home and the lack of a man's image and model for the son to follow. With the rise of sexual freedom and exploration, many men have been leaving their parenting duties behind in favor of sexual promiscuity, which left a lot of fatherless families. The father's role in the family is of primary importance, despite the claims of many women's rights movements that emphasize the ability of a woman to replace a man. The time has come for men to assume their responsibilities in the home and to lead their sons and daughters to success.

A person may wonder just how the lack of the man in the home contributes to the alarmingly rising rate of homosexuality that is rampant in our cities today. For an answer, think a moment about your childhood experiences and see if your recollections focus on the persons in your home that were the ones you patterned yourself after. Most daughters wanted to be like their mothers, and sons wanted to be like their fathers. This is true for the majority of normal families. Now when the father is not in the family who does the son have to follow and watch and to gain insight from on how to be a man? He watches his mother put on her makeup and she dresses up to look pretty and adoring for some man. All of these things contribute to the subconscious development of the child, which it is all right for a daughter, but detrimental to the son.

The long-term effect of two generations of broken homes when the daughter grows up in a broken home only later to have her own children in another broken home situation compounds the problems. Let us analyze what is happening for a moment. A daughter who has no father in the home to watch how he does things matures to raise her own son without really knowing what goes into making a man a man. Then she tries her best to be a mother and a father to her son, which is the exact situation found in the majority of the homes today, with little or no success. She raises her son according to the best possible example she has available to her. Many little subtle things that a child picks up from his home environment go unnoticed by even the best woman in the most ideal environment.

For example, a friend of mine and her six-year-old son were having dinner with me. The dinner menu included fresh steamed vegetables, Cornish game hen and milk. Ginger had been added to the food, and perhaps a bit too much which caused the mother to exclaim that her son would not be able to eat it.   In my opinion, the food was all right and good for the boy to eat, so I informed him of the advantages of eating the vegetables which were beneficial to his growth and nourishment and would insure his having strong muscles.   Her son agreed with me and wanted to eat the food without further comment. Here is an example of how a son could have been persuaded in the wrong direction   by an over-concerned mother.   There are many examples creeping into the everyday family routine which will support subtle messages being conveyed to the son causing slow, but detrimental effects on the son's masculinity.

Recent Government Programs

Positive influences of government legislation can be completely beneficial to the family.   More programs developed by politicians to help the family at the national, state and local levels are needed to bring harmony to American homes. Actually, governments of all countries are badly in need of an agenda that gives clear direction on how a nation should proceed to develop family unity.   Such a program would do alot toward counteracting the increasingly negative elements that are weakening the family.

Negative influences are undermining the court systems, national and local governments, and religious organizations. We can review the ways in which each one of these systems is in turn eroding the foundations of the family.

First, let us examine the court system and underline major areas of concern.   Three Supreme Court justices came before the voters of California for reaffirmation in the last election: Rose Bird, Cruz Reynoso and Joseph Grodin.   Chief Justice Rose Bird received an unprecedented attack on her role as Chief Justice from the conservative groups aimed at removing her from office.   The Governor of California was very vocal in his re-election   campaign tactics. He played upon the sentiments of victims of violent crimes, proponents of the death penalty, and, backed by big money groups, he successfully ousted one of the most concerned, dedicated, and humanitarian Chief Justices that the State of California has ever been fortunate enough to have on the bench.

The Chief Justice's defeat was a severe blow to the safeguards of the three-branch system wisely bequeathed to the people of California by their forefathers.   Many families failed to be counted on the side of an advocate of fair judgment for all people, either because they allowed themselves to be influenced by deceptive political advertising or because they were too lazy to leave their easy chairs and go out and vote.

Decisions that often had favored large corporations and rich and powerful people finally, in Rose Bird's court, were replaced by those that meted out just treatment to the poor, the elderly, women and minorities.   The rich and powerful corporations realized what was happening and had to act to return things to the good old days when financial institutions with all their muscle, money and clout insured that laws were interpreted in their favor and against the interests of the small families who had neither the time nor money required to get involved in the wheeling and dealing of the legislative process.

Large oil companies, industrial corporations, and many other special interest groups with their highly paid, well-placed lobbyists made sure that legislators were influenced to serve the needs of big business.   Gradually, steadily, unceasingly they chipped away at the many good laws designed to meet the needs of all the people as only they could with their well-qualified, finely tuned, full-time experts in political persuasion.

And these powerful interests saw to it that the three judges who stood in their path were mowed down, these three who dared vote against the death penalty, not to challenge the will of the people but to uphold the legal rights of every Californian.

Whatever the personal feelings of the three justices regarding the death penalty may be, I proclaim that the death penalty should never be invoked.   Is it so difficult to see that God gave life to men and women, and only He should take it away?   After giving the matter great thought, I focused my attention back in history to the time when Cain killed his brother Abel, and God was the Chief Justice.   God drove Cain from the Garden of Eden, but he did not take his life for the murder committed.   His example supports the precept of not taking a life for a life, and governments should not be justified in taking the life of a family member by citing laws and rules of court.

Another time Jesus Christ faced a very formal court proceeding in which he was condemned to be executed by a judge for purportedly violating the laws of the government of Rome.   Many people worship at Easter but choose to forget the unfair trial.   Has anyone ever stopped to wonder whether Jesus would have been executed if he were rich?

No one thinks that Saul would have been persecuted when he was following the orders of the prosecutor by persecuting Christians?   But after Saul converted from a prosecutor to a Christian, he too met a hostile government that eventually imprisoned and punished him, and finally took his life.

Or do not even mention the time when John the Baptist was ordered to be beheaded by the King, the law of the land, and only because of a woman's wounded vanity. The King feared divine reprisal, because he was well aware that John the Baptist was beloved by God; yet the King was loathe to go back on his word given before all the people. His fears, however, were well founded.

History has many examples of people receiving violent prosecution in the form of the death penalty from governments acting in the name of the law. But is it right?

Think about Hitler who had the full power of his government and the silence of the world behind him when he executed six million Jews.

Religious fanatics, dictators and other persons of power have carried out death penalties against many members of families in the name of justice. Yet, practice does not make it right.

Surviving victims of crime vented their frustration, grief and vengeance upon the three justices by arousing the emotions, sympathy, and compassion of the small percentage of people who voted in the election. Big money paid for the television ads displaying photos of the horrible murder scenes.

But if the state were to execute every one of the inmates on death row, would it bring back the person killed? If God killed Cain, would it have brought back Abel?

We have something else to think about nowadays. It is common news now to hear of a person who kills several people and then kills himself/herself. When the killer takes his/her own live, do the victims return to live again?

Special interest groups used their financial might and resources to send a message throughout California, the United States and the world by defeating the three judges. It was the first time in the history of the reaffirmation process that a judge has been removed from the bench.

The message was clear. A free nation has turned around and allowed politics to determine justice. If a particular judge is not liked by Pontius Pilate, get rid of him. That's the message. If a judge does not vote for the death penalty, chop his head off. If a judge does not rule in favor of the big corporation, nail him to the cross.

The sad message was also seen in the low voter turnout (37%). We are reminded of a statement Martin Luther King, Jr. said in a speech when he pointed out that the thing that bothered him the most was when good men remained silent and did nothing to eradicate evil. This is exactly what happened when the more than 60% of the very people being protected by Rose Bird remained intimidated, lazy and silent and refused to exercise their right and duty to vote, failed to exercise a freedom so precious that many lost their lives fighting for it.

Disenchantment with the political process was at the top of a long list of excuses of many family members who did not vote. The families of the world who have this precious right should never take it for granted.

There is general agreement among most of us with those we elect to office when they brag about how they are going to be tough on crime and bring to justice our family members who fall on the wrong side of the law. Many politicians boast about how they are going to bring into line the vast budgets of government by cutting services to the sick, poor and elderly. They take pride in appointing judges who are willing to give a family member a tough sentence for crimes that do not even reach the scale of the injustices of large corporations that charge us double the cost of their products or the auto makers that purposely keep us poor repairing the lemons they call cars. Do not mention the chemical companies that dump poison into our lakes and streams killing our fish, robbing us of our water supply, and causing cancer in our children.

The law books are silent about these crimes. Why? Because the corporations are giving so much money and support to the lobbyists who represent them, and the poor have no one to speak for them. We find ourselves pushed into a corner and forced to go to the polls to vote for yet another liar who is not concerned about the family.

An idea on how to increase the number of people voting has been put forth by a politician. He suggested that workers who voted be given a paid holiday. He was concerned about the steady decline in the numbers of family members who voted in recent elections.

Good shall win over evil! The evil spirit shall be extinguished and banished from good families all over the world. Drugs, murder and wrongdoing will be diminished. The good shepherd will guide us through these perils. We will not let evil prevail.

Good men, women and children must take a stand. They will have the courage to speak up for the good. The good spirit will grow and those who worship evil will vanish.

The Selling of the U.S.A. Many men and women have valued the power of freedom. They seek to preserve freedom and make it a right for all people on the planet Earth.

We in the United States have watched wealthy men, women and corporations buy our country and cast its dreams and principles to the winds. Major buildings from New York to California have been bought by foreigners from countries whose leaders dare brand our minorities as ignorant and stupid.

The United States has sold large buildings and land holdings to foreigners that will not allow U.S. citizens to buy property in their countries. Australia will not even allow an alien to get a job in the country whenever unemployment reaches 4 percent. Yet the U.S. spends millions of dollars in foreign aid while many of its own families are homeless.

The federal government in the U.S. has found ways to increase the tax burden on the middle class, but refuses to spend some of this money to provide shelter for the homeless.

The U.S. has made dictators in other countries rich, while the people in these countries remain poor to the point of starvation. We have supported politicians in these countries who purport to draw a salary of only $50,000 per year; yet they end up with millions of dollars in bank accounts around the world.

As long as politicians take money from hard-working people in the U.S. and give it to dictators and corrupt leaders of foreign nations, we will have suffering among our families.

We must stop this evil. First, we must reduce foreign aid to zero until every family in the U.S. has a home, food and a job. We have watched enough abuse as we have seen the corrupt get rich while the poor starve. Many city mayors are without adequate funds from the federal government because the money is going to corrupt foreign governments. We have seen too many banks in this country write off foolish loans to irresponsible nations and make up their losses through charges levied against the American people.

Second, we should begin a "Help the U.S.A." movement that provides money so that every citizen has good medical care.

Third, the U.S. and all countries should end the production of nuclear weapons. This money would more than provide adequate medical care for every citizen.

Fourth, we should stop destroying the farmer and the farm lands in the U.S. where we have warehouses with enough grain to feed every starving child in the world. But the helping hands must start at home first. Farmers have lost land because Congress and state legislators have joined in the butchery of America.

Fifth, the federal government should give back the tax breaks to the middle class which were recently lost. Every politician that joined the movement to take away all these tax advantages such as <u>interest</u> <u>deductions</u> should be voted out of office. We need politicians who are for the family, just as they are for big business.

Sixth, we need to end selling U.S. properties to foreigners and giving loans, tax breaks and other benefits unavailable to U.S. families. We need to support our citizens and make life more pleasant for our families before we open our doors to foreigners.

Seventh, we need to bring about an equitable justice system for the poor in the U.S. We need to stop the overcrowding in jails. If adequate jobs, homes and education are provided for the poor, more than half the crime would be eliminated.

Finally, we must remove the walls of the Iron Curtain, end apartheid in South Africa and eliminate every drug lord in the world.

Evil takes on many disguises. Many rich men and women in powerful places care only to enslave the homeless, poor and sick and condemn them to ruined lives. This evil shall stop. It is the duty of good families to oppose evil.

Silent, good men and women must speak out for fair laws, good liberal judges and equal rights for all family members. We shall not rest until the American dream becomes a reality for every family. We will eliminate racism, bigotry, and unjust legal systems. Then we will not stop until the earth is a safe place for every family. We of good spirit will prevail over evil. We shall be courageous until the end.

CHAPTER VII

VII. BEYOND MERE PLEASURE

BEYOND MERE PLEASURE

CELEBRATIONS

The time is now to start the momentum and let all know that the family is alive and well. We will strengthen the family.

Family Day (1987)

On July 29, 1986, Congress by Joint Resolution authorized and requested the President to designate the weekend of August 1-3, 1986 as National Family Reunion Weekend. This legislation was the result of a lot of letter writing to the entire Congress and the White House to dedicate a time for the family to be honored by all families throughout the land. It was a worthwhile effort for me and the end result was a true pleasure. Now that the precedent has been established for the family, the next step is to make this celebration an annual occurence in every state of the nation.

Let us be appreciative of all the members of Congress and the Executive Branch for bringing about a Family Reunion weekend. But this is only a beginning; we have more work to do, **more letters to write and calls to make.** We must not stop until we have made the world a better family community. Our fight is sincere and our effort relentless. That is our goal and we shall bring honor back to the family! I need your help in writing letters to the mayors, aldermen and alderwomen, councilmen and councilwomen of our cities. Write to the managers and supervisors of our counties. Write to every governor and to each elected official of our states. We must not stop there, we must write all the way to the White House, sparing no one the urgency of our letters demanding reforms for the family.

Congress and the Executive Branch of the federal government shall be notified that the time has come for the birth of legislation that is family-friendly. We need this legislation now, not tomorrow. If our voices go unnoticed we shall begin a massive voting campaign to remove every incumbent from office who fails to heed our cries.

Family Week (1988)

The **third week in June** is the week that we shall ask our legislators to designate as the week of the family when we write to them. We need to concern ourselves with the week this week to make a solid impression and bring about a permanent change to better the position of the family. The agenda for that week will be:

Sunday	1st day	. . . .	Son
Monday	2nd day	. . . .	Daughter
Tuesday	3rd day	. . . .	Baby
Wednesday	4th day	. . . .	Elderly
Thursday	5th day	. . . .	Father
Friday	6th day	. . . .	Mother
Saturday	7th day	. . . .	Family Reunion.

We seek to bring all the fragments, all of the broken dreams and all of the aspirations together in a one-week ceremony in every city. Parents are to bring home the prodigal child. Adult children will bring home the lost elderly from their homeless, friendless situation. Hurt feelings must give way to a birth of love and renewed faith. The way we would ask God to forgive us for our sins, wrongs and evildoing is the same way we will want to forgive our family members for their transgressions against us. This may be a painful task. I never have said it will be easy. But, it must be done -- now! We are all human beings deserving forgiveness.

Until family members can confront their own bigotry, racism, prejudice, hatred, stupidity, and dislikes, we have not begun to eliminate the forces of evil that prevail against the family. Until we do this needed housecleaning, we are basically saying that we are content with the increase in serious crime. We must take positive steps to make this a better world for the family.

The first day, Sunday, is dedicated to our sons. Our sons will be the fathers of the future. During family week we should take time out to spend an entire day on Sunday with our sons. The entire family joins in and makes a special effort to create a better understanding between the family and the son.

On Monday, the second day, we will do the same thing for the **daughter.** We want to let our daughters know that we need them to make good mothers someday.

On Tuesday, the third day, we will bring honor to the **little babies** of our families and cherish them for they are the future. Without them we need not concern ourselves about tomorrow. The babies cannot be forgotten.

On Wednesday, the fourth day, we will respect and honor our elderly. In some countries of the world, the elderly are respected and looked up to for their wisdom and knowledge. The older the person is in China, the more lavish the praise and respect he receives. But, in some societies the opposite is true. In North America, the elderly seem to be carted off to a corner of the world to be forsaken and forgotten.

Therefore, on the fourth day, which is Wednesday, we shall make a special effort to change the destructive attitude toward the elderly. We want to love, honor, and respect our elderly. If for some reason your family does not have anyone over 60 years of age, then go to the homes for the elderly and bring them gifts, flowers, clothes, and love. Spend the day helping another family bring love and happiness to its elderly. Nowhere will an elderly person be neglected. Go to the mental institutions and spend some time with the elderly there.

Do not stop there, go to the hospitals and make some elderly person feel better by letting him/her know someone cares. Become pen pals with these elderly persons. Go help an elderly person cross the street. More and more cities are making it virtually impossible for the elderly to cross the street in the short amount of time allotted for street crossing now. Write the legislatures about this lack of concern for the elderly.

Make a call for an elderly person and help dial his/her family. Since the destructive breakup of American Telegraph and Telephone Corporation, phone companies do not allow a person enough time to make a telephone call. Very rude messages disconnect the person from the call forcing him/her to start all over. A loud buzzer goes off in the phone. The phone companies are only interested in making more dollars by charging higher prices while providing less service. The phone companies are not in the business of making it possible for the elderly to keep in touch with friends and desperately needed health services. The public utilities that regulate the phone companies have sold out on justice and fairness to the elderly. We need to write to the legislators to change this disturbing trend, abuse, and insensitivity to the elderly. Let us make the fourth day a grand day for the elderly.

The fifth day is a Thursday in which we shall bring a deserved honor to our fathers. Unfortunately, fathers have not made their presence known in most families in a positive way. More and more fathers are opting for the easier way of filing for divorce rather than seeing the family through the hard times and sailing with the family during the good days.

The women's liberation movement has brought about some needed reforms, but it has dealt a severe blow to the family. Many a woman wants to be a man as well as a woman. They do not know the value of being a good mother and a good wife. So due to this state of confusion, many women have contributed to the collapse of the family. We need to bring back the respect for the father and for the woman's own role as mother.

Fathers have also been demolished by many over-zealous prosecutors in the area of child support. What is a reality here is the fact that many women purposely conceive children for many reasons: getting away from a poor home, hoping to make it big in another city or trapping a lover into marriage. So these women do not investigate their lovers to see if they qualify to be good fathers. They just bear children as a way out. When the man turns out to be the wrong mate for the woman, she lobbies the authorities with full force to make the father of her children pay for child support. This would not even be necessary if the woman had chosen the right mate in the first place.

Whenever a woman has to force a man to take care of his own children, it is a sad day indeed. The prosecutors have disregarded the family image by locking up these fathers. Many prosecutors seek publicity and media coverage of themselves arresting fathers on Father's Day. The prosecutors have no respect for the integrity of the family. What is necessary is a new program to bring about compliance that replaces the locking up of irresponsible men.

We need programs that teach men what it is to be good fathers, not just biological parents. We need to implement programs that keep the family intact as a unit even when divorce interrupts the family foundation. These programs are needed because this is where the most damage is presently being done to the family.

We need more psychological therapy for the children from broken homes. Many children blame one of the parents for the breakup. They really need help at this stage before the seeds of evil and destructive ways are born. These are needs legislators should be concentrating upon instead of passing more and more stupid, tough laws that are supposed to stop crime. The laws will never work. If these types of programs are not implemented soon, we will see that the stupid, get-tough laws only lead to an overflow of serious violence in society.

The young people that are going to be sick tomorrow will not even know how to read the laws, nor will they be tuned in to the news station that informs the public about these laws. The lawbreakers of tomorrow will be of a kind that have never been witnessed before in most societies. They will have no problems committing mass killings and turning the trigger on themselves. That is why we must turn to the fathers to return to the home, and stop leaving the home. We must vote out of office these sick prosecutors, governors, and legislators that seek to apply a pound of laws to cure the damage rather than an ounce of programs to prevent the crime.

It is not too late if these programs are enacted soon. We need father-friendly legislation. We need programs that will honor the father and bring the mother back to the home. The time is now for a good day of celebration of the father on the fifth day.

On Friday, the sixth day, we will honor our **mothers.** A good mother makes all the difference in family stability, knowing when to nudge and when to pull the rug out from under the transgressor. A good mother knows and practices proper nutrition for the family. She serves good hot cereal for breakfast, hot vegetables for lunch, and hot stew for dinner providing a balanced diet for the healthy development of the family. This is what the family needs.

Many schools and educational institutions are teaching women not to become domestic. Women are being taught to go out in the work place and compete against men. Many women do not even know how to cook. They pattern their lives after stupid soap operas that parade maids, cooks, and other servants doing all of the domestic work in the home. Television has some good, but many women are carrying their portable televisions to work for continuous feeding of the propaganda that gets them out of the home and into the market place.

Many of the academic institutions are providing more credence to the same notion that the woman's place is in the marketplace. It is all right to educate a woman on how to survive in the market place, but the education should also provide for her enlightenment as a homemaker. The academic community bears a large part of the blame for the destruction of the family. The theory and ideals that students learn are often taught by professors who have never entered the real world. They have gone to school all of their lives and have been sheltered by the universities. They are foolish in not trying to discover the world in which most of us reside.

The mother of the family has been further alienated from the home by the churches that promote bogus religious salvation. The preachers of these doctrines are merely trying to fatten their purses by making mothers emotionally dependent upon the church. The church is offering very little guidance and help in bringing the family together in a real sense. The ministers are not going to the home early enough to prevent the breakup in the family. Many ministers do not visit the homes of families at all. We need to see truly concerned ministers that preach the unity of the family. We need to see actual deeds with the ministers supporting the family through the finances of the church.

Mothers should be devoted to their husbands. They need to spend more time choosing a compatible mate and less time on an adventurous man. Many women even seek and stay with men who are abusive to them. They seem to love this type of disrespect. Women should be taught to choose men that will support the family even if the path is not on a continuous line, that is, even if a divorce does come to conclude the marriage. Mothers must be taught that divorce is not the end of the family; it may be the end of the marriage, but not the family.

A woman should pick as a spouse the man who loves her and who will honor his responsibility to the family. If the man does not measure up to these objectives, then she must avoid getting involved him. It should never be necessary to bring litigation against a well-chosen mate in the case of divorce. Litigation only proves that the woman was stupid for getting involved with the man in the first place. In the presence of this stupidity, the woman should never have had a child by such a man. There are too many ways to prevent an unwanted pregnancy if it should become necessary.

Let us not forget that the mother is the flower of the garden, the life-giver, and the sustainer of the family. We need more responsible women to take the home seriously and choose a proper mate for the development of the family. With such thought and care, many homes would never be broken. A good mother is worth God's praise.

On the seventh day, Saturday, we will celebrate the family reunion in which we <u>bring</u> all the <u>nuclear</u> <u>families</u> together within the extended family. This day culminates a week in which the family has been brought closer together. This closeness will last; it will only grow stronger.

There are many forces that will try to prevail against the family, but at this point they will be useless. We will never surrender the positive forces of the family to the evil, weak efforts of Satan. All good men and women will do the right thing and bring their children, relatives and extended family together for God. Now let us end the family week celebration with a short prayer:

> *Thank you God for bringing our family closer to thee this Week of the Family. Amen.*

Family Month (1989)

We shall keep going in the year of 1989, with an entire month dedicated to the family. We have chosen the month of June to be the **Month of the Family.** In 1989, let us again concentrate on the family with a power that is penetrating. Only good can emerge from this true concern for the survival of the family. Here is an outline of the month's activities:

Week	Day	Objective
First	Sunday	Prisons
	Monday	Jails
	Tuesday	Reform Schools
	Wednesday	Orphanage Homes
	Thursday	Half-way Houses

	Friday	Brigs	
	Saturday	Asylums	
Second	Sunday	Pre-school	
	Monday	Kindergarten	
	Tuesday	Elementary	
	Wednesday	Junior high	
	Thursday	High school	
	Friday	College	
	Saturday	Adult education	
Third	Sunday		Church
Monday		Marriage matters	
	Tuesday	Divorce concerns	
	Wednesday	Civil court	
	Thursday	Criminal court	
	Friday	Family Exercise	
	Saturday	Financial programs	
Fourth	Sunday	City government	
	Monday	County government	
	Tuesday	State government	
	Wednesday	Federal government	
	Thursday	Juvenile justice	
	Friday	Family Olympics	
	Saturday	Family communication	

Family month is designed to touch upon those areas that affect the family directly or influence the family in some indirect way, even if it is only an idea for the family to consider. The first week finds us in the middle of those members of our family who somehow have been ostracized by the system and locked up from the rest of us. We have a duty to seek the proper reform of these members of our family. Many of us may think that we will never be in the jails and prisons of the land. Let us hope not. And for the sake of our family members who are in the prisons, let us pray that they never return to those places of no compassion.

The first week recognizes that it is significant for the growth of a healthy country to make programs that are successful in rehabilitating those who are in prison. We have to examine the conditions of our family members who are placed in the most intolerable conditions. The family reunion concept is for the benefit of the weakest link in the family chain. If we cannot speak well of the least of us, then let us not say anything about the greatest among us. For what does it profit a society to promote the wealth of the few when the majority arise every day to poverty and intolerable conditions.

We must make sure that the members of all families throughout the world who are found locked up in jail cells watched over by prejudiced and unfair wardens are treated humanely.   In addition, we must demand that all of the officials of the penal system embrace a true program of rehabilitation.

Many wardens throughout the world will have society believe that the members of our families who are in the jail cells are incapable of being rehabilitated.   That is because the same system that locks up people is the system that rewards prison officials and makes the budget for them based on how many are locked up.   This whole process must be changed to make a program that centers around the successful rehabilitation of prisoners.   In another words, if the wardens make programs that prevent the return of convicts to the prisons, then the wardens are rewarded with   larger budgets to provide for the expansion of their successful programs.

Universities will help in the achievement of this goal. Scholarships, grants, and stipends will be made available to students who develop model plans that are worth giving a try. Many bright minds will be motivated to partake in such a program that will provide for the successful rehabilitation of convicts.   Not only will society benefit from programs like this by the reduction in crime, but the studies will also help prevent members of the family from ever entering the dehumanizing penal system in the first place.

Law enforcement personnel may not be aware of how they are contributing to crime in the country.   Subconsciously police and other law enforcement agencies are not really trying to eliminate all crime.   Why?   It is a basic principle of survival.   If crime were completely eliminated today, what would the police do?   How could they justify huge budgets when no crime abounds?

Legislators are in a similar position.   They have followed a path of making more and more laws.   Many of the laws are pointless and foolish.   Most of the legislators are not even concerned about living up to the laws that they pass.   In fact, if a law starts to bother the legislators, they will soon abolish it or seek ways not to be affected by it.   They leave the foolish laws to the frustration and capriciousness of judges to interpret and to render judgment.

A case in point is the situation a legislator found himself in when he was unable to coerce a California Highway Patrolman not to issue him a ticket for speeding.   After the officer treated him like a regular citizen, the legislator was in a position to block the California Highway Department from getting radar.   Now most regular citizens may have desired to do the same thing when they get moving traffic violations.

The point here is that legislators are making laws that they do not plan to have to abide by because of their status.

A solution to this problem is to reduce the time the legislators spend in the chambers of government. And make the legislators have to be subject to their own laws; then we regular family members will see a dramatic reduction in the number of foolish laws. Laws will also be made for the poor, not just for the rich.

Now let us get back to how legislators will be affected by the complete elimination of crime in a very direct way. They will be seen as nothing but an unnecessary drain of the taxpayer money. They will not be needed for the most part. What will they do? Out of pure survival, they will be forced to make nonsense laws. They are basically doing that now.

Thus we see that laws are being made to keep jobs in the law enforcement areas of employment. We can realize that a large part of the budget is dedicated to a few criminals. Huge sums of money will be lost if crime is not maintained. Think of all of the judges, senators, and police officers that will be out of jobs. It costs the State of California $60,000 to keep one prisoner in the penal system for one year. This is the same state that spends $1,500 a year on a full-time community college student.

So we can see that legislators will arrange it so wardens' budgets will be fattened by the number of prisoners that are in the systems. Then the work of police and judges is to populate the prison system. The legislators get in the act by restricting the flow of money to education and the private sector, especially to the minorities and low-income sectors of society. With few jobs available for the poor, crime is bound to rise. With a rise in crime the system works like magic.

More police and more judges will be needed and eventually more legislators will also be necessary. We can see that the family is up against a brick wall of resistance. The system must develop into a positive program of working for the benefit of all.

The first week will be for the change of a negative system into a positive one. It can and it will be done. Rewards, budgets, and programs will be made around the positive improvements and overhaul of the penal system during the first week. From the reform school to the prisons, we will make solutions that are workable and positive.

The second week we will look more closely at how the academic sector can improve the quality of education while at the same time strengthen the family bond. Preschools to colleges will be targeted for ways to implement programs that generate an understanding for the need to bring the parents into the educational process of their children.

Parents and teachers associations throughout the country are not attended by many parents. Some mothers have made a showing with a very few fathers ever being present to find out about the system that affects the progress of their children. We want all of us who are fathers to make our presence known to our schools. Our children need to know that their fathers care. The father is an important link in the family chain that has been absent or remiss in taking responsible roles and helping to make the family grow.

Most of the violence, terror, and problems that educators experience in many of the city schools would be eliminated if the fathers would get involved in their children's education. Fathers should share the responsibility for children completing their homework properly and on time. All too often the father leaves this care to the mothers. This is unfair and is a primary reason for juvenile delinquency.

Prayer must be returned to the schools. Too many concerned families are sitting around and allowing a few atheists to take prayer out of the schools. One must not be confused into thinking that the separation between church and state is the real issue here. The rulings of government are in no way jeopardized by allowing children to praise the creator, God. Now, good men, women and children of faith must rally for the necessary legislation to return prayer to the schools.

If amending the constitution is necessary to bring about this change, then let us organize to bring prayer back into the school. It is not impossible to achieve this goal. No wonder the schools are running rampant and discipline is at an all-time low. We need to bring prayer back in the schools. We can respect the beliefs of all faiths as well as the rights of atheists and agnostics by providing a time for silent prayer or meditation. This would be a first step toward reintroducing the instruction of values, basic moral conduct and personal responsibility to our children.

Corporal punishment is necessary to bring about discipline in the classroom. The level to be affected in a program to start in 1990, when spanking will be reintroduced, will be the first through the fifth grades. The sixth through the ninth will be included in 1991. And finally, with the tenth through the twelfth in 1992, we will have concluded the process of bringing the entire school system back to the control of the teacher and administrator, and not a few thugs who do not wish to learn anything.

Principals' and administrators' performances should be more closely connected with the success of the students. It has been proven by a principal in the Los Angeles school system that a principal who knows what he or she is doing can greatly improve the entire educational system. Many educators are only drawing a paycheck. They do not care anymore about students receiving a meaningful education than the hoodlums who terrorize the classroom care about being studious. This lack of concern by administrators can be stopped.

An overhead-heavy situation is creating a lot of jobs at the top for personnel in the academic system, but cutting back on the actual teachers who perform the real work inside the classrooms. The fancy cars that many of the administrators are riding around in can be eliminated completely and more teachers can be put in the classrooms. The fewer students per classroom will allow more attention to be given to each student.

Schools located in minority communities must be well-equipped with the same materials and quality of teachers as in the non-minority communities. With the elimination of violence, many of the inner-city schools frequented by a high number of minorities will be brought up to standards. Many programs have already been initiated to bring about some of these improvements. Busing has also been utilized to achieve the migration of disadvantaged youths to some of the schools the advantaged children attend. The positive developments in this area will make the improvement in the overall academic environment a reality.

Adult education at all levels of education is needed. Not enough is done to encourage and bring more adults back to school. Many adults dropped out of school for one reason or another. Pregnancy and supporting younger brothers and sisters are among the many reasons for not getting a high school diploma. Many states, notably California, have in recent years discouraged adults from returning for self-improvement studies and have promoted only degree-oriented programs, and to a lesser extent, vocational programs.

Employers should offer incentives to their adult work force to get an education. Pay raises, promotions, and time off from the work place to pursue an education should have a top priority on the corporate agenda.

The education level of the parents in a family have a lot to do with the family. The better the education, the greater the earning power, the less need there is for youths to be in the streets stealing. The decrease in crime will be noticed among young adults who are responsible for most of the law-breaking and crimes of violence.

When education is a focal point of the entire family it can be a pleasure for all of the family to be in school at different levels. From pre-school to graduate school, the entire family can join in the wealth of knowledge. We must go back to school and complete our certificates, get our diplomas, and bring home our sheepskins.

A difference can be made when parents, especially fathers,

get involved in the activities available to parents in the schools of our children. We must put more teachers in the classrooms and eliminate the waste at the top. Disciplining the disobedient youths who wish to ruin the educational process for the many must be done. And, finally, education should be an ongoing process for everyone.

The third week starts on Sunday with the church. All religious faiths, Catholic, Jewish, Protestant, Islamic, and all others not mentioned here, should provide for the family to renew its faith. There is a true need for the family to strengthen its belief in God now. More evil forces have made this earth their campsite. The family must pull all of its positive energy together to prevail against Satan.

Satanic worshipers are a bunch of fanatics who prefer to worship the devil instead of God. The family is being bombarded with youths disenchanted about traditional religion. They have witnessed much hypocrisy and have become full of despair. We must turn around this demonic force. It must be met with confidence and faith in God.

Go find all of our children and remove them from the grips of Satan. Stop crying and start praying for the complete end of satanic forces. Many do not wish to acknowledge this growing evil. The end is at hand for such idolatry.

The good prophets are persons who are busy uniting their own families and they are working to make the lives of other families more pleasant. They are not parading around in fancy cars when members of their parish are without food and shelter. They are on the front lines in the fight to eliminate drugs. They are often leading marches, protests and church services in opposition to the growing phenomenon of substance abuse.

We find the good prophets in the hospitals visiting the sick. They are at the homes for the elderly giving comfort and conversation. They do not forsake their friends who need help; instead they stand by their sides to provide the needed support. They are at the places in the world where sinners are found, to offer the word of the Lord for the salvation of the sinners' souls.

We need more good prophets in the land of racism, apartheid, and war. These prophets are not afraid to risk their lives in the land of strife and stand up against the forces of evil. They are not enriching their own lives with material wealth; instead they are giving financial aid to the needy.

Oftentimes, we are able to find good prophets in the church who spend a great deal of their time among the people doing the work of God. It is important for us to give aid to the good shepherds who sincerely love their sheep.

False prophets are on the rise. It is not unusual to read in the newspapers of churches being established purely for the tax advantages. These places established for the sake of profit and gain and not for the worship of the Lord are a vexation to the spirit of the Lord. We must make a difference and recognize true shepherds sent from God to lead us from false prophets who are not concerned about the souls of mankind. Let us focus on the qualities of the good prophets.

Fathers in the church are in short supply. It is quite all right for busy fathers of many of our families to attend the early services offered at 7:00 or 8:00 a.m., at the many churches that offer such services. Sunday schools, Bible classes, and prayer meetings need more fathers in attendance. Those of us who are fathers are forsaking our spiritual duties to our families. We are leaving church duties to the mothers.

We fathers must make our presence in the churches, temples and synagogues known by taking our families to worship and praise the Lord. Today is not too late, but tomorrow may be.

We have our eyes set on making the third week a time to bring religion back into the lives of family members.

Marriage matters. Why are marriages made to last forever? The bond of the very first marriage was cemented by God between Adam and Eve. The bond was meant to last forever. There are some things that a couple should do to make the dream a reality. More time before making the vows is needed, a more meaningful courtship with time to get to know each other, and a better economic program. These are only a few of the important matters that are needed to make the wedding last -- forever.

Many young adults are anxious to get married under the guise of love, which often turns out to be premature romance. If young adults would spend more time getting acquainted and would have at least three romances over a period of at least six years with a minimum of two years each, it would do a lot toward making true love everlasting. It usually takes a man at least two years of dating one woman to get to know the real woman. He will be able to make a genuine decision on whether the woman offers him the qualities he desires.

Only after the sharing of each other's dreams and getting to know each other in a romantic way can the man and woman get to know the person that resides inside of the shell. The facade will disappear.

The financial position of the couple prior to getting

married must be planned wisely. Sometimes the parents help the couple get a start, but this help must not be relied upon. The expectations must be realistic for both persons. If the dreams are realistic for the couple and they share common interests, then the chances are far better.

The young couple should consult a financial planner to help them make wise plans for their future wedding. A program should be based on the salary of the breadwinner with the salary of the other spouse used as a safeguard for emergencies. My thought is that the man plan to be the breadwinner so the woman can be at home with the children. This is the way it should be.

Children need their mothers at home with them for the first 13 years of their lives. The soap operas have made glamour a false concept for the average family. We do not want to make our children's dreams unrealistic. It is not the luxury of material possessions that the couple need; they need the true quality of a good family life, raising a family and helping the children in the right way.

Guidance is needed from the mother and love is needed from the father in the homes throughout the land today. Marriage statistics will improve with couples getting married at a more mature age (25 plus). Marriage will be a good institution for the helpful growth of the family.

Divorce concerns are making the news. Maturity in choosing a mate will help to decrease the divorce rate. Less stress on the family with better financial planning will make the marriage last longer. But we do want to review a positive way to make divorce less painful and dangerous for the children. Even the father and mother will benefit from positive programs.

Parents who get a divorce must realize that the mental pain children encounter is real. They need therapy to help them over this tragedy. They are very uncertain about the future. What can we do to make divorce a bit less painful for all?

The couple should break the physical relationship off if they can not handle their individual pain, but for sure, the couple should stay friends. Their friendship must have a realistic outlook. First, they should realize that each one of them is going to be looking for a new romance. Give each other room to get over the pain and understand that nothing is wrong with either of them; it just was a venture that did not work out well.

Second, remain a team for the needs and development of the children from the marriage. Teamwork can stop a lot of the children's sorrow that is a result of the divorce. The education, clothing, and financial needs of the children are still there, still joint responsibilities.   If the mother did her homework and established a friendship prior to getting married, the chances are good that the father of her children will be a good friend who will own up to his responsibilities.

Third, the rearing and disciplining of the children still requires the father to be present.   The father should know everything about his children.   What schools are they attending?   He should be involved in the children's spiritual growth too.   The father should know the sizes of the clothes and shoes, and when the children need to go to the dentist. He should know what time his children are due to be home from school and demand an explanation if the children are late. If the father did a good job in getting acquainted as a friend prior to becoming a lover, he will be able to have a partner in his divorce that will still respect him.   If not, the children will suffer because the mother of his children can be a real witch.

Divorce does not have to be such a nightmare if the couple entered the relationship mature, financially sound and as friends.   If not, the results will be disastrous for the children.   Let us stay a family even if we are no longer lovers to our spouses.   And above all, let us keep our children's welfare first in our concerns.

Civil courts have long been the dumping ground for family disputes.   These judges are constantly seeing and hearing the bad side of the family.   This is a thankless task for the judges.

But something must be done to balance the welfare of the children in a way that is fairer for the many fathers who are refused custody of their children. Confrontation in the courtrooms has further stripped the family of its dignity. Fathers are being ignored and even being taken advantage of by many courts.   This must be converted to a just situation where the awarding of child support, visitation rights, and property division is guided entirely by the need to keep the family intact.

The civil courts have a meaningful task to achieve in the family division of the legal system.   Now we can balance the scales of justice for the father and the mother to make the children's life better.

Criminal courts have the opportunity for the most challenging task of all of the courts.   Family members who have gone astray for one reason or another may end up here.

Some legislators believe that tougher laws, harsher sentencing, longer periods of confinement, and the death penalty will solve everything.   Elimination of a suspect's rights and denial of bail for the accused are other ideas the legislators hope to see in practice.   Well, they are wrong. If the legislators are successful in bringing about a police state, chaos and anarchy will be the result.   Again, these plans to take away the personal freedoms of a free society will not stand.   But, these legislators are hoping to shift the burden of enforcing these outrageous plans on the judges in the criminal courts of the judicial system.

Because the legislators do not have the responsibility of actually enforcing the laws, their lives are not in jeopardy. For the most part, the personnel of the court system suffer when laws become unreasonable.

Society pays a price too.   More jails, prisons, courtrooms, and the personnel to do the evil tasks are needed.   More tax dollars will be demanded when actually there is a need for legal reform.   If the courts, legislators, and law enforcement officials would simply concentrate effort where it is needed, a marked improvement in the judicial system would result.   This needed change will benefit families and provide for a safer society.   First, legislators would place violent crimes under the jurisdiction of the criminal courts and non-violent crimes in the civil courts.
Fraud, bad checks, and the like are crimes that could be punished by fines and by making restitution to the victims. There is no need to clog the penal codes with non-violent crimes.   Non-violent crime control belongs in the civil codes.   Second, jails, prisons, and brigs should be for those members of our society who are violent.   When violence is committed, then it is more appropriate to consider locking up people.

All the persons who are incarcerated for non-violent crimes should be paroled and put on probation with a plan to repay the debt owed.   The person should remain on probation until the debt is repaid.   Third, poor members of families should be afforded the same type of legal representation as the rich.   The judicial system is grossly unfair to the poor. Economic crimes are the primary category most poor felons commit.   When a family is starving, the likelihood of crime is inevitable.   The children from poor backgrounds face an almost insurmountable barrier caused by malnutrition, poor education, and lack of guidance from both parents.   These factors can be eliminated in America.   The criminal court system is made the pawn of oppressive legislation.   Law enforcement officials and personnel are caught in the middle. Reform of the system is a must.

Family Exercise.   The importance of exercise can be stressed over and over, and still that would not be enough. An entire day for the family to have fun is needed.   Try a short walk-a-thon with the entire family.   If possible, why not join another family for a good little walk. The result could be very therapeutic and release many anxieties. The family that exercises together is more likely to stay together.

Financial Programs. More marriages are wrecked because of excessive money problems than for any other reason that I know. Take a day to get sound financial advice on money management within the family. I know a woman who had to buy an expensive item for her family every other week. She had to have a television for every room, a rear-projection 52-inch set for the livingroom, and a new addition on the family home. She replaced the furniture constantly, and so it went. These expenses put a strain on the marriage. The family was affected.

If reasonable financial plans are made for the entire family, the family will stay together without excessive stress. Good money management is essential.

The Fourth Week. On the first day, Sunday, the city or town government should bring families to city parks and recreation centers in honor of the family. Cities should review all of their ordinances, regulations, and laws to conform with family unity. Mayors should make a sincere effort to issue a proclamation giving honor to the family on this day. City government can make the difference.

On the second day, Monday, county governments should work to provide homes, food, and clothing for the needy. Medical care should be available to all of those family members who are in need and unable to provide medical assistance for themselves. The agenda for this day is to encourage every county to eliminate unfair conditions for the poor.

On the third day, Tuesday, we should have the state government provide for a system of full employment. Jobs should be created to provide decent work with decent wages for every resident of every state.

The minorities and non-white family members are paying a high price to balance the budget. They are the ones suffering very high unemployment rates that are directly related to the very high crime rates. State officials in the government are directly to blame for this prejudicial situation. No good reason exists for this tragic condition of creating unemployment among the non-white members of our society. It is completely possible to eradicate unemployment.

On the fourth day, Wednesday, we call for a family reunion celebration at the federal level of government. A total shift in the priorities of the federal government must be achieved. Presently there is more money allocated for missiles than biscuits. The national defense budget must be surveyed for reduction. What areas must be reduced is important.

A vast sum of money is overspent on weapons, especially nuclear weapons. Nuclear research may go on; but there is no need to make another nuclear warhead for storage. Stop this waste now. There are enough nuclear weapons to destroy the entire world. We do not need to manufacture any more nuclear weapons. There should be a complete ban on the manufacturing of nuclear weapons. Nuclear research can go on, but a ceiling must be placed on the expense for this endeavor.

After a period of twenty years has passed, studies can be make to determine whether or not the existing nuclear system needs an overhaul.

Increasing the ranks with more men and women in uniform is acceptable. The armed services have been one of the few means available to the poor to escape from intolerable home conditions. Even though the armed service system is unfair to the poor, many poor youths would not have had a chance to better their conditions if it were not for the military.

Family members going into the military may get a chance to travel. The military provides for educational programs, training in the trades, and it offers a future for some family members. After an honorable discharge, many men and women go on to college with the financial benefits that the military offers to those who have completed their service duties. The military could eliminate a lot of the prejudice against the poorest and least educated personnel in uniform by rotating them into viable trades after spending half of their tour of duty in non-marketable skills.

After men and women have served half of the time in ground units, rotate them into office administration, supply administration, and computer technology. This should be a mandatory option available to all persons entering the service after this day, (the fourth day of the fourth week of the month of June).

Members from rich families have their choice of going to schools to make them officers while in the service. The same opportunities should be available to members of poor families after they have decided to re-enlist and make the military their career. The officer programs that these persons go through should be adapted to provide these personnel with whatever skills are necessary to make their completion satisfactory. If a man or woman has made a commitment to the military, then the military should make a program that will place that person in an officer's position.

The prejudicial system that now places rich members from

rich families in commissioned officer status while denying this opportunity to members of poor families must end this day.

The poor are the ones who die on the battlefields. Rich kids run to other countries or have their rich uncles pass legislation to keep them out of the military during times of war. The poor have no one to go to for legislation to give them decent promotions, officer status, and just treatment while in the military. This whole process must be changed now. The necessary change can be done this day of Federal Government Day.

Juvenile Justice. On the fifth day, Thursday, we need changes that will help bring successful solutions to the judicial system that deals with juveniles. We need to identify the origin of the problems and find solutions.

First, juvenile crime stems from the absence of the father in the child's early development. When the child reaches the teen-age stage, the damage has been done, and change for the better is more difficult. Second, youths that commit hard-core violent crimes may need to enter the adult justice system after the age of 13 years. However, these offenders should be segregated from the adult offenders over the age of 19 years. Third, programs like the ones developed in the state of Utah should be given serious study because these programs have been successful in reducing hard-core crimes among youths. The programs have also been successful in preventing the reoccurrence of other crimes among young offenders.

We should make programs to identify young children that show traits that may lead to a life of crime in the early stages. Early treatment will prevent government expense in dealing with criminal conduct later in these children's lives. Society benefits from these positive programs. Someone's life is spared, and homes and stores are not robbed by the children given help early in life. This kind of sense is difficult for most legislators to deal with. They think that more policies and tougher laws will solve everything. This is not the case.

More parks and recreational facilities must be built to provide areas where children can exercise and vent their hostilities. Cities are tearing down buildings to build large shopping complexes without requiring these developers to provide recreational areas within these facilities. Vacant lands are divided up into parcels for housing. But none of it is cultivated for parks and recreation.

Where parks exists, families fear allowing their children to play because the government fails to see the importance of providing armed park officers to patrol the parks on a twenty-four hour basis. They say it costs too much, but violence and crime are the result. Thus, government officials are directly to blame for the shooting sprees, mass murders, and other violent crimes that occur when hostility is held inside indefinitely until the seams burst, often in adulthood.

Not only is it necessary for the government to provide parks and recreational facilities, it is also necessary to provide security in these parks for families. After the government has done its part, then families need to do their part.

Many times we will get off from work, too lazy to take our children to the park. We do not volunteer our services for the various sports activities for children to participate in while visiting the parks. Tee-ball, baseball, track and swimming are only a few of the activities that need adult coaches and supervisors. We, the families, must do our part to help eliminate juvenile unrest also. Take your children to the park at least three times a week. Get them involved in recreational activities. Help donate money to support a Little League activity. Involve yourself in providing coaching, transportation, and other needed services. With government, developers, and parents pitching in together, we can eliminate juvenile problems.

Family Olympics.   The time is ripe for athletic competitions from all the corners of the world that create an air of friendly competition.   Unlike in the regular Olympic Games, politics, violence, and hatred shall be unacceptable.

The games should be conducted every four years starting in the year of 1992. However, the various committees shall be formed on this day of celebrating the creation of the Family Olympic Games. Professionals are not allowed to enter the competitions, but their participation in coaching, staffing and other needed services will be invited. Communities from around the world will contribute by providing the Family Olympics with several families from each nation to enter the competition.

Gold, silver, and bronze medals shall be awarded the 1st, 2nd, and 3rd place finishers. Trophies, certificates and other awards of appreciation may be given to those who contributed time and resources to make the whole affair work. Judges from all the nations participating in the Family Olympics shall appreciate a proper forum in which disagreements can be handled fairly. We need to provide for good competition for the Family Olympics.

Family Communication. We must learn to open the doors of communication between the members of our family. The single most important channel to family survival is communication. Fear, feelings of inadequacy, and a lack of confidence are some of the contributing factors preventing good verbal and written dialogue between the members of the family.

Fear of being physically abused or mentally ridiculed lies in the minds of many children and keeps them from expressing the problems in their lives. A dominant father figure or abusive mother frightens children. Children need to be disciplined but not abused. Open the door to the flow of dialogue between the children and the parent. Also, adult members of the family may not be speaking to other adult members of the family due to reasons that may be unknown to both. Those members of the family who are strong, big and loud-mouthed must not allow these attributes to intimidate other members of the family. A special effort is necessary to tone down the loudness of the voice, just enough to encourage talking with other family members.

Feelings of inadequacy among those of us who are not well-educated often discourage verbal expression. We limit what we have to say in order not to be called ignorant or stupid. Such remarks should not be made toward family members. All of us need encouragement and we should not have to be made to feel inferior because we are not highly educated. Education has its benefits, but for whatever reason some family members did not obtain a higher education it should not be cause to embarrass them. Incentives are better utilized to promote academic achievements.

Sometimes uneducated members are themselves to blame for their feeling of inadequacy. They are super-sensitive to their shortcomings. They feel that everyone is criticizing or demeaning them when it is not the case.

Therapy can best help diminish and eliminate this situation. Also, if the family member would go to college to acquire an education, the sensitivity would cease. The person would no longer suffer from a lack of confidence in this area.

Speech difficulties may contribute to a person's lack of confidence. Speech therapy with trained professionals in this area can be beneficial in reducing the problem. With patience and understanding, we can open the doors of communication and we can keep them open.

Written communication between family members is at a low point. For one thing, we have put ourselves in a box when it comes to writing. Now we are really afraid of what someone may say about our writing. We feel that they can see how stupid we really are. We can not spell, punctuate, or write a complete sentence. We feel that we have to write a book every time we write a letter. We often feel we must tell everything about our jobs, kids and hobbies when we write.

We get headaches at the very thought of picking up a pen to write a letter. We wonder about whether we should buy expensive stationery? Should it be scented? No wonder we do not write more often to our families. We are too busy trying to maintain the facade. I know a relative who told me that her husband refused a promotion to a higher management position because he did not want to take a position where he would have to write. Writing is a reality that must be dealt with now.

My first suggestion is to relax a minute. Get a piece of paper, pen, envelope and a stamp. Only one sheet of paper is required. It can be plain, scented or notebook paper. Now write the following letter to a family member:

Dear Family Member,

How are you and your family doing? My family and I are doing fine. We hope all is well with you. When you get a chance, please drop me a short note to let me know how things are with you and your family.

May God bless and keep you.

Love,

———————————————
Your name

The point here is to write brief letters. My relatives increased their letter writing when I sent them a 3" x 5" card to write to me a letter on. They began to realize that I was serious about writing a short note.

The main thing is to let family members know that we are still alive. We can add a detail or two each letter. The goal is for more frequent communication, not letters long enough that they become novels, that may come only once every two years.

Short letters erase a feeling of guilt from not writing. We must start writing again. Short letters are a good start and help us to continue writing on a regular basis.

We should also encourage children to write their grandparents, uncles and aunts at an early age. Let them print the letters while in kindergarten. If they only say "Hello, how are you? I love you. Bye," it is a good start.

The adults can send the young children a dollar as an

incentive to encourage the children each time they write. This also acts like a financial reward for learning how to write. This is only one of many ideas that are available to promote family members young and mature to write to each other.

We need to communicate with our family members more often. It can help reduce the chances that our family members will become an embarrassment to themselves. Verbal and written communication can bring the family closer together.

The month of the family is designed to concentrate totally on making this world a safer planet for the family. All of us must do our part to make this reality complete. We must have government, business and family work as a team. We can do this for the family.

The Year of the Family (1990)

In 1990, THE YEAR OF THE FAMILY, we will have an entire year to dedicate to the family. Every hamlet and village in every nation will join in this celebration. Each month will have a specific objective.

The following annual chart lists the topics to be focused upon by all of the world's governments, citizens and families. We can no longer delay. If we do not act now to stabilize and eliminate the world's continuing growth of violence, wars and tragedies in the home, **we will perish.**

Let no one be found lacking in their complete dedication to and full concentration on this unified world objective. We can, as a team, eliminate evil. We shall be triumphant. Now, review the annual chart for 1990, select a topic that your family will help with, and dedicate yourselves to a concentrated effort to make improvements for the families of the world.

Month	Objectives
January	United States Resolution Proclaiming 1990 as the year of the family. Elimination of All Wars month. End of apartheid in South Africa.
February	Continent of Australia's celebration of Family Reunion. Programs providing aid and assistance to the elderly.
March	Continent of Africa's celebration of

Family Reunion. Programs for the mentally ill.

April   Continent of Europe's celebration of Family Reunion. Programs for the visually impaired and the homeless.

May   Continent of South America's celebration of Family Reunion. Programs for the physically disabled and the jobless.

June   Continent of North America's celebration of Family Reunion. Space programs for travel in outer space by the family.

July   Continent of Asia's celebration of Family Reunion. Legislation for the family.

August   Continent of Antarctica's celebration of Family Reunion. Psychological and psychiatric concerns for the family.

September   Entertainment industry reform for the family.

October   Church and medical programs for the family.

November   Pets, Health, and Financial concerns for the family.

December   The international Family Reunion of the World.

All of the world stands to gain from having the global goal of bettering the conditions of the family. What can we lose? Nothing. We will gain success from the total dedication of the entire world to the elimination of evil from the family.

Where can we go? We can go directly to our goals. We will not have to be pawns of the devil. We do not have to be weak and helpless. We must believe that we are strong, and strong we will be. We must believe that we will achieve, and success will be ours.

AFTER THE FAMILY REUNION

Once all of the joy of meeting relatives, in-laws and friends has come and the reunion is over, we need to do something to keep the spirit alive.

Letters to the Family

Write a thank-you letter to all of the members who attended. This letter should be in the mail within seven days after adjournment.

Family Thank you Letter

Dear Family Members,

We enjoyed another occasion of family unity at our family reunion. We were glad to see all the young members of our family blend in with each other and become reacquainted. School progress, sports and spiritual growth were their topics.

The adults had many fishing stories, championship games in sports and fashion trends to discuss. We needed this time to keep in touch with each other.

We had a delicious barbecue, homemade ice cream and anniversary cake, enough to go around for seconds and to take home. We had a real feast.

The entertainment brought us gales of laughter as we watched the little ones bowling for the first time. The fun was doubled when we had a chance to see the video of the family bowling. The children played games and the adults had a fine time competing with each other.

The adults and children found Uno to be a real challenge. We had so much fun. We know that each year that we put our hearts into our family reunion it can only get better. We will soon be getting the word out about the details of our next family reunion. Until then, God bless each and everyone of us.

Sincerely yours,

_____
Honorable Chairperson

_____*FAMILY____ANNUAL REUNION*

Family Thank you Letter

Dear Family Members,

Thank you so much for your continued support of our family reunion.   We sincerely hope that each member of our extended family enjoyed himself/herself.

Very kindly yours,

_____

Honorable Chairperson

_____FAMILY____ANNUAL REUNION

Family Thank you Letter

Dear Loved Ones,

Let us put our hands together for having so much fun again at our family reunion this year. We appreciate all of those who took time out of their busy schedules to make the family reunion a big success. And, for those who were unable to come this year, we pray that God will bless them and make it possible for them to attend the next family reunion.

We hope everyone had plenty to eat, lots of fun and enjoyed the events offered at our family reunion this year.

Again, thank you for coming.

Love always,

Honorable Chairperson

_____FAMILY___ANNUAL REUNION

Letters to Committee Members

Letter to the Members of the Nutrition Committee

Dear Member of the Nutrition Committee,

Thank you for all of the energy and effort that you dedicated to providing the delicious food that we had at our family reunion this year.

Without all of the time and work that you put into making sure that everyone had plenty to eat, we do not know what we would have done. Your efforts paid off in many ways. The food was very tasty and we appreciate your devotion to our family reunion. Again, thank you.

May God bless and keep you.

Sincerely.

Honorable Chairperson

_____*FAMILY___ANNUAL REUNION*

Letter to Members of the Transportation Committee

Dear Member of the Transportation Committee,

Your accepting the real challenge of making sure that everyone had an affordable, dependable and reliable means of transportation to the family reunion was courageous.   Your help got us to and from the family reunion.   Without you, how would we all have made it to this year's celebration?

Sincerely yours,

Honorable Chairperson

_____*FAMILY___ANNUAL REUNION*

Letter to Members of the Communication Committee

Dear Member of the Communication Committee,

The word was clear: you wanted us there and you let us know it.   We thank you for making each of us feel loved, needed and important by the way you chose such kind words to invite us to the family reunion.

We thank you for keeping us informed in advance on a regular basis of all the plans for our family reunion.

Sincerely,

<u>Honorable Chairperson</u>

_____*FAMILY____ANNUAL REUNION*

Letter to Members of the Entertainment Committee

Dear Member of the Entertainment Committee,

Fun, laughter and excitement were all rolled into one in all of the events that you provided for entertainment at our family reunion this year.

Games, prizes, and friendly competition were provided by you for the children and the adults. Consideration was given to the physically disabled and the elderly in the activities that you selected for all of us. No one felt left out.

Your ideas brought us close together as a family. We salute you.

Truly yours,

Honorable Chairperson

_____*FAMILY___ANNUAL REUNION*

Letter to Members of the Spiritual Committee

Dear Member of the Spiritual Committee,

Only someone like you could have managed to bring all the members of our family who are spiritually dedicated so close to God. You were able to arrange church services for all of the different denominations and faiths within our family.

Such a delicate and sensitive task requires the skills of an angel. These gracious skills you possess. You made sure we were able to provide in our family reunion services a time to praise the Lord.

We thank you for your sensitivity to our spiritual needs.

God's blessing,

Honorable Chairperson

_____*FAMILY___ANNUAL REUNION*

Letter to Members of the Ceremonies Committee

Dear Member of the Ceremonies Committee,

Awards, certificates and trophies were given to the members of our family who had made achievements worthy of honor and praise. We thank you for making an untiring effort to develop a program and attend to all of the details to award those who were deserving.

Your humility was so genuine. Many times we find ourselves seeking attention from the world, and we would thank God a million times if only our family loved us and gave us the praise that you gave to the members of the family in honor of their achievements.

We need you, our family loves you and will always remember you.

Very Sincerely yours,

_____

Honorable Chairperson

_____*FAMILY____ANNUAL REUNION*

Letter to the Host Committee

Dear Host Committee Member,

Your sacrifices for the overall planning and success of the family reunion made it a joyful one. We honor your devotion and the unselfish contribution of yourself. Your ability to work with everyone in the family did not go unnoticed. Each and every member of the family sincerely loves you.

As a result of your work and good deeds our family is just a little bit closer, and we know that we are also moving closer to God.

Now, at the close of this year's family reunion, we thank you so very much. May God bless and keep you.

Love always,

_____

Honorable Chairperson

_____FAMILY____ANNUAL REUNION

Changing of the Guard

What about the changing of the guard?   In other words, we need to write a letter to the next Host Committee.

Letter to the new <u>Host</u> Chairperson

Dear New Host Chairperson of the ___ Annual Family Reunion:

We were proud of your election to the Host Committee, and we are equally proud of the fact that you were selected to be the Chairperson by the votes of the committee and the family. We know that your best is what you always give to every situation.

We honor you.

_____
Honorable Chairperson

_____*FAMILY____ANNUAL REUNION*

These letters are only examples and you will want to adapt them to fit your own style and the needs of your family. Remember to give thanks to as many members as possible for their devotion to the family reunion. We need these devoted members of our family to keep us together as a unit. Their efforts makes crime disappear.

Family Style

The Family Color that the family chooses to represent it is significant. The color stands for something. The family historian will have records telling the meaning and history behind the family color. This is more likely to be the case in established families. Now we need to establish our family color, if we have not already done so.

The color may only be significant to your family. It does not have to be universal. However when selecting a family color, call the entire Host Committee together for the purpose of trying to make a selection for the entire extended family.

What purpose is there in having each nuclear family make a color selection? Some large family reunions provide each nuclear family with a tee-shirt. Each nuclear family may have a different color. It is possible for two nuclear families to have the same color tee-shirt if it is agreed upon. We will speak more about the tee-shirt later. The colors are very good for picture-taking and for identifying all of the members present from different families.

The colors of an individual family may have a history or have significance for a particular year only. Most families will probably want to make a color selection and keep it year after year. That is possible. But do not let the individual colors take away from the meaning of the family reunion -- family unity. It would be better to have different colors every year than to let such a matter cause ill feelings within an extended family.

My only purpose in even mentioning family color is to acquaint our families with an idea that may add a little sparkle to the family reunion. Let us examine a color scheme that I just made up from the top of my head.

```
Blue ....... for the sky or beautiful ocean.
Green  ..... for the green meadows and lovely trees.
Gold ....... for the precious metal from the mother earth.
Brown ...... for the mother earth herself.
Red ........ for the fire from the sun that heats the earth.
Black ...... for the pure in heart, justice, and long life.
White ...... for the clouds that are in the sky.
Pink ....... for the meek and humble.
```

```
Amber ...... for the righteous.
Orange ..... for the sake of happiness.
Yellow ..... for the subtle and kind ones.
```

The color scheme is limited only by the imagination of the Family Reunion Executive Board. Jot it down and let the family vote on the various colors for the nuclear families. Also, the family can make a combined effort to choose a color that will be symbolic of the entire extended family. This is a color that will represent the entire family, with all of the branches sharing this color in common.

Perhaps the color chosen to represent the entire family will not be a color that any one family will wear for nuclear family tee-shirts. This color belongs to all of the family. But if it is agreeable with the Board, then any family chosen can wear it. Maybe it will be a good idea to allow the host family of each family reunion to wear the extended family color.

Having a family color can be fun and never should lead to hard feelings, resentment or withdrawal. It would be better to do without a family color if peace will be disturbed. There is nothing to stop any family from deciding to have a tee-shirt for its branch of the family tree.

The tee-shirt may be artistic and carry a nuclear family logo on it. It may also have the extended family logo. The tee-shirt may combine the logo, nuclear family name and extended family name or color. A silk-screening machine is used to make the family logo and name. An artist in the family can sketch the artwork initially. If the family is without an artist, use the yellow pages to locate a reasonably-priced artist who will take pride in doing the family logo.

The family emblem can be artistically rendered by the family artist or one can be obtained from the commercial art industry. The emblem will have the essence of the family represented in a very simple form. Simplicity is the key to clarity in the artwork of the emblem.

The emblem may be the one item that is unique to the family history, a family coat of arms. Some families already have a coat of arms which they have discovered by tracing their roots. If after researching the family history it is determined that no coat of arms exists, then one may be created after the devotion of a considerable amount of thought to the project. It will be the emblem for the whole extended family. The extended family emblem is a testimonial to the closeness of the entire family. Because if it is close, it will be easy for the extended family to agree upon the design of the emblem. The opposite may be true of a family which is just coming together; more difficulties may be encountered.

However, the emblem for the extended family will be something that will have to be agreed upon, even if it is necessary for compromise. Every family should give serious thought to having a family emblem. It does not have to be done today; sometime in the near future will be fine.

A name to be used for the extended family name may be another point of contention. Usually the family name takes on the name chosen by the Chairperson of the Family Reunion Executive Board. It is the root of the family tree formed from the family name of the most senior member from which all of the branches extend.

All the nuclear families can have the extended family name on their nuclear family tee-shirts. They can also include in smaller lettering the nuclear family name on the same tee-shirt. The designs will have a unified appearance, meaning everyone will have a tee-shirt with the same basic design. This is possible even though the tee-shirts may have different colors and different nuclear family names. We do not want to look like an unorganized bunch, now do we?

Although different words may be used to denote the family emblem, like family crest or family coat of arms, it is an emblem we want to be proud of and wear with integrity. The family will want to start on the design, color and artwork which represent the family style about **ten months before** the family reunion. Family style is the phrase I use to refer to what characterizes that particular family and will be represented by:

> *Name
> *Crest
> *Color

We want to make an artistic rendering of the family style that we will be proud of for generations to come. And, we want to record in the family history books the significance and meaning inherent in the family style.

Family Historian. After each family reunion, the historian of the family will want to be sure to have pictures of each nuclear family. Perhaps, if the family budget allows it, a professional photo of the family tree could be taken. Photos do wonders; the family can look back through time and see the growth of its members. The historian will identify each person in the panorama.

The historian will want to order several prints of the extended family formal picture. This picture is something like the one we had taken of the entire class in grade school. It is like the ones of the entire football team, cheerleaders, and platoon at graduation. We will want to keep this picture in a safe place. The historian will want to keep the master prints, negatives and slides in a safe deposit box. The Chairperson of the Family Reunion Executive Board will want to consider providing this necessary expense in the ongoing budget of the family reunion.

Today we are able to make a video of the family reunion. A copy should made available to each nuclear family that desires it for their home video entertainment. The master video should be put in the safe deposit box for safekeeping.

Why the safe deposit box? It is less likely to be destroyed in a fire. Many a treasury of family pictures has been destroyed in a fire. We may have thought of the perfect place to store the pictures in the home, only to have a raging fire destroy that which is irreplaceable. Some of the pictures are of members of the family that are deceased. We will never be able to re-photograph that once-in-a- lifetime smile. Or, the pictures of the babies cannot be retaken because they grow too fast. The safe deposit box is not perfect, but it is the best place I know for a family to keep negatives, videos and slides of the family reunion.

Choosing a family historian is fun because there is always at least one member of the family that desires to please the group by keeping track of all of the joy of each reunion throughout the years. The family historian will become the cornerstone of the entire family, and will remain a very valued and revered member.

A Family Photographer will catch through his/her lens all the special moments of the reunion. The creativity of a clever photographer will make the work of the Communication Committee easy by allowing them to distribute throughout the entire family warm, funny, moving photographs of reunions past.

Special occasions like weddings, baby showers, graduation, and even funerals should be captured by a good photographer too. The family photo album can be a full-time hobby. The video camcorder will further add to the family's treasury of remembrance. The importance of a devoted family photographer cannot be overemphasized.

FAMILY EDUCATIONAL AND FINANCIAL CONSIDERATIONS

Academic Motivation Awards

Families can provide incentives to start the young and mature adults in the right direction. Most of us can think of several good suggestions to create interest in our family members. Here is an example of an idea put into effect by me some years ago to help encourage and motivate my family members to strive for their very best without placing unnecessary stress and tension on their systems. My plan was called the financial motivator which was very successful in bringing about a dramatic change in the grades brought home by my younger brothers, sisters, nephews, and nieces.

At first I thought about some way to punish my family members into making better grades, but this idea would end up creating stress and possibly doing more damage than good. There must be a better way I thought, but just what? Here, then, is the layout of the result of much thought and analysis:

Kindergarten level:

```
        Outstanding........................$    .25
        Good...............................$    .15
        Honor Roll.........................$   1.00

        Attendance:
          Outstanding/Excellence...........$    .15
          Good.............................$    .10

        Special Subject Bonus:
          Arithmetic
            Grade Outstanding..............$    .30
          Reading
            Grade Outstanding..............$    .40
          Writing
            Grade Outstanding..............$    .40
```

Elementary School:

```
        Grade  A...........................$    .40
        Grade  B...........................$    .30
        Honor Roll.........................$   1.50
      Attendance:
          No Absenteeism...................$    .75
          1 - 2 Absences...................$    .50
          3 - 4 Absences...................$    .30
```

Additional Bonus:

```
Mathematics/Arithmetic-
   Grade A.........................$   .50
English
   Grade A.........................$   .60
```

Junior High School:
```
Grade  A...........................$  1.00
Grade  B...........................$   .75
Honor Roll.........................$  2.00
Attendance:
No Absenteeism.....................$  1.05
1 - 2 Absences.....................$   .95
3 - 4 Absences.....................$   .70

Additional Bonus:
Mathematics/Arithmetic
   Grade A.........................$   .90
English
   Grade A.........................$  1.00
```

High School:
```
Grade  A...........................$  1.35
Grade  B...........................$  1.00
Honor Roll.........................$  5.00
Attendance:
No Absenteeism.....................$  1.75
1 - 2 Absences.....................$  1.20
3 - 4 Absences.....................$   .90

Additional Bonus:
Mathematics
   Grade A.........................$  1.15
English
   Grade A.........................$  1.30
```

College/University:
```
Grade  A...........................$ 15.00
Grade  B...........................$ 10.00
Honor Roll.........................$ 30.00
```

Additional Bonus:
```
Mathematics/Arithmetic-
   Grade A.........................$  3.00
English
   Grade A.........................$  5.00
```

This system allows the person to choose how much additional money he/she wants by making the best of the educational system.   To explain how the system works, let us review an example of a child in kindergarten.   If the report card looked like this:

```
Arithmetic..........'O'
English.............'G'
Art.................'O'
Music...............'S'
Reading.............'O'
```

We would give the child money for his/her achievement by making the following computations:
Example #1-

```
'O' = $ .25;
'G' = $ .15;
 3  @ $ .25  = $ .75;
 1  @ $ .15  = $ .15;
```

After we have computed the amounts for each category, then we added the totals together to derive a figure to give to the child which would be in the amount of $ .90.

Let us take another example of a child in high school who has made the honor roll.   What calculations would we make if we used the McKinzie Financial Motivator Chart?   Here are the grades to compute from:

Example #2 -

```
Arithmetic..........'A'
English.............'A'
Art.................'B'
Music...............'A'
Reading.............'A'
Writing.............'A'
Science.............'A'
Social Studies......'B'
Physical Education..'A'
Cooperation.........'B'
Work Habits.........'B'
Attendance..........'no absences'
```

We would give the child money for his/her achievement by making the following computations:

```
'A' = $1.35;
'B' = $1.00;

 7  @ $1.35  = $9.45;

 4  @ $1.00  = $4.00;
```

Here we have to add to the computation the additional
bonuses earned:

```
-English bonus for grade of        'A' = $1.30;
-Mathematics bonus for grade of    'A' = $1.15;
-Attendance bonus for 'no absenteeism' = $1.75;
-Honor Roll bonus would be             = $5.00;
```

Then we total all the figures to determine the amount of
$22.65.

From the amounts above, we can see how the McKinzie Financial Motivator Chart will definitely make some improvements
in the way our family members perceive their education.   Each
one of us has ideas that we could use to encourage our family
and other families to pursue worthwhile goals.

Career Motivation Awards

In addition to applying the system above, a family can
provide incentives by utilizing the McKinzie Career Motivator
System which provides financial incentives for members of the
family who go into   certain fields, professions or trades.
For example, let us say we want to make a chart to help
direct our family into areas that will be beneficial to the
family first and then to the neighborhood, community, and
country. (In the case of my family, I feel we are most in
need of lawyers, so I have placed them at the top of the
chart. But your family may have different priorities.)

McKinzie Career Motivator Chart for the Family

```
Lawyer.......................$2,000.
 (after passing the bar)
Medical Doctor...............$1,500.
Doctorate Degree (Ph.D.).......$500.
Master's Degree ..............$300.
Bachelor's Degree.............$200.
Associate Art's Degree........$150.
High School Diploma.  ........$100.
Registered Nurse..............$200.
Computer Programmer.  .........$500.
Writer (book published) ......$895.
```

Trades:
```
Plumber......................$105.
Electrician..................$120.
Carpenter....................$109.
Heating and Refrigeration.....$112.
```

Entertainment
```
Sports Figure.................$123.
Singer.......................$130.
Movie Celebrity..............$135.
```

The combined effects of the McKinzie Financial Motivator and the McKinzie Career Motivator Charts will provide positive incentives for our families to make a contribution to the family and to our communities.

There are many examples of poor kids who decided to take their education seriously by going to school to better themselves and obtaining degrees in various professions. Abraham Lincoln was a splendid example of a poor kid that kept to the books to become a lawyer and later on was considered one of the best presidents of the United States.

Gandhi's thirst for knowledge led him to seek an education for the benefit of his family and his nation, and he rose to become a great leader of his country. The importance of an education is profound and the benefits are enormously significant to the family and the nation. If we are going to be a world of peaceful people, then we owe it to the future to make an investment in the education or our family members.

Family Financial Considerations

In some families, many of the elderly do not have the means to attend the family reunion. Funds are provided by the family so that they may be a part of it. The money is a gift, and no repayment is expected.

The family may want to help a few of its members who live very far from the reunion site and must expend large sums each year to attend. In such cases, each family unit within the whole might be asked to contribute a certain amount to help defray the expenses of these especially hard-hit members.

Investment

The average family does not make special arrangements for investment. But it can be a worthwhile outgrowth of reunions. Families can unite and form investments together with larger returns than are ever possible on an individual basis. Each family unit could contribute a certain amount per month or the amounts could be varying percentages depending on the desires of each. Even small families can start trusts by contacting their bankers, financial advisors and financial institutions that specialize in family money matters for advice.

Something like a family financial kit

What if a single, widowed or divorced family member is injured and is unable to attend to financial affairs? How do we get help for those members of the family who are stricken by an illness that incapacitates them for an indefinite length of time? The **Family's Financial Survival Kit** will provide pertinent information about the family member's personal finances. The kit should be kept in a safe deposit box. Another trustworthy member of the family should have access to the box just in case the need should arise. The following forms should be filled out as completely as possible for the security of the family.

Take out your pen, print clearly, and complete the forms with the requested information. Do a page a day, twice a week with the entire immediate family participating. It may be wiser to be over-prepared than to be caught unorganized.

LIFE INSURANCE

COMPANY

STREET ADDRESS

CITY   STATE   ZIP

TELEPHONE: AREA CODE   NUMBER

POLICY NO.   TYPE

AMOUNT   DATE OF POLICY

BENEFICIARY

LOCATION OF POLICY

AMOUNT OF REGULAR PAYMENTS   DUE DATE

AGENT

STREET ADDRESS

TELEPHONE: AREA CODE   NUMBER

COMPANY

STREET ADDRESS

CITY   STATE   ZIP

TELEPHONE: AREA CODE   NUMBER

POLICY NO.   TYPE

AMOUNT   DATE OF POLICY

BENEFICIARY

LOCATION OF POLICY

AMOUNT OF REGULAR PAYMENTS   DUE DATE

AGENT

STREET ADDRESS

TELEPHONE: AREA CODE   NUMBER

BANK ACCOUNTS

BANK

STREET ADDRESS

CITY   STATE   ZIP

ACCOUNT NO.

TYPE OF ACCOUNT

BANK

STREET ADDRESS

CITY   STATE   ZIP

ACCOUNT NO.

TYPE OF ACCOUNT

BANK

STREET ADDRESS

CITY   STATE   ZIP

ACCOUNT NO.

TYPE OF ACCOUNT

BANK

STREET ADDRESS

CITY   STATE   ZIP

ACCOUNT NO.

TYPE OF ACCOUNT

SAVINGS AND LOAN ASSOCIATIONS

REGULAR SAVINGS ACCOUNTS

ACCOUNT NO.	NO. SHARES	NAME OF SAVINGS AND LOAN

INVESTMENT SAVINGS ACCOUNTS

ACCOUNT NO.	NO. SHARES	NAME OF SAVINGS AND LOAN

INDIVIDUAL RETIREMENT ACCOUNTS

CREDIT UNION ACCOUNTS

NAME OF CREDIT UNION
_____

STREET ADDRESS
_____

CITY   STATE   ZIP
_____

TELEPHONE: AREA CODE   NUMBER
_____

LOAN OFFICER
_____

REGULAR SAVINGS OFFICER
_____

MANAGER
_____

SHARE ACCOUNT NUMBER
_____

NAME OF CREDIT UNION
_____

STREET ADDRESS
_____

CITY   STATE   ZIP
_____

TELEPHONE: AREA CODE   NUMBER
_____

LOAN OFFICER
_____

REGULAR SAVINGS OFFICER
_____

MANAGER
_____

SHARE ACCOUNT NUMBER
_____

NAME OF CREDIT UNION
_____

STREET ADDRESS
_____

CITY   STATE   ZIP
_____

TELEPHONE: AREA CODE   NUMBER
_____

LOAN OFFICER
_____

REGULAR SAVINGS OFFICER
_____

MANAGER
_____

SHARE ACCOUNT NUMBER
_____

SECURITIES

COMPANY

COMMON   PREFERRED   BOND   DEBENTURE

DATE BOUGHT   CERTIFICATE NUMBER

UNIT PRICE $ NO. OF SHARES   AMOUNT $

LOCATION OF CERTIFICATE

BROKER

STREET ADDRESS

CITY   STATE   ZIP

TELEPHONE: AREA CODE   NUMBER

COMPANY

COMMON   PREFERRED   BOND   DEBENTURE

DATE BOUGHT   CERTIFICATE NUMBER

UNIT PRICE $ NO. OF SHARES   AMOUNT $

LOCATION OF CERTIFICATE

BROKER

STREET ADDRESS

CITY   STATE   ZIP

TELEPHONE: AREA CODE   NUMBER

MUTUAL FUNDS

NAME

STREET ADDRESS

CITY   STATE   ZIP

DATE BOUGHT   FUND CERTIFICATE NUMBER

SHARES   PRICE $ AMOUNT $

LOCATION OF CERTIFICATE

CUSTODIAN BANK

STREET ADDRESS

CITY   STATE   ZIP

TELEPHONE: AREA CODE   NUMBER

NAME

STREET ADDRESS

CITY   STATE   ZIP

DATE BOUGHT   FUND CERTIFICATE NUMBER

SHARES   PRICE $ AMOUNT $

LOCATION OF CERTIFICATE

CUSTODIAN BANK

STREET ADDRESS

CITY   STATE   ZIP

TELEPHONE: AREA CODE   NUMBER

SAVINGS BONDS

DATE	SERIES NO.	COST	MATURITY VALUE	MATURITY DATE

SAFE DEPOSIT BOX

BANK

STREET ADDRESS

CITY   STATE   ZIP

TELEPHONE: AREA CODE   NUMBER

BOX NO.   KEY NO.

THOSE HAVING ACCESS TO SAFE DEPOSIT BOX

NAME

STREET ADDRESS

CITY   STATE   ZIP

TELEPHONE: AREA CODE   NUMBER

LOCATION OF KEYS

BOX CONTENTS AS OF: DATE: MONTH   DAY   YEAR

1.

2.

3.

4.

5.

6.

7.

8.

9.

10.

11.

12.

BUSINESS

NAME OF FIRM
_____

STREET ADDRESS
_____

CITY   STATE   ZIP
_____

TELEPHONE: AREA CODE   NUMBER
_____

PRINCIPALS
_____

_____

_____

_____

MY ASSOCIATION: OWNER   PARTNER   EMPLOYEE
_____

POSITION
_____

LENGTH OF SERVICE   DATE
_____

INCOME
_____

_____

_____

_____

RETIREMENT BENEFITS
_____

INSURANCE BENEFITS
_____

SOCIAL SECURITY
_____

OTHER BENEFITS
_____

ADDITIONAL INFORMATION MAY BE OBTAINED FROM
_____

_____

REAL ESTATE

DESCRIPTION
_____

STREET ADDRESS
_____

CITY   STATE   ZIP
_____

LEGAL DESCRIPTION
_____

_____

PURCHASE PRICE $ DEED IN NAME OF
_____

LOCATION OF DEED
_____

AMOUNT OF MORTGAGE $ TYPE OF MORTGAGE
_____

MORTGAGE PAYMENTS $ DATE DUE
_____

NAME OF MORTGAGOR: 1ST TRUSTEE
_____

OFFICER
_____

STREET ADDRESS
_____

CITY   STATE   ZIP
_____

TELEPHONE: AREA CODE   NUMBER
_____

ASSESSED VALUATION $
_____

REAL ESTATE TAX PAYABLE ON
_____

OTHER ASSESSMENTS DUE ON
_____

NAME OF 2ND TRUSTEE HOLDER
_____

STREET ADDRESS
_____

CITY   STATE   ZIP
_____

LOCATION OF NOTE
_____

AMOUNT OF LOAN $ INTEREST RATE
_____

TYPE OF LOAN   YEARS
_____

AMOUNT OF MONTHLY PAYMENT $ DATE DUE
_____

REAL ESTATE (CONTINUED)

PROPERTY LEASED TO

STREET ADDRESS

CITY   STATE   ZIP

TELEPHONE: AREA CODE   NUMBER

GROSS INCOME $ NET INCOME $

INSURANCE ON PROPERTY

COMPANY

STREET ADDRESS

CITY   STATE   ZIP

TELEPHONE: AREA CODE   NUMBER

POLICY NUMBER   TYPE

AMOUNT $

DATE OF POLICY   RENEWAL DATE

LOCATION OF POLICY

AGENT

STREET ADDRESS

CITY   STATE   ZIP

TELEPHONE: AREA CODE   NUMBER

REAL ESTATE IMPROVEMENTS

DATE	DESCRIPTION	COST
	DO NOT INCLUDE MAINTENANCE COSTS	

PROFESSIONAL ADVISORS

ATTORNEY

STREET ADDRESS

CITY	STATE	ZIP

TELEPHONE: AREA CODE   NUMBER

TRUSTEE OF ESTATE

STREET ADDRESS

CITY	STATE	ZIP

TELEPHONE: AREA CODE   NUMBER

EXECUTOR OF ESTATE

STREET ADDRESS

CITY	STATE	ZIP

TELEPHONE: AREA CODE   NUMBER

ACCOUNTANT

STREET ADDRESS

CITY	STATE	ZIP

TELEPHONE: AREA CODE   NUMBER

SOCIAL SECURITY -- ACCIDENT INSURANCE

SOCIAL SECURITY NO.

LOCATION OF SOCIAL SECURITY CARD

MY SOCIAL SECURITY PROVIDES

NEAREST SOCIAL SECURITY OFFICE

STREET ADDRESS

CITY   STATE   ZIP

ACCIDENT INSURANCE

POLICY NO.

AMOUNT

POLICIES LOCATED AT

AGENT

STREET ADDRESS

CITY   STATE   ZIP

TELEPHONE: AREA CODE   NUMBER

OBLIGATIONS

FAMILY:
_____
_____
_____
_____

FRIENDS:
_____
_____
_____
_____

JOB:
_____
_____
_____
_____

OTHER:
_____
_____
_____
_____
_____
_____
_____
_____

RECOMMENDATIONS

_____

_____

_____

_____

_____

_____

_____

_____

_____

_____

_____

_____

_____

_____

_____

_____

_____

_____

_____

_____

_____

_____

_____

_____

FINANCIAL COMMITTEE

NAME
_____

STREET ADDRESS
_____

CITY   STATE   ZIP
_____

TELEPHONE: AREA CODE   NUMBER
_____

NAME
_____

STREET ADDRESS
_____

CITY   STATE   ZIP
_____

TELEPHONE: AREA CODE   NUMBER
_____

NAME
_____

STREET ADDRESS
_____

CITY   STATE   ZIP
_____

TELEPHONE: AREA CODE   NUMBER
_____

NAME
_____

STREET ADDRESS
_____

CITY   STATE   ZIP
_____

TELEPHONE: AREA CODE   NUMBER
_____

NAME
_____

STREET ADDRESS
_____

CITY   STATE   ZIP
_____

TELEPHONE: AREA CODE   NUMBER
_____

THE FINAL WORD

If I Had It To Do All Over Again, What Would I Do Differently? What would we do if we had it to do all over again? Many times our minds will wonder about the past. The good and the bad are unequally present there. If we could just turn back the hands of time, we could set our life back on the right course.

The times we played hookey from school instead of learning our lessons kept us out of college. Our whole future was altered by making this mistake in the past.

Or the day everything was going wrong, the awful headache and then the accident that no one will ever believe was not our fault. We were innocent, but the jury and the court did not see it our way. Now if we could have another chance to return to the moment before the fatal accident that reduced our lives to a total shamble. If I had one more chance to do it all over again...

The family historian tracks the events of time and records them. The family photographer records our lives on film. The pen writes the good and the bad for our ancestors to read for generations to come.

How difficult it is to alter the single event that takes a son from his mother forever, that causes a pain so great that it sends a tender daughter away from her father's home. If we could mend the war between two cousins and wash away the pain they have caused one another. **We must try.**

Pencils have erasers and wrongs can be forgiven. Every family must deal with pain, hate and sorrow. We must find a way to mend the wrongs that divide our family.

The scholarships and investment programs will mean nothing if we forget or fail to change our hearts from hate to forgiveness and love. Family Day, Week, Month and the Year of the Family will be meaningless if we do not learn to forgive. Our forgiveness must be quick and come soon after the offending deed to keep the hurt from leaving its indelible marks.

We must understand that our own ill deeds have caused untold hurt and grief to others in our family. **We must forgive and forget!**

If I had it to do all over again, I would forgive and forget. **FOREVER!**

APPENDIX

FAMILY REUNION QUESTIONAIRE

INSTRUCTIONS

Please print with dark ink or use the typewriter for answering the attached questionnaire. If you do not have enough space to answer a question, please attach a separate page. Whenever you desire to include photographs, write a brief description of:

Who?
Where?
When?

Any documents that are attached will be treated with care. If you desire the return of any documents, please make a note to that effect. Otherwise, all documents will become the property of McKinzie Publishing Company.

Please be aware that any or all information, pictures, documents, etc. will be considered for publication and that your submission of the above and or any additional information will be understood to be your express permission to release any or all of the above.

It is further understood that you will designate any information you regard as confidential and it will not be published, printed or quoted.

The information you submit will be of considerable service in making this nation and all nations stronger. Strong, good families help eliminate the need for war.

Do your part today. Fill out and mail this questionnaire now!!

GENERAL PLANNING

1. Has your family had a family reunion?
   ____Yes
   ____No
2. If you have not had a family reunion:
   a. When will you?
   b. What time of the year?
3. Would you like help in planning your family reunion?
   Answer:
4. Would you like to purchase the book on family reunions at a discount?
   ____Yes
   ____No
5. If you have had a family reunion:
   a. Are all members of your immediate family invited?
      ____Yes
      ____No
   b. Are all members of your extended family invited?
      ____Yes
      ____No
   c. If "No" to either "a" or "b", explain why not:
      Answer:
6. Approximately how many people attend your family reunions?
   ____ Less than 50.
   ____ 50 to 100.
   ____ How many?
7. When was your first family reunion?
   ____ Less than 1 year?
   ____ l to 2 years?
   ____ Other
8. What made you decide to have a family reunion?
   Answer:
9. What difficulties did you encounter during your initial planning for your first family reunion?
   Answer:

a. How were these difficulties resolved?
Answer:
b. Who was instrumental in resolving the difficulties?
Answer:
10. When was your last family reunion? _____
11. How often do you plan to have a family reunion?
Answer:
12. What were the contributing factors in determining how often your family will meet?
Answer:
13. In your opinion, what is the most significant rea-son for planning a family reunion?
Answer:
14. Do you plan your family reunion around:
    ____ Holidays
    ____ Special occasions
    ____ Certain seasons
    Please elaborate:
    Answer:
15. What season of the year do you find best for having a family reunion?
    ____a. Winter
    ____b. Spring
    ____c. Summer
    ____d. Fall
16. What was the reason for your family choosing the season that was selected?
    Answer:

COMMUNICATION

17. What communication system is utilized to get the word?
    ____A. Telephone
            ____1. AT&T
            ____2. Western Union
            ____3. SPRINT
            ____4. Other a._____
                        b._____
    ____B. Letter
            ____1. Mail
            ____2. Telegram
            ____3. Electronic mail
            ____4. Other a._____
                        b._____
    ____C. Other 1._____
                 2._____

HOUSING ACCOMMODATIONS

18. What kind of housing accommodations are made:
A. Homes:
    ____1. Local family members.
    ____2. Friends.
    ____3. Homes rented for the occasion.
    ____4. Tents.
B. Hotel
    ____1. Holiday Inn.
    ____2. Hilton.
    ____3. Westin.
    ____4. Sheraton.
    ____5. La Quinta.
    ____6. Other. a._____
                 b._____
C. Motel
    ____1. Motel 6.
    ____2. Travelodge.
    ____3. Motel 8.
    ____4. Best Western.
    ____5. Other. a._____
                 b._____
                 c._____
D. Campgrounds
    ____1. National Campground
            a. Name _____
            b. Address_____
                       _____

____2. State Campground
     a. Name_____
     b. Address_____
     _____

____3. Private Campground
     a. Name_____
     b. Address_____
     _____

E. ____ Lodge.
F. ____ Boarding homes.
G. ____ Other a._____
          b._____

FOOD PREPARATION
19. What planning is made for food preparation?
Answer:

20. Did your family reunion made food planning for special diets:
____ a. Low calorie.
____ b. Low cholesterol.
____ c. Heart ailments.
____ d. Sodium free.
____ e. Other 1. _____
          2. _____

21. Did your family reunion make special preparation for meals for:
____ a. Pets
____ b. Other 1._____
          2._____

22. Did your family include any food preparation ideas or suggestions that you would like to mention to help other people?
Answer:

TRANSPORTATION
23. What modes of transportation are primarily used by your family to travel to and from the family reunion?
A. Airlines
____ 1. TWA
____ 2. American
____ 3. PSA
____ 4. Delta
____ 5. Chartered Airline
    Name_____
    Address_____
    _____
____ 6. Other
    a._____
    b._____
B. Bus
____ 1. Greyhound
____ 2. Continental
____ 3. Trailways
____ 4. Chartered Bus
____ 5. Other a._____
        b._____
C. Train
____ 1. Amtrak
____ 2. Southern-Pacific
____ 3. Other a._____
        b._____
D. Cruise
Name _____
Address_____
_____
E. Sailboat. Size _____
F. Auto
____ 1. Budget
____ 2. Dollar
____ 3. Thrifty
____ 4. Avis
____ 5. Hertz
____ 6. Private
____ 7. Other
    ____ Van
    ____ Camper

____ Trailer
____ Other a._____

               b._____

G. Private airplane.
    ____ l. Cessna.
    ____ 2. Beach craft.
    ____ 3. Other a._____
             b._____

24. What kind of group tour travel arrangements are made?
    Answer:
25. What tour service is utilized for family tours of the local area?
    Name _____
    Address_____
    _____
    Who plans the tour?
    Answer:
26. Does your family use experts in making travel arrangements?
    ____a. Tour operator.
    ____b. Travel Agent.
    ____c. Other (l) _____
             (2) _____
27. Does your family use any of the following in making travel arrangements?
    ____a. American Express Travel
    ____b. Southern California Automobile Club
    ____c. May Co. Travel
    ____d. Bullocks Travel
    ____e. Other 1._____
             2._____

FAMILY LOCATION
28. Where are the majority of your family members located in the USA?
    ____ a. North.
    ____ b. South.
    ____ c. East.
    ____ d. West.

29. In what cities and states have your past reunions been held?
    A. _____
            city\state
    B. _____
            city\state

30. Where will your next family reunion be held?
    _____
            city/state
31. In what country are your reunions scheduled?
    a. _____
    b. _____

ACTIVITIES

32. What kind of group tour travel arrangements are made?
    Answer:
33. What tour service is utilized for family tours of the local area?
    Name _____
    Address_____
    _____
    Who plans the tour?
    Answer:
34. What kind of activities does your family engage in while together?
    A. Physical activities include: (Check each one that is applicable.)
    ____ l. Racquetball. ____ 5. Rollerskating. ____ 9. Horseback riding.
    ____ 2. Swimming.   ____ 6. Dancing.   ____10. Shopping.
    ____ 3. Tennis.   ____ 7. Ice skating.   ____11. Other.
    ____ 4. Boating.   ____ 8. Bowling.   a._____
                                                       b._____
    B. Mental Activities
    ____1. Chess.
    ____2. Poetry reading.
    ____3. Games
         ____a. Monopoly.
         ____b. Trivial Pursuits.
         ____c. Computer games.

```
____4. Arcade Games.
        ____a. Dig-Dug.
        ____b. Centipede.
        ____c. Other_____
____5. Other. a. _____
              b. _____
   C.  Spiritual Concerns
        ____1. Church.           ____4. Meditation.
        ____2. Prayer meeting.   ____5. Other. a._____
        ____3. Bible reading.                 b._____

   D.  Entertainment
        ____1. Theater
        ____2. Movies.
        ____3. Symphony.
        ____4. Opera.
        ____5. Fashion shows.
        ____6. Other a._____
                    b._____
```

CHILD CARE

35. What arrangements are made for babysitting?
    Answer:
36. Are children in attendance at all events?
    ____Yes
    ____No
37. If no, name the events from which they are excluded:
    Answer:
38. Why are children excluded?
    Answer:
39. Are special food arrangements made for toddlers?
    Answer:
40. What financial investments are made for minors?
    Answer:
41. What family trusts are made for minors?
    Answer:

EDUCATION

42. What education plans do your family provide?
    ____ A. Scholarship
            Name _____
            Address _____
                    _____
    ____ B. Educational award or stipend
            Name _____
            Address _____
                    _____
    ____ C. Educational activities
            Name 1. _____
                 2. _____
43. Who contributes to the scholarships and awards?
    Answer:
44. What are the amounts of the scholarships and awards?
    Answer:

SECURITY

45. Does your family require any special security arrangements?
    ____Yes
    ____No
46. If yes, who is responsible for making the security arrangements?
    Answer:
47. Who pays for the security arrangements?
    ____ a. Individual(s) requiring security?
    ____ b. Family reunion committee?
    ____ c. Government?
    ____ d. Other l._____
                 2._____
48. Do the security personnel hamper the family reunion?
    ____Yes
    ____No

FINANCIAL

49. What financial considerations are made for family members who may need money in order to attend the reunion?
    Answer:
50. How is the money repaid?
    Answer:
51. What action does the family take if the money is not repaid?
    Answer:
52. What qualifies a family member(s) to receive money?
    Answer:
53. Please provide a copy of the application form used.

INVESTMENTS

54. Has your family made family investments together as a unit?
    Answer: (Feel free to attach examples.)
55. How is trust established, controlled, or arranged on money-handling matters? Please elaborate:
    Answer:
56. Does your family seek the help of professionals in handling money matters?
    ____Yes
    ____No
57. What professionals are utilized in money matters?
    ____ 1. Attorney.
    ____ 2. Stockbroker.
    ____ 3. CPA.
    ____ 4. Tax consultant.
    ____ 5. Financial planner.
    ____ 6. Banker.
    ____ 7. Other. a._____
                   b._____

INDEX

BIBLIOGRAPHY

REFERENCES

Adler, Jack. The Consumer's Guide to Travel. Santa Barbara, Calif.: Capra Press, 1983.

Barthel, Joan, "Family Reunions," Ladies' Home Journal, August, 1978, 71-72+.

Bennett, Lerone, "The 10 Biggest Myths About the Black Family," Ebony, August, 1986, 123-128+.

"Christmas in July," Ebony, September, 1964, 94-100.

Coffin, Patricia, "Boy Meets 416 Cousins," Look, September, 1959, XXIII, 84-88.

Cosby, Bill. Fatherhood. Garden City, N. Y.: Doubleday & Company, 1986.

"Deep South Reunion: Some 3,500 Expatriate Black Meridians Converge on Their Mississippi Hometown," Ebony, June, 1984, 85-88+.

"Dude Ranch Getaways," Harper's Bazaar, January, 1985, 110+.

"Family Reunions Needed to Trace Roots: Haley," Jet, September 11, 1980, 26.

Formanek, R. and Gurian, A. Why? Children's Questions; What They Mean and How to Answer Them. Boston: Houghton Mifflin, 1980.

The Great Ideas Today. Chicago, Encyclopaedia Britanica, 1986.

Green, Maureen. Fathering. New York: McGraw-Hill, 1976.

Greenberg, Keith, "Family Reunion: the Martin Clan Retains Its Roots, 160 Years and 1,500 People Later," The Detroit Free Press, July 11, 1984, 1+.

Haley, Alex, "We Must Honor Our Ancestors," Ebony, August, 1986, 134+.

Hetherington, E. M. and Parke, R. D. Child Psychology; A Contemporary Viewpoint. New York: McGraw-Hill, 1979.

Hiking Map To the San Jacinto Wilderness. Sacramento: California Dept. of Parks & Recreation, c1986.

Hutchins, Robert M., ed. Great Books of the Western World. Chicago, Encyclopaedia Britannica, 1952.

The History of Our Family. Secaucus, New Jersey: Poplar Books, c1977.

"Inventory of the Contents of Your Home." Bloomington, Ill: State Farm Fire and Casualty Co.

Kantor, D. and Lehr, W. Inside the Family. New York: Jossey-Bass, 1975.

Kaufmann, F. "Recognizing Creative Behavior," in The Gifted Child, the Family and the Community. New York: Walker, 1981, 83-91.

Klein, D. M. and Hill, R., "Determinants of Family Problem-Solving Effectiveness," in Contemporary Theories About the Family, v.1. New York: Free Press, 1979, 495-498, 500-517.

Leshner, Marty. Trouble-Free Travel. New York: Franklin Watts, 1980.

Lewis, J. How's Your Family? New York: Brunner/Mazel, 1979.

McCandless, B. R. and Trotter, R. J. Children; Behavior and Development. New York: Holt, Rinehart and Winston, 1977.

McKinzie, Harry. Names from East Africa. Los Angeles, Calif., McKinzie Publishing Company., c1980.

The New Encyclopaedia Britannica. Chicago, Encyclopaedia Britannica, c1984.

The New English Bible. New York: Oxford University Press, c1976.

The 1984 Kelsey Family Reunion, August 10,11,12, 1984.   Program.

Orlick, Terry. The Cooperative Sports and Games Book: Challenge Without Competition. New York: Pantheon Books, c1978.

Pierpont, Margaret. "The Big Switch: Why Walking's Hot, Running's Not," Self, May, 1987, 162-166.

Portnoy, Sanford and Portnoy, Joan. How To Take Great Trips With Your Kids. Boston: Harvard Common Press, c1983.

Reed, Roy, "In Tennessee: A Family Goes to Camp Meeting," Time, September 6, 1982, 12-13.

Rule, S. "Black Divorces Soar; Experts Cite Special Strains," New York Times, May 24, 1982, A17.

Sanderson, Jim, "The Liberated Male: Taking the Time to Honor the Living," The Los Angeles Times, May 15, 1986.

Stewart, Gordon W. Things Your Travel Agent Never Told You. Montreal: Grosvenor House Press, 1983.

"Thirty Ways to Make the Most of Summer: #1 Reunite Your Family," Essence, June, 1981, 93-94+.

Ulrich, H. H. and Yandle, T. B., Jr. Managing Personal Finance. Dallas, Texas: Business Publications, Inc., 1979.

What Determines a Safe Speed? Los Angeles, Calif.: Automobile Club of Southern California, c1985.

ACKNOWLEDGMENTS

DEDICATION

This book is dedicated to all the families of the world; free and not so free. It is our hope and desire that all people become free to raise their families in peace and harmony in free societies, regardless of the political or economic systems of their governments.

This effort would not have been possible if it were not for the support, encouragement, and assistance of special friends in the many tasks of making a project like this a reality.

Special Thanks

I will always be very grateful to **my mother and father** for their prayers and love. To those **members of my family** who expressed their belief in and need for such a project to help us plan and continue our annual family reunion, I shall be forever appreciative.

Special thanks go to those special friends who would surrender only to victory.

Elisabeth K. Campbell * Sheila Langley * Frank W. Donaldson

In addition, thanks to these persons:

Deborah Rugley . Dr. S. M. El Farra . Milford Bliss . Don Nicolson . Mary Cobb . Anne Powers . Bob Lansdowne . Pamela F. Brownie . Vilma L. Potter . Senator Ted Kennedy . Valerie-Jean Hume . G. D. 'MAC' McReynolds . William F. Buckley, Jr. . President Ronald Reagan . Senator Dianne Watson Vice President George Bush .

Sketches: Maurice Walker
Artwork: ReadyRepro, Inc
Cover Design: Harry Mc Kinzie

FAMILY CARE

Let our family's hearts rejoice,
Let all who are near hear our voice.

Our family will make the time to share,
In a peaceful way without a big flare.

****

HARNESS HOSTILITY,
DON'T HARBOR IT.

****

2089 MISCONCEPTION MINUS A CENTURY"

What you get,
Which you wearing thing.
Tri-Laser Derringer,
At home at the car.

Medical science,
Not at par.
Miscegenation without reservation,
Accepted so far.

A day in the daze,
Possibly a gaze.
Crimes a maze,
Don't be amazed.

The discreet one of power,
Still fresh as a flower.

This hour imagined,
See no pageant.
Little tots,
Within the slots.

****

A community is only as strong
as the families that reside
within it.

The family is only as strong
as its weakest members.

****

STRAYED SHEEP

If one gets lost along the way,
We all help him or her today.
Whether it be a cause for metal,
Or injury from a bike's pedal.
Indignation and pride behind us,
Glory, joy and prayer will make a plus.

Let us reach out to bring
In all our family's lost sheep
A step closer to our deepest spring,
So we made all find a good night's sleep.

Forgiveness is definitely an order,
Even though we find ourselves the shorter.
Give glory to God, first and last,
Then exalt the glory of our past.
None meets the standards of the perfect eye,
Repent for our sins as we decide.
The one above will be our goal,
Now, help bring in our lost sheep.

****

I AM NOT

I am not a saint.
So do not expect me to be holy.

I am not a preacher.
So do not expect me to give a sermon.

I am not a pastor.
So do not expect me to be a good shepherd.

I am not a husband.
So do not expect me to be faithful.

I am not a good parent.
So do not expect me to have good children.

I am not a scholar.
So do not expect me to be knowledgable.

I am not without sin.
So do not expect my record to be blameless.

I am not known to be wise.
So do not expect me to have wisdom.

****